The Jewish Idea and Its Enemies

The Jewish Idea and Its Enemies

Personalities, Issues, Events

Edward Alexander

Transaction Publishers
New Brunswick (U.S.A.) and London (U.K.)

First paperback reprint 1991
Copyright © 1988 by Transaction Publishers,
New Brunswick, New Jersey 08903

Library of Congress Catalog Number: 87-13956
ISBN: 0-88738-175-8 (cloth); 0-88738-873-6 (paper)
Printed in the United States of America

Library of Congress Cataloging-in-Publication Data

Alexander, Edward, 1936–
    The Jewish idea and its enemies.

    1. Jews—Politics and government—1948–
2. Antisemitism—History—20th century. 3. Israel—
Politics and government. 4. Lebanon—History—
Israeli intervention, 1982–   —Foreign public
opinion. 5. Public opinion. I. Title.
DS143.A34   1987   305.8'924   87-13956
ISBN 0-88738-175-8

In Memoriam
Irvin Ehrenpreis

Contents

Acknowledgments

For help and suggestions of various kinds I received while writing this book, I would like to thank Leah Alexander, David M. Alexander, Avraham Balaban, David Bar-Illan, Yehuda Bauer, Maier Deshell, Emil Fackenheim, Robert B. Heilman, Erich Isaac, Rael Jean Isaac, Sholom Kahn, Shmuel Katz, Yaakov Keinan, Neal Kozodoy, Dorothea Krook, Ron Nettler, Cynthia Ozick, Marie Syrkin, and Donald W. Treadgold.

For support of my work in the form of a summer fellowship, I am grateful to the Jewish Studies Program of the University of Washington.

For typing the manuscript, I am grateful to Janice Goldstein, Sherry Laing, Ellen Polsky, and Marianna Wright.

The author gratefully acknowledges the following publishers and publications for permission to use previously published material:

Ohio University Press: "John Stuart Mill: A Post-Holocaust Retrospect," from *The Victorian Experience, The Prose Writers,* Richard Levine, editor, 1982.

Jewish Chronicle, "Body-Snatching in Rishon Lezion," 4 January 1985.

Congress Monthly, "Rationalizing Evil: The Journalistic Explainers," "Converts in Zion," "Jewish Self-Hatred," condensed reprint from vol. 53 (1, 4, 7). Copyright 1986 by American Jewish Congress. Reprinted by permission.

Midstream—A Monthly Jewish Review: "Stealing the Holocaust" (November 1980); "Terror at Home" (August/September 1984); "We Will Drive this Country Crazy" (October 1984); "Denis Goldberg, Jerry Falwell, and the Wise Men of Chelm" (August/September 1985); "Lionel Trilling" (March 1983); "Isaac Bashevis Singer" (January 1987).

Commentary, "Operation Moses" (July 1985); "Liberalism and Zionism" (February 1986); "Shcharansky's Secret" (October 1986); "Off Balance" (January 1987). Reprinted by permission; all rights reserved.

Encounter, "The Journalists' War against Israel" (September–October 1982). Americans for a Safe Israel: "NBC's War in Lebanon: The Distorting Mirror" (1983).

Introduction

By "the Jewish idea" I mean nothing abstruse or original but only the familiar view that the Jews were called into existence as a people by a covenant with God that is as real and living today as it was at its inception. "I will establish My covenant," says God to Abraham, "between Me and thee and thy seed after thee throughout their generations for an everlasting covenant" (Gen. 17:7). According to this simple and traditional idea, the Jews were chosen by God in order to achieve the universal salvation of mankind: "In thy seed shall all the nations of the earth be blessed; because thou hast hearkened to my voice" (Gen. 22:18). Israel has been chosen, but chosen by a God who keeps admonishing Israel to love the stranger "as thyself; for you were strangers in the land of Egypt" (Lev. 19:34). The chosenness of Israel, therefore, is directed toward the ultimate unity of mankind.

These simple notions would hardly require emphasis were it not for the fact that the Jews' chosenness has so often been presented by their enemies as something the Jews themselves initiated for their own aggrandizement, and still more often travestied by spurious aspirants (medieval Roman divines, German Nazis, and Dutch Boers) to the title of "the true Israel" or "chosen people" who wanted to justify their domination of another people. So great is the possibility for confusion on this point that, as I note in my essay in this book, "The Attack on Holocaust Studies," even so highly instructed a critic as George Steiner cannot recognize the distinction between a people chosen by God so that *all* "the nations of the earth be blessed" and a nation that chooses itself so that it may destroy several of the nations of the earth and subjugate all the rest.

The idea of the Jews as a covenanted people chosen to receive the law (Torah) is present, usually implicitly, sometimes explicitly, in many of the essays that follow. It takes the form of an assumption that Jewish life can lead somewhere only so long as Jews remember that it began somewhere.

1

At Sinai (or Horeb) God made his covenant, not only with our fathers, "but with us, even us, who are all of us here alive this day" (Deut. 5:3). According to this doctrine, further elaborated in a psalm and a midrash, every Jew, no matter in what valley of dry bones he finds himself, whether the Gehenna of Hitler's Europe or the atheistic wilderness of the Soviet Union, was present in the imagination of those with whom the covenant was originally made. No matter how deaf Jews may have become, the voice from Sinai continues to sound and is forever available to those who can put away their idolatries and respond, as they did when Joshua enjoined them to choose to be chosen: "Now therefore put away the strange gods which are among you, and incline your heart unto the Lord. . . . And the people said unto Joshua: 'The Lord our God will we serve, and unto His voice will we hearken' " (Josh. 24:23–24).

The Jewish idea of chosenness is inseparable from the belief in a divinely revealed moral code. "Thou shalt have no other gods before me" (Deut. 5:7) prohibits idolatry not merely in the worship of graven images but in the worship of one's own mind. Systems of morality that originate in the human mind (or in human minds gathered together in social science congresses) can never raise man one inch above his earthly level for the simple reason that in morals as in physics the stream cannot rise higher than its source. The coolness with which the Enlightenment, in both its gentile and Jewish forms, is treated in some of the essays in this collection, derives from the conviction that Moses Mendelssohn and other enlighteners undermined the idea of chosenness by making Judaism "the religion of reason," thereby depriving the moral law of its efficacy by reducing it to the level of secular philosophy. Delighted with the Enlightenment's promise to grant them everything as individuals but nothing as a nation, many Jews quickly forgot that it was only *as a nation* that they could be "a light of the nations" (Isa. 42:6).

The uneasy relation between Enlightenment liberalism and Jewish collective existence is explored in several of the essays in this collection, starting with the least "Jewish" and most personal of them all, that on John Stuart Mill, the greatest of nineteenth-century liberals, which I have included as a kind of preamble. The theme of antagonism between progressive ideologies and Jewish interests and beliefs is further developed in the portraits of Lionel Trilling and Isaac Bashevis Singer and in the more polemical essays on "Liberalism and Zionism" and "Jewish Anti-Semitism, Enlightenment Evenhandedness, and the Arab-Israeli Conflict."

In essays dealing with various aspects of the Holocaust, the idea of chosenness appears in another guise, shocking yet familiar. The Holocaust was the most terrible event in Jewish history and yet, paradoxically, was an event that confirmed to religiously Orthodox and even many non-

Orthodox Jews the very idea of chosenness it was intended to uproot, for it reiterated more pitilessly than any previous Jewish disaster the terrible promise of the covenant: "You only have I known of all the families of the earth; Therefore I will visit upon you all your iniquities" (Amos 3:2). In my essay on "Stealing the Holocaust" I describe the attempt to take from the Jewish people even this murderous, mocking travesty of their chosenness, and in "The Attack on Holocaust Studies" I discuss the still more desperate attempt by certain Jewish scholars to remove the Holocaust from the central place it now commands in Jewish memory.

Throughout the book, I shall be concerned with the triumphs and tragedies, the heroisms and follies, and the friends and countless enemies of the state of Israel. This state and the Zionist movement from which it sprang have always stood in a complex and ambiguous relationship to the idea of Jewish chosenness. Most (not all) of the early Zionist ideologues repudiated the idea of chosenness in favor of something they called "normality." Yosef Haim Brenner, the Zionist journalist and novelist who moved to Palestine in 1909, wished that he could "blot out from the prayer book of the Jew of our day the 'Thou hast chosen us' in every shape and form." Yet Zionism, rightly called by Hannah Arendt the only ideology in which Jews have ever taken seriously the hostility directed against them, understood that the Jews had been chosen by history, by the world if not by God, and could only continue to make their mark in the world by renewing their national existence in a reconstituted homeland. The continuing power of the Zionist ideal to inspire Jews to make great, heroic sacrifices in order to return to the homeland is described in the essays devoted to two recent arrivals in Israel—the Beta-Yisrael, the black Jews of Ethiopia, and the Russian Jew Anatoly Shcharansky.

Whether, by returning to Zion, the Jews will be able to recover the inner world and culture and sense of Jewish destiny they once had, or whether, as gloomy Israelis are wont to say, the maladies of exile have taken up residence in Zion itself, is a question raised in many of the following essays. "Strangers in the Land of Israel" examines the problems of Zionist converts to Judaism. "The Quandaries of Terrorism" analyzes the Jewish terrorist underground and the difficulties of balancing national security against the rescue of individual lives and the maintenance of legal procedures. " 'We Will Drive this Country Crazy' " weighs the importance of the election to the Knesset of Rabbi Meir Kahane in relation to the other results of the Israeli election of 1984.

In all three sections of this book, considerable attention is given to what I have called enemies of the Jewish idea. Some of these are anti-Semites opposed to Jewish collective existence or to Jewish existence in any form. Some, especially among the half-educated intelligentsia in the communications industry, are people without much overt hostility to Jews who have been infected by a body of clichés, indirectly derived from anti-Semitic ideology, about Jews and Israel. Some are Jews. This last category among the enemies of the Jewish idea includes Jews who believe that the Jewish mission to the nations is to disappear as a nation, thereby setting the world on the road to internationalism; it includes Jews whose dedication to Enlightenment ideas of infinite tolerance and relativism leaves them intellectually helpless in the face of fanatically intolerant movements whose goals include the elimination of Israel; and it includes Jews who merely serve to remind us that anti-Semitism, not being genetically caused, is not limited to gentiles.

Anti-Semitism is important as a threat to the Jewish idea, but it cannot define that idea, any more than it can define Jews. The thesis, originating with Spinoza but especially popular in modern times since its articulation by Jean-Paul Sartre and Georges Friedmann, that anti-Semitism itself creates Jewish consciousness, Jewish peoplehood, and Jewish persistence, can be convincing only to those who consider very narrow and tendentiously interpreted evidence. This thesis, as observers ranging from Arendt to Robert Alter have pointed out, fails to explain why other peoples in the ancient Near East who suffered misfortunes similar to those of the Jews interpreted those misfortunes as proof that their national god had failed them and chose to surrender their religious loyalties and assimilate into the surrounding cultures. The Jews, also conquered, banished, and persecuted, chose to cling to their religion and national identity. The real question, therefore, is not how external hostility created Jewish consciousness but, on the contrary, how the Jews, unlike other unfortunate nations, remained loyal to their god—to God—*despite* persecution. And then there is the question about the anti-Semites themselves: Why, in a world in which 997 people out of every 1,000 are not Jews, do they persist in a hostility toward this "smallest of peoples" (Deut. 7:7–8) that keeps the Jews at the center of world affairs?

Part I
PERSONALITIES

1

John Stuart Mill: A Post-Holocaust Retrospect

> *The French* philosophes *of the eighteenth century were the example we sought to imitate, and we hoped to accomplish no less results. No one of the set went to so great excesses in this boyish ambition as I did. . . .*
> —John Stuart Mill, *Autobiography*

> *The dream which Western man conceived in the eighteenth century, whose dawn he thought he saw in 1789, and which, until August 2, 1914, had grown stronger with the progress of enlightenment and the discoveries of science—this dream vanished finally for me before those trainloads of little children.*
> —François Mauriac,
> foreword to *Night*, by Elie Wiesel

Several years ago I heard a survivor of Auschwitz speak to a group of students for two hours about her experience of Nazi terror from the time that she and her family were arrested in Hungary in 1944 and deported to the death factories until the day of her liberation at the war's end. She spoke movingly but also precisely of the murder of her whole family, of the obliteration of the world she had known, and of the destruction of her innocence. "In the camps," she said, "I learned that men are born evil." In the ensuing question period, one student asked whether, during her decades in the United States, she had experienced any "insensitivity" on the subject of the Holocaust. "I have experienced," she replied, "almost nothing except insensitivity, because for thirty years nobody would listen to my story." To epitomize what she meant, she told an anecdote about a very close friend of hers, a lawyer for the American Civil Liberties Union. "During all the twenty-five years of our friendship," she said, "he had never wanted to hear about my life during the war years. It was too

7

painful—too painful, that is, for him. I remembered this recently when he was holding forth at our home on the subject of the ACLU's vigorous support of the right of the Nazi Party of America to demonstrate in Skokie. He quoted John Stuart Mill, and spoke of the sanctity of the First Amendment, and expressed his impatience with the Jewish inhabitants of Skokie because they wanted to prevent the Nazis from marching past their houses." The Jewish inhabitants of Skokie (a suburb of Chicago) are, of course, themselves mostly survivors of the death camps. This ACLU activist and self-proclaimed devotee of Mill had studiously protected himself from learning anything of the experience and inner life of the people whom he now berated for the insufficiency of their devotion to "freedom."

What struck me about the story was not primarily the inadequacy of ACLU ideology to deal with a case like that in Skokie. Many commentators have remarked on the inanity or worse of a policy that defended a Nazi march through a community of survivors of Hitler as "symbolic political speech" and exhorted the local residents to draw their blinds and hide indoors while the Nazis tramped past inciting their murder. Others have remarked on the double standard of the ACLU and on its politicization and openly asked whether "it is time for the American Civil Liberties Union to undertake a test case for a Jew who views himself directly assailed by a program calling for his murder."[1]

What was far more disturbing to me in this woman's remarks was the implied question about the relevance of John Stuart Mill—a writer to whom I had devoted a considerable amount of time, attention, and, indeed, loyalty over many years—to the Holocaust, the systematic destruction of European Jewry. In fact, this survivor's remarks immediately put me in mind of a comment made to me by one of the leading Mill scholars in the world when she visited our campus as a Phi Beta Kappa lecturer. After her seminar dealing with *On Liberty,* Mill's most influential work, we discussed privately whether *On Liberty* was a representative or an aberrant work in Mill's corpus until she noticed—from the books on my desk—that I was immersed in reading about the Holocaust. "Oh, forgive me," she said, "alongside *that* subject everything having to do with John Stuart Mill is trivial."

Yet, if we are to speak of Mill's contemporary relevance, we can hardly evade the question of the link between the liberalism that claims descent from Mill and the central event of our times. Anti-Semitism and the "final solution" of the Jewish question are not merely Jewish concerns. In her classic study of modern totalitarianism published in 1951, Hannah Arendt pointed out that "the Jewish question and antisemitism, relatively unimportant phenomena in terms of world politics, became the catalytic agent first for the rise of the Nazi movement and the establishment of the organizational structure for the Third Reich, in which every citizen had to prove that he was *not* a Jew, then for a world war of unparalleled ferocity, and finally for the emergence of the unprecedented crime of genocide in the midst of Occidental civilization." The destruction of the Jews involved not only Jewish victims and German or Austrian criminals, not only what a Christian theologian has called the mass apostasy of millions of baptized Christians, but also the destruction of European civilization itself. If most people, including most historians, refuse to face up to the enormity of this event, that, asserted Arendt, is because "there is a great temptation to explain away the intrinsically incredible by means of liberal rationalizations. In each one of us, there lurks such a liberal, wheedling us with the voice of common sense."[2]

The actual involvement of European liberalism with the development of anti-Semitic ideology is not my concern here. In the introductory chapter of *On Liberty* Mill explicitly dissociated himself from the statist tendencies of European liberalism, the whole thrust of which had, in his view, come to identify the interest and will of democratically elected rulers with the interest and will of the nation itself. "The nation did not need to be protected against its own will. There was no fear of its tyrannising over itself."[3] It would not have surprised Mill to learn that modern anti-Semitism originated in the German Liberal party just after his death in 1873, or that by the 1880s (under the leadership of Georg von Schoenerer) the Liberals had begun to organize the first closely knit university students' organizations on the basis of open anti-Semitism.

Whether Mill could have understood what was objectionable and dangerous in the attitude of liberal "friends" of the Jews like Wilhelm von Humboldt, whose ethical idealism is celebrated in chapter 3 of *On Liberty,* is a more delicate question. For Humboldt considered the disappearance of the Jews as an ethnic group a condition for taking up the cause of their "emancipation." In this attitude, he was representative of the Enlightenment and the French Revolution, which professed its readiness to grant everything to the Jews as citizens, but nothing to the Jews as Jews. These harried people were asked to choose between their individual identity as "human beings" and their collective identity as members of their own people. Now, with the wisdom of hindsight, we can recognize the insidious link between this liberal principle and Hitler's insistence that every single person in Europe had to prove that he was *not* a Jew in order to be considered "human" and receive the basic human right, the right to live.

Even in the aftermath of the Holocaust, orthodox liberalism has generally shown itself incapable of recognizing, much less comprehending, what it was that happened in the Holocaust. Liberal discourse about the

Holocaust—as Hannah Arendt implies in her reference to "liberal rational-izations"—typically treats the plan to murder every single member of the Jewish people as a crime against "humanity" and "life" itself, thus making of the destruction of the Jews a blurred and indiscriminate example of "man's inhumanity to man." This is partly a historical error, an obfusca-tion of the difference between the terrible crimes committed by the Nazi regime against Poles, Russians, Czechs, and Gypsies, on the one hand, and against Jews on the other. Yehuda Bauer has stressed "the difference between forcible, even murderous, denationalization, and wholesale, total murder of every one of the members of a community."[4] The Jews alone were singled out to die for the sole "crime" of having been born.

This historical error is not accidental, but derives directly from the metaphysical premises of modern liberalism. In her essay, "A Liberal's Auschwitz," Cynthia Ozick writes that "the liberal is a humanist—which is to say, he is an anthropomorphic idolator; his god is called *humanity*. And because he is a humanist, the liberal is also an egalitarian—which is to say, he is a leveler: like death."[5] The modern liberal who, in contemplating Auschwitz and Treblinka and Majdanek, weeps over "mankind" and "humanity" but not the Jews, is the true heir of his Enlightenment ancestors who would grant everything to the Jews as citizens or as "men" but nothing to the Jews as Jews.

For Cynthia Ozick, the liberal's preference of abstraction to specificity is, like his anthropomorphic idolatry, a sign of spiritual hollowness. Liberalism, as a child of the Enlightenment, has always faced the problem of how to make systematic negation, fashioned to destroy an oppressive reigning philosophy, into the organic basis of a living culture. A recent critic of the Enlightenment, Robert Loewenberg, shrewdly observes that "enlighteners have spent the past two centuries seeking out what they oppose, and, in quiet times, studying ways to turn the instruments of attack into philosophies in order to discover what it is they favor."[6] Indeed, the Skokie affair produced a stunning illustration of this problem in one of the few subjectively honest responses to the affair among those who took the "liberal" side in the controversy. An editorial in the *New Yorker*, a magazine famous for the sophisticated confusion of its political utterances, came to the predictable ACLU conclusion that, paradoxical though it might seem, the best way of opposing the Nazis in the long run was to support them in the short run. But then the writer, in a burst of candor, said:

> In short, freedom's strange emptiness—its maddening refusal to favor the body or the soul, to choose between tolerable and intolerable music, or even to tip the scales of the political system against unfreedom and in favor of itself—is not a flaw in freedom but, rather, its essence. Just this lack is its most precious treasure, just this emptiness its surest foundation.[7]

Such a statement summons from the vaults of death not only the specter of Weimar Germany, where liberalism did a memorable job of *not* tipping the scales against freedom's enemies, but the specter of John Stuart Mill himself. It serves to remind us just how far modern liberalism has departed from the spirit of its founder, who did indeed celebrate the freedom of the secular society, but expressed dread of, and sought means to forestall, its emptiness.

The Skokie affair sharpened the uneasiness my readings in the Holocaust had already aroused about Millite liberalism, and made me cast a retrospective glance over my experience of Mill during a period of over twenty years. I hoped that the conclusions I drew from examining my subjective experience of Mill would prove to be not only an exercise in self-awareness, but a means to self-correction. Of one thing, at least, I could be certain: the constant calling into question of the first principles of liberalism would surely recommend itself to John Stuart Mill. For he believed that however true any doctrine may be, "if it is not fully, frequently, and fearlessly discussed, it will be held as a dead dogma, not a living truth."[8]

In the first period of my interest in Mill, which extended from the late fifties, when I was in my early twenties, to the mid-sixties, he was for me primarily the Mill of chapters 2 and 3 of *On Liberty,* the apologist for nearly unbridled liberty of thought and discussion, and for individuality of character, even to the point of eccentricity. He struck me as the most articulate spokesman since Milton for the perennially beleaguered intellectual whose heretical ideas incurred the disapprobation and often punishment of a temporal authority unjustly extending its arm into the spiritual and intellectual realm. Like most "thinking" teenagers of the fifties, I held the conviction that McCarthyism was an enormous danger to the liberty and democracy of this country, a far greater danger than the communism it pretended to battle. At Columbia College, where I was an undergraduate, professorial wisdom had it that the true inheritor of the totalitarianism of Nazi Germany was not the Soviet Union or its satellites but the "Cold War ideologists" and McCarthyites of the United States. Liberalism, often so defined as to make socialism its natural accompaniment, was the reigning orthodoxy at Columbia, and I was far from immune to its influence. Perhaps out of deference to Mill's own insistence on the desirability of a devil's advocate, Columbia's standardized social-science curriculum for the first two years of college allowed for the reading of one dissenter every year—an antiliberal like Arnold or an antisocialist like F. A. Hayek—so that it was possible, however difficult, to believe that someone besides the ignorant, antiintellectual majority of the citizenry called into question the first principles of liberalism and socialism.

The liberalism inculcated at Columbia was distinctly the twentieth-century version, with its very un-Millite receptivity to governmental interference in the economy and in education. It would have come as a shock to me if, in those days, I had come upon Mill's warning that "a general State education is a mere contrivance for moulding people to be exactly like one another: . . . in proportion as it is efficient and successful, it establishes a despotism over the mind, leading by natural tendency to one over the body." Mill's *Principles of Political Economy,* one of the four classics of laissez-faire economic theory, with its insistence that "Wherever competition is not, monopoly is" and that "monopoly, in all its forms, is the taxation of the industrious for the support of indolence, if not of plunder,"9 would also, had I read it as an undergraduate, have struck me as remarkably illiberal for a founding father of what we were taught to think of as liberalism. Indeed, it did come as a shock to me, when I began to write about Mill, to discover that not only his *Examiner* essays of 1831, "The Spirit of the Age," but also his correspondence with Harriet Hardy Taylor, had been collected and edited by none other than F. A. Hayek, one of the most articulate and contentious advocates of a free-market economy as against the welfare-state ideology of modern liberalism.

Nevertheless, we who believed that the essential concern and conflict of modern America was the struggle of a minority of liberal intellectuals, doggedly devoted to free speech, against an unthinking majority, who lived only according to custom, prejudice, and conformity, were not wrong to find in Mill our most eloquent spokesman. Northrop Frye has correctly pointed out that the underlying opposition, posited as almost a permanent one in *On Liberty,* is between the majority of people living in what Burke had called a continuum of habit and prejudice, and the much smaller liberal opposition, a highly individualized group who are said to initiate all wise and noble things.10 If one shared such assumptions about the plight of democratic society in the United States, it was also natural to respond sympathetically to the schemes that Mill at various times in his career propounded for diluting the power of the numerical majority in democratic societies, for the simple reason—so it seemed to Mill—that "the great majority of voters, in most countries, and emphatically in this, would be manual labourers."11 Mill's *Considerations on Representative Government* despaired of the operation of equal and universal suffrage unless it were combined with the proportional representation of all minorities. The scheme he himself preferred, however, was plural voting, in which everyone would have a voice, but not an equal one. When I first read *Representative Government,* I not only shared the common liberal feeling of those days that "we" were outnumbered and beleaguered by "them," but I had not yet myself become a member of the academic community, not yet lived among those officially certified to be what Mill calls "superior . . . in knowledge and intelligence" to the rest of the community and therefore entitled to two or even more votes. Neither had I much attended to the startling revelations of the disproportionate role played by professors and intellectuals in the establishment and running of concentration camps, death factories, and all the other institutions of totalitarian rule. Perhaps because he never taught or even studied at a university, never entered a learned profession, and worked mostly in isolation, Mill could believe that "wherever a sufficient examination, or any serious conditions of education, are required before entering on a profession, its members could be admitted at once to a plurality of votes."[12] One does not need to be a fanatical believer in "one man, one vote, one vote, one value" to recognize that as between this proposal and the suggestion sometimes made (for example, by Eric Hoffer) that professors should not be allowed to vote at all, the latter is by far the more prudent.

When, in this first stage of my attraction to him, I read Mill along with the other Victorian thinkers, his liberalism served me as a kind of litmus paper for the detection of what was dangerous, dogmatic, and in some cases (most notably Carlyle's) violent in their thought. The seemingly self-evident truth of Mill's claim, in the introductory chapter of *On Liberty,* that advanced thinkers had, throughout history, "occupied themselves rather in inquiring what things society ought to like or dislike, than in questioning whether its likings or dislikings should be a law to individuals,"[13] was confirmed by my reading of Mill's contemporaries. Carlyle derided individual liberty at every opportunity, preferring a well-fed Gurth bound in a brass collar to a hungry one at liberty, and explosively rejecting *On Liberty* with these words: "As if it were a sin to control, or coerce into better methods, human swine in any way; . . . Ach Gott im Himmel!" Newman represented the Catholic church as believing that "unless she can, *in her own way,* do good to souls, it is no use her doing anything." Ruskin boasted that "My own teaching has been, and is that Liberty, whether in the body, soul, or political estate of men, is only another word for Death, and the final issue of Death, putrefaction." Arnold, though very far from a strident opponent of individual liberty, saw it as no more than a piece of machinery, like coal or population, and was not notably distraught when accused of violating its spirit. When his sister Jane told him he was becoming as dogmatic as Ruskin, he "told her the difference was that Ruskin was 'dogmatic and wrong.' "[14]

In varying degrees all of these thinkers were heretics within Victorian society, even so sober a figure as Arnold taking pleasure in the awareness of how frequently he had "startled" Oxford with his "heresies." But Mill pointed out, in *On Liberty,* that heretics, with whom he tended naturally to sympathize, were in respect of liberty no better than the established authorities who badgered or censored or oppressed them. For they aspired to bring the rest of mankind around to their own way of thinking rather than making common cause with heretics generally, in defense of freedom itself. Starting from the principle that all silencing of discussion and all interference with individual behavior that does not primarily concern other people are assumptions of infallibility, Mill argued in *On Liberty* (and elsewhere) for complete liberty of expressing and publishing opinions, for the liberty of "doing as we like, subject to such consequences as may follow," and for the liberty of "combination among individuals . . . for any purpose not involving harm to others."[15]

It was in the middle and late sixties that my relationship to Mill's work and personality began to undergo a change, arising from a variety of causes and not easy to define. Under the pressure of demands for racial quotas in admission and hiring, and for organized opposition to American involvement in the Vietnam War, academic communities everywhere demonstrated that their liberalism was highly selective and often blatantly political. With remarkable ease, universities yielded themselves to the seeming exigencies of politics (sometimes to merely trendy idolatries), and the academy was soon the very last place in America where one could find freedom of speech. Rather, it had become the instrument for inculcating and enforcing what Lionel Trilling once called the "orthodoxies of dissent."[16] I marveled at the way the majority of the university community continued to pay a kind of ritual obeisance to the libertarian doctrines of Mill while doing the will of explicitly antidemocratic enemies of tolerance and of Mill like Noam Chomsky and Herbert Marcuse, who spoke before large and adoring campus audiences. Chomsky insisted that "By entering the arena of argument, by accepting the presumption of legitimacy of debate on certain issues, one has already lost one's humanity."[17] Herbert Marcuse, as early as 1965, condemned tolerance on the ground that it is a veil for subjection, a rationale for maintaining the status quo; and he demanded that "regressive" elements of the population be suppressed lest they impede social liberation. In something of an understatement, Irving Howe remarked at the time that "Such theories are no mere academic indulgence or sectarian irrelevance; they have been put to significant use on the American campus as rationalizations for schemes to break up meetings of political opponents and as the justification for imaginary *coups d' etat* by . . . enraged intellectuals."[18]

Since Mill was a progressive and a social reformer as well as a lover of liberty, I returned to his work to see how he reconciled the principles of liberty with the exigencies of practical political action. He did not disappoint me. Indeed, in the essay called "Civilization," he paid particular attention to the problem of sectarian teaching in the universities of

England, and asserted that this evil would never be removed by altering the form of sectarianism taught, for "the principle itself of dogmatic religion, dogmatic morality, dogmatic philosophy, is what requires to be rooted out; not any particular manifestation of that principle."[19] It was precisely his own ability to rise above disagreements over particular issues to shared first principles that enabled him to learn so much from Coleridge and other conservative thinkers. The primacy of principle over party now seemed to me one of the strongest elements in Mill's work. The party might be one's own, might in addition be—or proclaim itself to be—the party of humanity and altruism. But if it invoked the dogmatic principle, Mill was as firm in his rebuke of it as he had been when his political and philosophical antagonists acted on their assumptions of infallibility.

Mill, I now recognized, had gone further yet in placing liberty above reformism. He had gradually come to see that it is precisely in our most generous wishes and most moral passions, rather than in the selfish ones, that the greatest dangers to liberty and the human spirit lie. His account of the origin of *On Liberty* located the chief threat to liberty and individuality not in governments but in movements of social reform. Writing from Rome in 1855 he told Harriet that "On my way here . . . I came back to an idea we have talked about, and thought that the best thing to write and publish at present would be a volume on Liberty. So many things be brought into it and nothing seems more to be needed—it is a growing need too, for opinion tends to encroach more and more on liberty, and almost all the projects of social reformers of these days are really liberticide—Comte's particularly so."[20] Mill was indebted to Comte for many things, including a theory of history, the so-called law of the three stages, the conception of altruism (Comte's word), the theoretical groundwork of sociology, and, above all, the Religion of Humanity, in which the great benefactors of the human race were to inspire the religious devotion formerly called forth by supernatural figures. But by the time he came to compose his definitive estimate of Comte and positivism (published in 1865), Mill admitted that the dogmatic principle had rooted itself in positivist sociology. Comte, believing that the time had arrived for the final truths of sociology to be formulated and applied, had acquired a powerful conviction in his own infallibility and proposed the establishment of an intellectual dictatorship, headed by himself, to enforce distinctions between indispensable and merely frivolous intellectual pursuits and to direct all the mental resources of a nation to the solution of the most pressing question of the moment.

Within *On Liberty* itself, Mill several times insisted that the spirit of liberty and the spirit of reform were not the same, and were perhaps even naturally incompatible. He saw England as a country by no means averse to change, so long as everyone changes at once:

> The spirit of improvement is not always a spirit of liberty, for it may aim at forcing improvements on an unwilling people; and the spirit of liberty, in so far as it resists such attempts, may ally itself locally and temporarily with the opponents of improvement; but the only unfailing and permanent source of improvement is liberty, since by it there are as many possible independent centres of improvement as there are individuals.

Social reformers were an impatient and therefore frequently intolerant lot. Mill knew them firsthand; he had, indeed, been nurtured by them and even trained as their secret weapon. From personal experience he knew that "spontaneity forms no part of the ideal of the majority of moral and social reformers, but is rather looked on with jealousy, as a troublesome and perhaps rebellious obstruction to the general acceptance of what these reformers, in their own judgment, think would be best for mankind."[21]

If reformers in general were, in Mill's view, prone to the temptations of liberticide, revolutionary socialists were committed to it in principle. Mill was a qualified adherent of socialism, as of the Religion of Humanity, but just as he opposed the establishment of the latter through suppression of opinion and intellectual dictatorship, so he opposed the institution of the former through insurrectionary violence. Both were violations of what he understood to be the moral code of liberalism. What made revolutionary socialism still more terrifying than its explicit doctrines was the emotional character of the revolutionaries. In his posthumously published "Chapters on Socialism" Mill maintained that the introduction of socialism by a revolutionary takeover of the whole property of the country "could have no effect but disastrous failure." But the prospect of such failure and the bloodshed it would bring would be no deterrent but rather an incentive to the revolutionaries. Spectacular and bloody failure would bring to them "only the consolation that the order of society as it now exists would be involved in the common ruin—a consolation which to some of them would probably be real, for if appearances can be trusted the animating principle of too many of the revolutionary Socialists is hate."[22]

The firmness with which Mill condemned reformers who invoked the aid of tyranny and socialists who wedded their cause to terror (and came to prefer terror to the cause), and his ability to recognize barbarism dressed in the slogans of liberation, made him seem the perfect antidote to the sleazy opportunism and selective morality of late-sixties progressivism. On a few occasions, in print and on the lecture platform, I had the temerity to prescribe this antidote to others. Rarely did it find acceptance, except among certain of the more senior members of the academic community. One of my old professors, for example, told me that when his younger colleagues accused him of having become an anachronism, by virtue of his old-fashioned liberal opposition to violence and his unresponsiveness to progressive fashion, he replied by pointing out that "young Alexander" held the very same retrograde views. More typical of the reaction to the Mill who preferred liberty to "improvement" was the professor at Boston University who said, or rather shouted, to me that nothing could be less immediate to the needs of our historical moment than "another elitist-fascist snob like Yeats and Eliot." The fist that he waved at me, I can still recall, was clenched symbolically around a copy of the *New York Review of Books,* which had by 1968 already become what Ruth Wisse calls "the *Women's Wear Daily* of the American intelligentsia."[23]

It was in reaction to an atmosphere created by intellectual desperadoes like Marcuse, Chomsky, and I. F. Stone that I began to teach Mill, as I still do, as that rarest of all creatures, the radical who is able to dissent from the conformity of dissent and to be truthful with himself about his own politics. This was the Mill who, despite having been trained by his father and Bentham to believe that in the total mobilization of virtue for the purpose of reforming the world lay the only prospect of happiness for himself and others, awakened from this "dream" in 1826 at the behest of a terrifying question: "Suppose that all your objects in life were realized; that all the changes in institutions and opinions which you are looking forward to, could be completely effected at this very instant: would this be a great joy and happiness to you?" I would ask students to imagine contemporary versions of Mill's question, to suppose that their own desiderata were realized—that Vietnam was united under a Communist regime, the Shah of Iran was overthrown, and Israel was reduced to sandy wastes—and then to ask themselves whether "this would be a great joy and happiness to you?" Few students, even in those days, could fail to appreciate the unique force of Mill's candor in allowing "an irrepressible self-consciousness distinctly [to answer] 'No!' "[24] Few could fail to respond to his discovery in literature of the means of rescue from the desert of political abstraction.

It was comforting to me to discover that Mill could be decisively set apart from his wayward disciples, and effectively invoked against the totalitarian tendencies of radicalism. Yet the quarrel with others served also to exacerbate the quarrel with oneself. Millite liberalism, after all, had once been, for most of the now militantly illiberal academics, a kind of substitute religious faith. How much, I now asked myself, could such a faith be worth if its central doctrines were hastily hidden from view at the first emergency that tested them? Was it not, after all, true that liberty in itself, being only a procedure rather than a good, could never be elevated above things of intrinsic value and made the basis of a philosophy of life and society? The rapid disintegration of academic liberalism (and liberals) under pressure from leftist bullying was provoking the more thoughtful liberal philosophers like Emil Fackenheim to ask whether contemporary events did not indicate that "secularist liberalism itself stands in secret need of Biblical inspiration for its liberalism? If bereft of this inspiration, or subjugating and thus perverting it, may secularism not become illiberal and totalitarian or even a demonic pseudo-religion?"[25] I began, in short, to return to the essentially religious critique of Millite liberalism made by Mill's Victorian contemporaries, and especially by Matthew Arnold. Only now, instead of using Mill's liberalism as a standard by which to judge Arnold's doctrine of culture, I was more inclined to use Arnold's culture as a touchstone for judging the spiritual sufficiency of Mill's liberalism.

Arnold's criticisms of Mill seemed to me especially potent because they were not entangled in peculiarly Victorian issues, but penetrated to the most enduring questions that separate liberal from idealist modes of thought. When Carlyle and Ruskin accused Mill of fostering anarchy under the cloak of liberty, they were attacking his laissez-faire political economy as much as his doctrines of free speech (for which Ruskin even expressed a grudging admiration before he wrote *Unto this Last*). It was Arnold alone who recognized that the real, the permanent danger implicit in Mill's world view was that of spiritual anarchy, of what Arnold also called atheism. Except when he took offense at Mill's references to the Church of England as nothing more than "the dominant sect" in English religion, Arnold chose to challenge Mill on the enduring questions of whether there is such a thing as a truth that can be known and made to prevail, and whether man or God is ultimately the measure of all things.

In Arnold's view Mill was wholly blind to one indispensable dimension of human experience—religion. "How short," he facetiously asked Clough in 1848, "could Mill write Job?" In other words, could a man whose entire education and philosophy were predicated on the desirability of realizing "the greatest happiness of the greatest number" appreciate the wisdom that was inseparable from suffering? Could this advocate of individual freedom and untrammeled self-development appreciate the ambiguous self-assertion of the Job who says, "Behold, he will slay me; I have no hope; but I will defend my (godly) ways before Him" (13:15). The implication of Arnold's question was that a utilitarian liberal devoid of artistic feeling as well as religious sensibility could make nothing of Job except a logical outline. Arnold was also quick to pounce upon what seemed to him the unconscious acknowledgment, in Mill's *Autobiography,* of the power of religion: "Mr. Mill tells us . . . that his father 'looked upon religion as the greatest enemy of morality.' Eighteen pages farther on, where he is descanting on the lamentable absence, in English society, of any high and noble standards of conduct, he adds that this absence prevailed everywhere *'except among a few of the stricter religionists.'* "[26]

Arnold at first responded to *On Liberty* with cautious approval, recommending it to his sister as "worth reading attentively, being one of the few books that inculcate tolerance in an unalarming and inoffensive way." But by 1863 Arnold felt called on to criticize *On Liberty* because it attacked the negativism of Christian morality and recommended a philosophical, which is to say a man-made, morality, over a religious, or revealed, one. This, in Arnold's view, showed a misunderstanding of the emotional springs of action, a failure to recognize that a purely rational morality can appeal only to the few, not to the many—and is not likely to appeal to anyone on a death bed.[27]

In *Culture and Anarchy,* Arnold condemned Mill as a "rabbi," and probably took the title of his second chapter, "Doing as One Likes," from Mill's argument in *On Liberty* for "doing as we like, subject to such consequences as may follow." Although rarely mentioned by name, Mill appeared to be a target throughout Arnold's work. Mill's contention that past thinkers had grossly erred in inquiring what things society should like or dislike instead of questioning whether those likes and dislikes should be a law to individuals was countered by Arnold's insistence that "culture indefatigably tries, not to make what each raw person may like, the rule by which he fashions himself; but to draw ever nearer to a sense of what is indeed beautiful, graceful, and becoming, and to get the raw person to like that." What Arnold deplored as British atheism was illustrated by a quotation from the *Times* that came almost verbatim from Mill's *On Liberty:* " 'It is of no use,' says the *Times,* 'for us to attempt to force upon our neighbours our several likings and dislikings.' " All the social and political manifestations of anarchy denounced by Arnold derived from the spiritual anarchy of Millite liberalism, "a kind of philosophical theory . . . widely spread among us to the effect that there is no such thing at all as a best self and a right reason having claim to paramount authority."[28] Mill ought not to have been surprised—he was—at "Matthew Arnold enumerating me among the enemies of culture."[29] According to Arnold's definition, culture did not consist only of knowledge, even prodigious knowledge like Mill's, but of the perfection of reason—"right reason"—under the aegis of authority.

Yet despite these severe criticisms of Mill, Arnold recognized that he was something more than a garden-variety liberal, and took pains to set him apart from his disciples, from those "in whom there appears scarcely anything that is truly sound or Hellenic at all." Arnold's concessions to Mill did have something of the condescending air of Ruskin's well-known praise of Mill for "inadvertently disclaiming the principles which he states, and tacitly introducing the moral considerations with which he declares his science has no connection." Yet it was clear that they were more than a

rhetorical gesture designed to show Arnold's flexibility and concessive-
ness. They represented a genuine respect of the kind that Mill could evoke
from even his most resolute enemies. It was because, for all his shortcomings, Mill had attained to the perception of certain truths about human
nature that he was, "instead of being, like the school from which he
proceeds, doomed to sterility,—a writer of distinguished mark and influence, a writer deserving all attention and respect." Mill was neither the
great spirit nor the great writer that his admirers supposed, yet "was a
singularly acute, ardent, and interesting man, . . . capable of following
lights that led him away from the regular doctrine of philosophical radicalism."[30]

Everything in my mature experience now seemed to confirm that the
school of Enlightenment radicals—"philosophical radicals," as they once
were called—was "doomed to sterility." In the twentieth century the
liberalism of Mill's followers had either taken a leftward turn into statism,
or had ended in the empty self-contradiction of the "honest doubters," like
the well-known author of the following:

> All the previous ages . . . had something they could take for granted. . . . We can
> be sure of nothing; our civilization is threatened, even the simplest things we
> live by. . . . In our present confusion our only hope is to be scrupulously honest
> with ourselves, so honest as to doubt our own minds and the conclusions they
> arrive at. Most of us have ceased to believe, except provisionally, in truths, and
> we feel that what is important is not so much truth as the way our minds move
> toward truths.[31]

That is to say, there are no truths, but it is terribly important to search for
them in the most scrupulous way.

Yet I remained convinced that Mill had indeed, as Arnold said, followed
lights that kept him from the dark corridors in which other philosophical
radicals lost themselves. One of these lights had revealed to Mill, decades
before Arnold's critique, that the philosophy of the Enlightenment was
destructive of the essence of culture. In his essays on Bentham and
Coleridge, essays that F. R. Leavis long ago singled out as more indispensable to knowledge of Victorian literature than *Sartor Resartus* or *Unto
this Last*,[32] Mill preceded Arnold in making "the philosophy of human
culture" the vital center of conservative, religious, and idealistic philosophy, just as it was the great deficiency in infidel Enlightenment radicalism.
Not even Arnold (who frequently expressed admiration for Voltaire) ever
spoke as harshly of the spiritual emptiness of Enlightenment monism,
naturalism, and relativism as did the Mill of 1840 who wrote of the
exponents of "the French philosophy":

To tear away was . . . all that these philosophers, for the most part, aimed at: they had no conception that anything else was needful. At their millennium, superstition, priestcraft, error and prejudice of every kind, were to be annihilated; some of them gradually added that despotism and hereditary privileges must share the same fate; and, this accomplished, they never for a moment suspected that all the virtues and graces of humanity could fail to flourish, or that when the noxious weeds were once rooted out, the soil would stand in any need of tillage.[33]

The conservatives, on the other hand, understood that every living culture, every society committed to continuance, is held together by something more than "freedom," something that does not come into existence by itself, but through human cultivation. Coleridge and the philosophers of his school had grasped the root meaning of the word and the idea of *culture*. Mill, at least in 1840, was entirely in sympathy with the Coleridge who, when his liberal friend Thelwall expressed the view that it was "very unfair to influence a child's mind by inculcating any opinions before it should have come to years of discretion, and be able to choose for itself," at once led Thelwall into his garden:

I . . . told him it was my botanical garden. "How so?" said he, "it is covered with weeds." "Oh," I replied, "*that* is only because it has not yet come to its age of discretion and choice. The weeds, you see, have taken the liberty to grow, and I thought it unfair in me to prejudice the soil towards roses and strawberries."[34]

The conservatives, with their respect for history and for the collective experience of the human race, grasped what Mill called the three requisites of a civil society, one in which men obeyed as citizens, not as slaves. The first was a system of education in which "one main and incessant ingredient was *restraining discipline*." The second requisite of permanent political society as defined by the conservatives and approved by Mill, was "the feeling of allegiance, or loyalty," the establishment in the very constitution of the state of "*something* which is settled, something permanent, and not to be called in question." The third requisite was "a strong and active principle of cohesion among the members of the same community or state."[35]

In reweaving the fabric of Mill's thought to make it proof against the onslaught of Arnold's criticism, I found that the essays on Bentham and Coleridge were the strongest and most durable elements. They represented no mere compromise between the conservative idealism of Coleridge and the radical utilitarianism of Bentham, but a creative union of vital forces at war with each other, then and now. They were a pure exercise of mind, operating free of attachment to sect and party, a perfect realization of what Arnold was later to call "disinterestedness." In them resonated the ideal that Mill had, according to his autobiography, been striving to achieve since the early 1830s—the union of the best qualities of the critical with the best qualities of the organic periods of history for the structure of the future society of Europe. Far from celebrating what the *New Yorker* rhapsodically calls the "strange emptiness" of freedom, Mill looked beyond the unnatural "transitional" era in which he lived to a society that would incorporate not only "unchecked liberty of thought, unbounded freedom of individual actions in all modes not hurtful to others; but also, convictions as to what is right and wrong, useful and pernicious, deeply engraven on the feelings by early education and general unanimity of sentiment. . . ."[36]

This perfect balance between freedom and conviction posited in the Bentham-Coleridge essays was an idea that eluded Mill nearly as often as it did the world for which he wrote. The excessive stress on the blessings of dissent and uncertainty in *On Liberty,* and the arrant dogmatism and intolerance of Mill's championship of women's rights, served in opposite ways as reminders that Mill did not always achieve the perfection of his own ideal. But I was now convinced that he came closest to realizing the balance he recommended for society as a whole when, in these dazzling essays of 1838 and 1840, he undertook to show that the great radical and the great conservative of his time, "these two sorts of men, who seem to be, and believe themselves to be, enemies are in reality allies. The powers they wield are opposite poles of one great force of progression."[37]

Mill's thought model was almost invariably a debate, either between individuals or between historical periods. Typically, he linked a theory of controversy and of the way to extract the whole truth from "the noisy conflict of half-truths" with a theory of history. Thus Bentham and Coleridge were made the spokesmen of historical epochs as well as of philosophical schools. History was a perpetual oscillation between conflicting modes of thought, a process in which progress consisted in approaching closer to the center of equilibrium. This newly structured apologia for Mill satisfied me until I came to study the Holocaust. It was only then that I began to have doubts about what Mill called the "historical" method of seeking truth, and about the source of that spiritual authority he invoked as a necessary complement to freedom of expression.

Prior to the twentieth century, the nearest parallel to the Holocaust, both in actuality and in Mill's perception of history, was the Reign of Terror of the French Revolution. Here, for a brief time and on a small scale, a sentence of death was pronounced and executed upon a class of people for no other "crime" than that of having been born into a certain class, the aristocracy. (It may be noted parenthetically that the aristocracy shared certain strongly held life principles with the Jews: both were inter-European, even international in their loyalties; for both, national allegiances often took second place to allegiance to a family scattered over Europe; and both "shared a conception that the present is nothing more than an insignificant link in the chain of past and future generations."[38]) I had always had a vague sense that, despite Mill's insistence that the French Revolution was a watershed event in history, its place in his historiography and his political ethos was something of a mystery, and perhaps a mystery with a meaning. I therefore decided to reexamine all his historical writing, using the French Revolution as a kind of litmus paper for detecting the moral underpinning of Mill's historiography.

According to the young Mill's historical theory, the outbreak of the French Revolution was the first spectacular manifestation of Europe's entry into an age of transition. Reading its history at age seventeen, he "learnt with astonishment, that the principles of democracy . . . had borne all before them in France . . . and had been the creed of the nation." For the next decade Mill immersed himself intellectually and emotionally in the revolution. Sometimes he identified himself with the early revolutionists and dreamed of becoming "a Girondist in an English Convention"; at other times, "the French *philosophes* of the eighteenth century" were the example he and his friends sought to imitate.[39] By 1832 the largest segment of his private library consisted of materials on the revolution, and everyone reported that it was his favorite subject of conversation. Henry Crabb Robinson stated that Mill "is deeply read in French politics, and bating his . . . unmeaning praise of Robespierre . . . and . . . the respect he avowed for the virtues of Mirabeau, he spoke judiciously enough about French matters. . . ."[40]

In 1828 Mill made the French Revolution the subject of his final and most ambitious article for the original *Westminster,* a detailed rebuttal of that part of Scott's *Life of Napoleon* that gave a history of the revolution. This elaborate defense of the early revolutionists against Scott's Tory calumnies was for Mill both "a labour of love" and the natural reaction of one who intended writing the history of the revolution against the premature effort of a biased and ignorant interloper. Mill at this time believed that he alone of all living Englishmen could do justice to the subject, a considerable claim in view of the fact that early in this essay he wrote that no one short of a universal genius could adequately convey so unprecedented and unimaginable an event.[41]

One might suppose that in April 1828 the Mill who had recently recovered from his mental crisis by an exercise of literary imagination would seek in imaginative literature an instrument for fathoming a historically unique event, incredible not only to those who did not witness it but often even to those who, having acted or witnessed, tried to record their experiences "when the genuine impression of the present events" had faded and they had returned to the realm of normal experience. Yet Mill asserts that Scott's novelistic gifts are among his prime disqualifications for writing the history of the revolution. Mill assumes a disjunction between the objective chronology of naked facts and a novelistic presentation of them, which he derides as the "dressing up" of reality according to the writer's idea. A still more serious shortcoming of the novelistic approach to the events of the French Revolution is that of moral judgment. Scott's history presents the revolutionists as free moral agents, fully responsible for their misdeeds. Ignoring the contingent nature of human actions, Scott "blames men who did the best they could, for not doing better; treats men who had only a choice of inconveniences, as if they were the masters of events."[42]

Mill does not, by deploring Scott's propensity for moral judgment, seek to exonerate the Terrorists. He refers to "the opprobrium which is justly due to the terrorists alone," and to the absolute separation between "all the more ardent and enthusiastic partisans of the Revolution" and "the party called the Terrorists." Yet it is also true that he tries to keep the Terror and the moral ambiguities linked with it decently out of view, that he flirts with the liberal idea that everyone is guilty of a crime except the person who happens to commit it, and that he wants to see the whole revolution as a "great experiment" in the laboratories of history and human nature.[43]

Why, then, having invested tremendous amounts of time and energy in a study of the revolution, and having convinced himself that the cause of human improvement itself hinged on vindication of the revolutionary experiment and that England, too, would feel the revolutionary "hurricane," did Mill abandon the project of writing the history of the revolution and consign it, along with many of his books on the subject, to Carlyle? His own explanation was that he found it impossible to declare to English readers that Christianity was historically, perhaps even biologically, obsolete and unsuited to the species in its present state of development. "One could not, *now,* say this openly in England, and be read at least by the many . . . *A propos* I have been reading the New Testament; properly I can never be said to have *read* it before." That Mill should simultaneously own up to the secret vice of gospel-reading and complain of Christian prejudice against truth-telling suggests that it was his own rather than the public's doubts about the adequacy of a purely historical judgment of historical events that kept him from writing the history. If Christianity had indeed been, in Mill's words of 1833, "the greatest and best thing which has existed on this globe,"[44] was not one forced to question the view that the

French Revolution was a great milestone in an infinitely progressing historical sequence? Or was progress distinct from improvement?

These questions pressed upon Mill's mind in 1833. History, he now argued, had both a scientific and a moral aspect. As a scientific enterprise, it "exhibits the general laws of the moral universe . . . and enables us to trace the connexion between great effects and their causes"; as a moral enterprise, it displays "the characters and lives of human beings, and calls upon us, according to their deservings or to their fortunes, for our sympathy, our admiration, or our censure." Yet the French Revolution challenged the historian's ability to reconcile his scientific and moral functions. In an angry review of Alison's *History of Europe* Mill calls the revolution "one turbulent passage in a progressive revolution embracing the whole human race" and derides the historian exclusively concerned with "the degree of praise or blame due to the few individuals who . . . happened to be personally implicated in that strife of the elements." The figure implies that the revolution was as irresistible as—what he had already called it in 1831—a "hurricane," and as little liable to moral judgment. Admitting that the revolution immersed itself in "Immediate Evil," Mill seeks refuge in the idea that it served the cause of improvement toward which history seems to be aiming. As for the moral questions raised by the Terror, Mill pleads that "We have not now time or space to discuss the quantum of the guilt which attaches . . . to the . . . revolutionary governments, for the crimes of the revolution." Yet he feels constrained to confess that "Much was done which could not have been done except by bad men." A few months earlier he had so far forgotten his devotion to the scientific aspect of history as to complain of French historians of the revolution that they had arrived at "the annihilation of all moral distinctions except *success* and *not success*."[45]

The strife between the scientific and moral principles in Mill's speculations on revolution was not primarily a conflict between the "radical" and the "conservative" Mill. That an amoral progressivism could coexist with Mill's newly discovered reverence for conservatism is indicated in the language and sentiments of the following 1831 letter to Sterling:

> If there were but a few dozens of persons safe (whom you & I could select) to be missionaries of the great truths in which alone there is any well-being for mankind individually or collectively, I should not care though a revolution were to exterminate every person in Great Britain & Ireland who has £500 a year. Many very amiable persons would perish, but what is the world the better for such amiable persons. But among the missionaries whom I would reserve, a large proportion would consist of speculative Tories. . . .[46]

The real argument is between two differing views of the source of authority for these "great truths." The "scientific" Mill tends toward the historicist view that history is the sole source and arbiter of truth and values; the Mill leavened by suffering and by literature seeks (without ever finding) a more absolute and eternal basis of intellectual and spiritual authority.

The years immediately following the abandonment of the French Revolution project were for Mill years of intense speculation on the nature of the historical enterprise. During the late 1830s and 1840s he began to substitute perpetual antagonism for perpetual movement as his metaphor for history. From Coleridge, especially, he learned that the well-being of society and politics demanded a balanced antagonism between radical and conservative sympathies, the interests of progression and permanence, with each party to this fruitful conflict tempering its opposite. The Enlightenment thinkers and their revolutionary disciples had forgotten that without contraries there is no progression. Their intolerance of the conservative party to the historical dialogue found its natural expression in the enormities of Robespierre and Saint-Just. These organizers of terror persuaded themselves (as did the originators of modern totalitarianism) that they murdered not as criminals but as executors of death sentences passed by history itself on unprogressive classes and ideas. What other conviction, Mill asked in 1838, "could lead any man to believe that his individual judgment respecting the public good is a warrant to him for exterminating all who are suspected of forming any other judgment, and for setting up a machine to cut off heads, sixty or seventy every day, till some unknown futurity be accomplished, some Utopia realized."[47] Mill had come to the recognition that utopianism is not love but hatred of mankind.

Hannah Arendt, in her magisterial study of the subject of totalitarianism, has located its origins in "the tremendous intellectual change which took place in the middle of the last century . . . in the refusal to view or accept anything 'as it is' and in the consistent interpretation of everything as being only a stage of some further development." She shows how totalitarian movements built themselves on the idea of a "law of nature" that eliminated everything unfit to live or a "law of history" that eliminated unprogressive classes in the "class struggle." Those who impede the movement of history or nature are the objective enemies of the natural or historical process that has passed judgment over inferior races, individuals "unfit to live," dying classes, and decadent peoples. According to totalitarian ideology, as perfected by Hitler and Stalin, the practitioners of terror are subjectively innocent because "they do not really murder but execute a death sentence pronounced by some higher tribunal. . . . Terror is lawfulness, if law is the law of the movement of some suprahuman force, Nature or History."[48]

I confess that, in this rereading of Mill, I very much wanted to find conclusive evidence that he eventually rejected historicist notions of inevitable forces that override human will and render moral judgment pointless. But I found that alongside the exhortations to the will that flow from his belief that in this world we make our own good, or our own evil, were invocations of the principle of historical law and inevitability. In the 1840s Mill continued to equate historical with natural causes, though he was now more likely to speak of raging rivers, which man could harness to his use, than of hurricanes, which he could not.

What kept Mill—fortunately, in my view—from being a consistent historicist was his experience of literature, whose proper role in historiography had troubled him from the time of his attack on Walter Scott. After being "cured" of his spiritual illness by Wordsworth, Mill tended to associate literary experience with the joy and wisdom that derive from stationariness. From the poets and novelists one learned little or nothing of the law of historical progress, but one could gain moral and psychological knowledge of what Mill in the *Autobiography* calls "the perennial sources of happiness." Since Mill's historical theory insisted that the laws of historical evolution required validation by correspondence with the laws of human nature to become scientific, literature posed the question of whether human nature matches the (supposedly) progressive character of European history. Mill's progressive theory, both of history and of the human intellect, was contradicted by his deep-seated belief in the stationary character of human nature. What kept laws of history from becoming laws of nature was not a flaw in Victorian historiography—as the youthful Mill had supposed—but a flaw in human nature itself. This grim discovery invaded Mill's writings in the 1850s. In 1852 he praised the Greeks because they "decided for an indefinite period the question, whether the human race was to be stationary or progressive," but "that the former condition is far more congenial to ordinary human nature . . . experience unfortunately places beyond doubt. . . ." *On Liberty* assumed that truth often fails to survive persecution, that history makes appalling "mistakes" and is often the record of wrong triumphant. In 1854 Mill confided to his diary: "It seems to me that there is no progress, and no reason to expect progress, in talents or strength of mind. . . . But there is great progress . . . in feelings and opinions. If it is asked whether there is progress in intellect the answer will be found in the two preceding statements taken together."[49]

These unresolved antinomies indicate that Mill's retreat from the organic and necessitarian view of history was a partial yet substantial one. That he had hit upon one of the most dangerous elements in nineteenth-century thought, one whose full destructiveness would become apparent only in our own time, is evident in his growing reluctance to accept "natural" metaphors for historical action. In the essay "Nature," written between 1850 and 1854, Mill returns briefly to the Reign of Terror and compares it, as he had done twenty years earlier, to "a hurricane and a pestilence." But the point of the comparison has entirely changed. Previously, Mill had used the analogy to explain the Terror as the agent of a historical progression as inevitable as a natural force. Now his aim is to reveal the moral enormity of political murderers who masquerade as the innocent executors of a law of nature: "Pope's 'Shall gravitation cease when you go by?' may be a just rebuke to any one who should be so silly as to expect common human morality from nature. But if the question were between two men, instead of between a man and a natural phenomenon, that triumphant apostrophe would be thought a rare piece of impudence. A man who should persist in hurling stones or firing cannon when another man 'goes by,' and having killed him should urge a similar plea in exculpation, would very deservedly be found guilty of murder."[50]

I believe that now, in the aftermath of the Holocaust, and for some time to come, Mill's exploration of the relation between history and terror, rather than his advocacy of liberty, individuality, sex reform and electoral reform, should compel the attention of scholars and students. Mill never wholly freed himself from the belief that the law of historical progression is of necessity a law of improvement. But to the extent that he incorporated into his thought an ability, which he had gained from the poets, to imagine the world as always in its beginning, the influence of historicism over his mind waned. His retreat from historicism arose from a recognition that human beings, truly to be free, had to be liberated from the service of history and nature as well as from the service of the state. He saw that a principle of progression that assigned to whole groups of human beings the role of raw material for the development of a more perfect mankind was a crime against the human status itself.

Notes

1. Marie Syrkin, "Sadat, Skokie & Cosmos 954," *Midstream,* 24 (March 1978): 66.
2. Hannah Arendt, *The Origins of Totalitarianism,* 3 vols. (New York: Harcourt, Brace, and World, 1951), 1: x; 3: 137–38.
3. J. S. Mill, *On Liberty,* in *Autobiography and Other Writings,* ed. Jack Stillinger, Riverside ed. (Boston: Houghton Mifflin, 1969), p. 353.
4. Yehuda Bauer, *The Holocaust in Historical Perspective* (Seattle: University of Washington Press, 1978), p. 35.
5. Cynthia Ozick, "A Liberal's Auschwitz," in *The Pushcart Prize: Best of the Small Presses,* ed. Bill Henderson (Yonkers, New York: Pushcart Press, 1975), p. 125.
6. Robert J. Loewenberg, "The Theft of Liberalism," *Midstream,* 28 (May 1977): 24.
7. *New Yorker,* 21 August 1978, p. 17.

8. Mill, *On Liberty,* in *Autobiography and Other Writings,* p. 383.
9. Ibid., p. 453; J. S. Mill, *Principles of Political Economy,* ed. J. M. Robson (Toronto: University of Toronto Press, 1965), 2: 794.
10. Northrop Frye, "The Problem of Spiritual Authority in the Nineteenth Century," in Richard Levine, ed., *Backgrounds to Victorian Literature* (San Francisco: Chandler, 1967), pp. 129–30.
11. J. S. Mill, *Considerations on Representative Government,* Everyman ed. (London: J. M. Dent, 1910), p. 283.
12. Ibid., p. 285.
13. Mill, *On Liberty,* in *Autobiography and Other Writings,* p. 357.
14. Alexander Carlyle, ed., *New Letters of Thomas Carlyle,* 2 vols. (London, 1904), 2: 196; John Henry Newman, *Lectures on Difficulties of Anglicans,* Lecture 8, 1850; John Ruskin, *Works of John Ruskin,* ed. E. T. Cook and A. Wedderburn, 39 vols. (London, 1903–12), 18: 402; Matthew Arnold, *Letters of Matthew Arnold,* ed. G. W. E. Russell, 2 vols. (New York: Macmillan, 1900), 1: 233.
15. Mill, *On Liberty,* in *Autobiography and Other Writings,* p. 362.
16. Lionel Trilling, *The Liberal Imagination* (New York: Viking Press, 1950), p. 7.
17. Noam Chomsky, *American Power and the New Mandarins* (New York: Pantheon Books, 1968), p. 17. In this connection, it is worth noting that Chomsky became in 1980–81 one of the most vigorous defenders of Robert Faurisson's inalienable right to propagate, from a university chair, the Nazi lie that the Holocaust is a Zionist invention. He also wrote a preface to the English edition of the book in which this French professor sets forth his argument. Apparently, since Chomsky takes an "agnostic" view of the question of whether the Jews of Europe really were murdered, he does not fear that his humanity is endangered by neo-Nazism. Either he is a late convert to Millite liberalism, or his zeal for free speech swells in proportion to the anti-Zionism of the speaker.
18. Irving Howe, "The New York Intellectuals," *Commentary,* 46 (October 1968): 45.
19. J. S. Mill, "Civilization," in *Dissertations and Discussions,* 2 vols. (London, 1859), 1: 201.
20. F. A. Hayek, *John Stuart Mill and Harriet Taylor* (Chicago: University of Chicago Press, 1951), p. 216.
21. Mill, *On Liberty,* in *Autobiography and Other Writings,* pp. 417, 404.
22. J. S. Mill, "Chapters on Socialism," *Essays on Economics and Society* (Toronto: University of Toronto Press, 1967), p. 749.
23. Ruth Wisse, "The Anxious American Jew," *Commentary,* 66 (September 1978): 50.
24. J. S. Mill, *Autobiography,* in *Autobiography and Other Writings,* p. 81.
25. Emil Fackenheim, "On the Self-Exposure of Faith to the Modern-Secular World," *Daedalus,* 96 (Winter 1967): 199.
26. Matthew Arnold, *Letters of Matthew Arnold to A. H. Clough,* ed. H. F. Lowry (London and New York: Oxford University Press, 1932), p. 75; Matthew Arnold, *A French Eton* (London: Macmillan, 1904), p. 122.
27. Arnold, *Letters of Matthew Arnold,* 1: 111; Matthew Arnold, *Lectures and Essays in Criticism,* ed. R. H. Super (Ann Arbor: University of Michigan Press, 1962), pp. 133–34.
28. Matthew Arnold, *Culture and Anarchy,* ed. J. Dover Wilson (Cambridge, 1960), pp. 50, 120.

29. J. S. Mill, *Later Letters of John Stuart Mill,* ed. F. E. Mineka and D. N. Lindley, 4 vols. (Toronto and London: University of Toronto Press, 1972), 3: 1324.
30. Matthew Arnold, *Dissent and Dogma,* ed. R. H. Super (Ann Arbor: University of Michigan Press, 1968), p. 126; Arnold, *Lectures and Essays in Criticism,* p. 136; Arnold, *A French Eton,* p. 100.
31. Bonamy Dobree, *Modern Prose Style* (Oxford: Clarendon, 1934), p. 220.
32. F. R. Leavis, Introduction to *Mill on Bentham and Coleridge* (London: Chatto & Windus, 1959), p. 1.
33. J. S. Mill, "Coleridge," in *Autobiography and Other Writings,* pp. 273–74.
34. Samuel Taylor Coleridge, *Table Talk,* in *Inquiring Spirit: A Coleridge Reader,* ed. K. Coburn (New York: Minerva Press, 1968), p. 75.
35. Mill, "Coleridge," in *Autobiography and Other Writings,* pp. 275–77.
36. Mill, *Autobiography,* in *Autobiography and Other Writings,* p. 100.
37. Mill, "Coleridge," in *Autobiography and Other Writings,* p. 289.
38. Arendt, *The Origins of Totalitarianism,* 1: 31.
39. Mill, *Autobiography,* in *Autobiography and Other Writings,* pp. 40, 66.
40. Henry Crabb Robinson, *The Diary of Henry Crabb Robinson: An Abridgment,* ed. D. Hudson (London, Oxford University Press, 1967), p. 114.
41. Mill, *Autobiography,* in *Autobiography and Other Writings,* p. 79; J. S. Mill, "Scott's *Life of Napoleon,*" *Westminster Review,* 9 (April 1828): 256.
42. Mill, "Scott's *Life of Napoleon,*" pp. 275, 258, 276.
43. Ibid., pp. 275, 296, 312n., 262–63.
44. J. S. Mill, *Earlier Letters of John Stuart Mill,* ed. F. E. Mineka, 2 vols. (Toronto and London: University of Toronto Press, 1963), 1: 182.
45. J. S. Mill, "Alison's History of the French Revolution," *Monthly Repository,* 7 (August 1833): 513, 515–16; Mill, *Earlier Letters,* 1: 139.
46. Mill, *Earlier Letters,* 1: 84.
47. J. S. Mill, "Poems and Romances of Alfred de Vigny," *London and Westminster Review,* 29 (April 1838): 39.
48. Arendt, *The Origins of Totalitarianism,* 3: 162–63.
49. Mill, *Autobiography,* in *Autobiography and Other Writings,* p. 89; "Grote's History of Greece," *Edinburgh Review,* 98 (October 1853): 428; *Letters of John Stuart Mill,* ed. H.S.R. Elliot, 2 vols. (London: Longmans, Green and Co., 1910), 2: 359.
50. J. S. Mill, *Essays on Ethics, Religion and Society,* ed. J. M. Robson (Toronto and London: University of Toronto Press, 1969), pp. 384–85.

2

Lionel Trilling

It is clear to me that my existence as a Jew is one of the shaping conditions of my temperament, and therefore I suppose it must have its effect on my intellect.

—Lionel Trilling (1944)[1]

In his critical study of Matthew Arnold, published in 1939, Lionel Trilling discussed a series of incidents in Dr. Thomas Arnold's life rarely mentioned by his admirers although thoroughly documented in Arthur Stanley's 1844 edition of Arnold's letters. These were incidents in which the famed historian of Rome, headmaster of Rugby, and leader of the Liberal or Broad Church movement within the Church of England, had given vent to his hostility against Jews, at least against Jews in England. Trilling, in the course of elucidating Dr. Arnold's theory of the state, stressed Arnold's opposition, both in principle and emotion, to the presence of Jews in England. Jews, in Arnold's view, had no right to full citizenship or to the privileges attendant on it, such as entry to the universities. England was the land of Englishmen, not of Jews, who as "lodgers" had claims to nothing more than an honorary citizenship. Arnold, in accordance with the Broad Church policy of blurring doctrinal definition and opening the Anglican communion to as many Christians as possible, had given his support to the nonsectarian London University, which, because it was ready to admit Dissenters and did not formally teach theology, was the epitome of a bad university for High Church or Roman Catholic writers on education like Newman. But even Thomas Arnold's "broadness" had its limits. " 'Religion,' in the king's mouth," Arnold insisted, "can mean only Christianity." Trilling points out how "the notion of a Jew as one of the Governors of Christ's Hospital infuriated him and he dreaded the possibility of examining a Jew in history at the University of London. . . ." To a friend, Arnold admitted that "every single member of the Senate except myself was convinced of the necessity . . . of giving the

31

Jews Degrees." Eventually, as Trilling surely knew (though he does not
mention it), Dr. Arnold resigned (in November 1838) from his position on
the university's board of examiners rather than countenance the admission
of Jews. He could no longer be part of a scheme that would mark "the first
time that education in England was avowedly unchristianized for the sake
of accommodating Jews."[2]

The incident must have had a special immediacy for Trilling. The son of
a mother who had been born and educated in the East End of London,
Trilling had discovered in 1936 that even in the American academic world
Jews had not yet been granted full and unequivocal citizenship. In that
year, four years after he had been appointed an instructor of English at
Columbia College, Trilling was dropped by the department because "as a
Freudian, a Marxist and a Jew" he was not, and could not be, "happy"
there. (The irony of commiserating with a Victorian scholar, a student of
Carlyle, over his not being "happy" in his destined work does not seem to
have dawned on the English department spokesman.) Diana Trilling, in her
essay on "Lionel Trilling: A Jew at Columbia," remarks that the documen-
tation produced by the department to justify its decision—that is, *their*
"unhappiness" with Trilling—"revealed that Jews were people who made
the Columbia faculty uncomfortable, Freudians were people who made the
Columbia faculty uncomfortable, Marxists were people who made the
Columbia faculty uncomfortable. It is in this sense, circumscribed but
charged enough, that in dismissing Lionel, Columbia can be accused of
anti-Semitism. . . ."[3]

The story, as everybody now knows, ended "happily." Trilling's protest
of the department's decision resulted in his retention until the time he
completed his dissertation, the magisterial book on Matthew Arnold that
so impressed Nicholas Murray Butler, Columbia's president, that he
personally appointed Trilling an assistant professor of English, the first Jew
to become a member of that department's faculty. Neither did Butler fail to
draw the apparent moral of the story for the benefit of the chairman of the
English department by remarking, in his presence, that at Columbia,
unlike the University of Berlin (which had recently refused to receive a
visiting Jewish professor from Columbia), "we recognize merit, not
race."[4]

Many such stories have by now been told of young Jews who in the
1920s, 1930s, and even 1940s were discouraged from entering graduate
English studies or excluded from employment after they had completed
them. Irving Howe has observed that for American Jews one of the most
"treacherous" paths to professional advancement was the teaching of
English literature. "Jews, it was often suggested, could not register the
finer shadings of the Anglo-Saxon spirit as it shone through the poetry of

Chaucer, Shakespeare, and Milton."[5] One of the most distinguished Milton scholars of our day was told, when he asked the senior Renaissance scholar of a famous New England university to supervise his dissertation, that a Jew could not write a dissertation on this preeminently Christian poet. The man who would later become the biographer of Jonathan Swift was effectively discouraged from embarking on graduate study in English when a leading figure in eighteenth-century studies persuaded him that it was unrealistic to expect that a Jew could receive a university appointment in English.

All of these prohibitors and discouragers of Jewish entry into the academic world of English history and literature, from Dr. Arnold through the 1940s, must strike us today as little better than ogres or Hesperidean dragons preserving what Tennyson called "the treasure/of the wisdom of the west" from the barbarous intruder. To Trilling and his contemporaries, they must have seemed far worse, for these young men could not readily differentiate between their own exclusion on social or cultural grounds and the Nazi policy of excluding Jews on racial grounds (and then moving from exclusion to isolation, expropriation, deportation, and murder). And yet, though we can hardly approve the actions of those who sought to exclude Jews from full rights of academic citizenship in the humanities, we must acknowledge that their prejudice rested on a grasp, at least a partial grasp, of a truth that the Jews tended to miss altogether.

"If you have gone through college as an English or history major," Cynthia Ozick has written, "it will one day strike you that what you have been studying all along is not simply poetry and revolutions, but the mind of western Christianity."[6] Dr. Arnold understood that a Jew who studied English history and literature, even at nonsectarian London University, must perforce submit to a whole world of assumptions that were alien and presumably offensive to him, namely, that the Jewish God is a fierce, tribal one who was supplanted in the progressive movement of the world by the gentle and "universal" Christian one; that what Jews call Torah is an Old Testament that had to be interpreted, complemented, and fulfilled by the New Testament; and that Jewish collective existence since the inception of Christianity is a diversionary ripple leading away from the mainstream of Western civilization into sand and dust. Few have expressed these assumptions about the universality of Christian civilization better than Dr. Arnold's son, the subject of Trilling's first book, Matthew Arnold:

> M. Albert Réville, whose religious writings are always interesting, says that the conception which cultivated and philosophical Jews now entertain of Christianity and its founder, is probably destined to become the conception which Christians themselves will entertain. . . . Now, even if this were true, it would still have been better for a man, during the last eighteen hundred years, to have

been a Christian and a member of one of the great Christian communions, than to have been a Jew . . . because the being in contact with the main stream of human life is of more moment for a man's total spiritual growth, and for his bringing to perfection the gifts committed to him . . . than any speculative opinion which he may hold. . . .[7]

For Arnold, eighteen hundred years of Jewish existence, the collective life of millions of people bound by covenant to the living God and by history to one another, was nothing more than "speculative opinion." And Arnold was not less, but more, sympathetic to Jews than most of his contemporaries. He was only making explicit the assumptions already implicit in the world of English letters.

Although it would be foolhardy to discount Jew-hatred as a motive for the exclusionary policy of Dr. Arnold and for the fear of the Columbia English department that Trilling would be unhappy in it, we must also remember that gentiles, who knew little of the extent to which "emancipation" had eroded Jewish self-definition, would not have understood how readily the supposedly stubborn Jews could assent to assumptions that ought to be anathema to them. A typical example of these assumptions, one that anyone who looks into Matthew Arnold's religious writing must soon encounter, is that the Pharisees were precisely the narrow-minded hypocrites depicted in the New Testament accounts. In his book, Trilling duly notes that for Arnold the typically "Pharisaic" error is to make conduct an end in itself rather than the means to the larger end, the good life. He does not try to counter the bigoted though "traditional" image of the Pharisees, but does indicate in a footnote that "Arnold, of course, is using the common conception of the Pharisees which two modern scholars—George Foot Moore in *Judaism* (1927–1930) and R. Travers Herford in *The Pharisees* (1924)—have rejected."[8] This may not seem much of a challenge to the Christian version of the Jewish world that obtains in English studies unless one happens to be aware that Arnold's erroneous account of Pharisaism has gone unchallenged in virtually all of the dozens of articles and books that have been published on his religious writing since 1939.

The reason for stressing the Christian character and assumptions of English and, indeed, Western literature is not to exonerate those who once sought to exclude Jews from its province or who today complain that one or another branch of literary creation or study has been "taken over" by Jews. Rather it is to stress the need for a relative rather than absolute view of the Jewish dimension of Trilling's mature work. He had entered a profession in which merely to retain a sense of Jewish honor, without ever intending to serve any Jewish purpose, required (perhaps still does require) considerable fortitude.

Lionel Trilling's formal association with the Jewish community lasted from 1925–31, during which time he contributed stories and reviews to the *Menorah Journal.* In 1929–30 he served as an assistant editor to Elliot Cohen. In his 1966 afterword to a reprint of *The Unpossessed* ("A Novel of the Thirties") by Tess Slesinger, Trilling recalled that it was his hostility to the ideals of the Ethical Culture Society that led him naturally to the *Menorah Journal.* Ethical Culture was, and is, an organization whose membership rolls clearly indicate the truth of the saying that universalism is the peculiarly Jewish form of parochialism. Trilling's reaction was in the direction of what would later be called "ethnic" identity. He was not drawn to the *Menorah Journal* either by religion or Zionism ("we were inclined to be skeptical about Zionism and even opposed to it, and during the violence that flared up in 1929 some of us were on principle pro-Arab") but by "authenticity." Trilling was seeking, he says, "a 'sense of identity,' by which is meant . . . that the individual Jewish person recognizes naturally and easily that he *is* a Jew . . . finding pleasure and taking pride in the identification. . . ."[9]

Looking back from the distance of nearly four decades, Trilling saw the effort made by himself and his friends as an attempt to "normalize" the Jewish present by showing that it was "not only as respectable as the present of any other group but also as foolish, vulgar, complicated, impossible, and promising." This was very far from normalization as understood by the Zionists, and it is doubtful that Trilling was even aware that he was using an idea (or slogan) beloved of Zionist ideology. He did not mean that the Jews were a people or a nation like all other peoples and nations but that American Jews could more clearly recognize themselves as Americans by first recognizing themselves as Jews; the benefits of this kind of normalization were inward and private rather than public and national. "The discovery, through the *Menorah Journal,* of the Jewish situation had the effect of making society at last available to my imagination. It made America available to my imagination, as it could not possibly be if I tried to understand it with the categories offered by Mencken or Herbert Croly, or, for that matter, Henry Adams."[10]

The contribution that Lionel Trilling's sense of himself as a Jew made to his thought is not greatly in evidence in his contributions to the *Menorah Journal.* This is not only because they are youthful productions but because they are often disfigured by that affected alienation from things Jewish that was wont to creep into his utterances before Jewish audiences (and only before them). The character he assumes in his numerous *Menorah* book reviews and short stories is not far from that of the protagonist in his short story called "Chapter for a Fashionable Jewish Novel." Of him the narrator says: "He merely wished to enjoy for a

moment the pleasure of feeling like those clever young Jewish artists of
Zangwill's whom he had admired when he was a boy, who were so
Anglicized and cosmopolitan and yet said such clever things about the
Jews." The narrator of Trilling's first published story, "Impediments,"
expresses fear that a certain classmate of his (perhaps an alter ego) will
break down "the convenient barrier I was erecting against men who were
too much of my own race and against men who were not of my own race
and hated it." In a review of *Success*, by Lion Feuchtwanger, Trilling
defends the popular idea of art as a force "opposed to the evil, the greed,
the blindness and stupidity of the world," against the coterie idea of pure
art, and even asserts that the artist "must make it at least part of his
function to be a propagandist for political decency and against injustice."
Yet in a review of Hugo Bettauer's *The City Without Jews,* he complains
that the book is "pro-semitic propaganda" because it opposes—in the year
1927—the policy of expulsion of Jews. From a strictly literary aspect,
Trilling's most important *Menorah* essay is his review of Charles Reznikoff's *By the Waters of Manhattan,* praised as "the first story of the
Jewish immigrant that is not false." This piece introduces the critique of
realism that is at the core of Trilling's later attacks on Dreiser and Sinclair
Lewis. Here he argues that Reznikoff's finely crafted poetry captures the
reality that always eludes "realists" because it represents "the mind of
man . . . in all its complexities."[11]

The most ambitious literary essay that Trilling composed for the *Menorah Journal* never appeared there, but is typical of his approach in the
numerous short book reviews. "The Changing Myth of the Jew," written
in 1931 and published posthumously in 1978, surveys the mutations of the
Jewish myth in English literature in an intelligent and discriminating
manner. But the discriminations are historical rather than evaluative and
political. No distinctions are made either among the varying degrees of
truth in versions of the myth or among their varying consequences in
actuality. Dickens's Riah *(Our Mutual Friend)* is quite as bad as his
Fagin—if anything, worse, because it is well known that Victorian England
did have a Jewish criminal class but few Victorians had met a Jewish
tsaddik in the East End. The implications of Dickens's casting Fagin as the
devil himself, and this in the year 1837, are lost upon Trilling the Jew
precisely because Trilling the English graduate student is so keenly aware
of the traditional basis in English literature, from the ballads onward, for
the figure of the Jewish devil. Here as in later comments (for example, in
Matthew Arnold), Trilling has little patience with *Daniel Deronda,* though
he does admit that it is the first work in English literature in which Jews are
visualized not as gentiles see them "but in terms of their own life and their
own problems." Trilling responds with warmth (and implicit sympathy) to

the Jewish anti-Semite who is Daniel's mother, but rejects the other Jewish figures as "unanimously noble" (which they are not) and therefore mythical.[12]

Even as a literary exercise, the essay has several weaknesses. It proceeds on the assumption, especially odd for Trilling, that only "realistic" novels, bare of every hint of myth, symbol, or allegory, can truthfully represent Jews. It consistently overlooks the truth that Trilling himself would admirably state eight years later: "The value of any myth cannot depend on its demonstrability as a fact, but only on the value of the attitudes it embodies, the further attitudes it engenders and the actions it motivates."[13] From a Jewish point of view, the essay seems grudging and meanspirited, especially in its assumption that a literary demonstration of the "mythical" character of the Jew in English literature should be sufficient to quiet the fears of those Jews who bother themselves about organized Jew-hatred and wish critically to examine its sources, including literary ones. Many years later, Trilling would write of Isaac Babel that "sometimes he affects a wondering alienation from the Jews, as when he speaks of 'the occult crockery that the Jews use only once a year at eastertime.' "[14] He might have said the same of the Trilling who wrote for the *Menorah Journal*.

In the thirties Trilling immersed himself in Freud, Marx, and Matthew Arnold. None of them was for him, nor can be for any intellectually honest person, an essentially Jewish figure. Trilling would sometimes, when he came later to write about Freud, mention Freud's "ethnic situation" as a useful barrier against the influences of his society ("he was a Jew, and enough of the Jewish sub-culture reached him to make a countervailing force against the general culture"[15]), but he was not prepared to go beyond this toward the dismal practice of enlisting Freud among "the great Jewish thinkers." He was equally cautious with respect to Marx, although he could succumb to the temptation of rationalizing the anti-Semitism of Marx and Engels by alleging (mistakenly) that it "has its source in the Jewish connection with money and banking."[16]

Arnold was a more complicated matter. Trilling was not merely a student of Arnold's work; he had penetrated the innermost recesses of Arnold's mind (characteristically, he wrote a biography of Arnold's mind, not of Arnold) and eventually fashioned himself after Arnold as a critic of literature and society and liberalism.[17] In the 1930s Arnold became for him the culture hero whose stress on objectivity and reason stood in absolute contrast to the madness of Nazi *kultur*. In his preface to *Matthew Arnold,* published on the eve of World War II, Trilling contrasted Arnold's ideal of "seeing the object as it really is" with the position enunciated by Hitler's minister of science, who urged a "new science" to replace the old one that had valued the disinterested and "unchecked" effort to reach the truth.[18] There was even a sense in which Trilling thought of Arnold as possessing "Jewish" impulses and intuitions. In his discussion of Arnold's theology, Trilling maintained that in his definition of God as "a term of poetry and eloquence, a term *thrown out,* so to speak, at a not fully grasped object of the speaker's consciousness," Arnold was actually denying all the centuries of Christian intellectual tradition and reaching "back of all Christianity for his theology to the God of the Old Testament Jews."[19] More startling is Trilling's description, in his 1949 introduction to the *Viking Portable Matthew Arnold,* of Arnold's habit, embodied in his notebooks, of meditating on "sayings" that encapsulated discovered truth. He calls it Arnold's attempt to obey as literally as a non-Jew could "the commandment to fasten the truth upon the doorpost of his house and upon his hand, and to set it as a frontlet between his eyes."[20] Arnold may, then, have been for Trilling a more "Jewish" writer than Freud or Marx, but finally we cannot say much more about the effect of Trilling's Jewish identity on his treatment of Arnold than that a few of his most striking insights into Arnold's religious temper and thought are not likely to have occurred to a non-Jew.

In February 1944 Trilling was one of a number of young Jewish intellectuals who participated in a symposium on the state of Jewish "identity" that appeared in the *Contemporary Jewish Record,* a precursor of *Commentary.* The tone of his essay must have irritated, must indeed have been intended to irritate, the Jewish readers of the magazine. In it Trilling insists that Jewish religion in its modern forms has failed to provide "a single voice with the note of authority—of philosophical, or poetic, or even of rhetorical, let alone of religious, authority." He further alleges that the American-Jewish community is utterly incapable of giving spiritual sustenance to the American artist or intellectual who is born a Jew. He even warns that writers who consciously aspire to be Jewish will abort their creative impulse and shorten their careers. "I know of writers who have used their Jewish experience as the subject of excellent work; I know of no writer in English who has added a micromillimetre to his stature by 'realizing his Jewishness,' although I know of some who have curtailed their promise by trying to heighten their Jewish consciousness."[21]

One may justifiably fault this statement of belief (or rather nonbelief), not only for its haughtiness of tone but also for the author's scholarly failure to be aware that among the authoritative modern Jewish religious voices that a willing ear might have heard in 1944 were Gershom Scholem (whose epoch-making lectures on Jewish mysticism were delivered in 1938 not far from where Trilling lived), Martin Buber, Franz Rosenzweig, S. Y. Agnon, and many of the Yiddish writers whom Irving Howe would share with the American public (in translation) nine years later. But perhaps the failure is not so much scholarly as spiritual. Light is a quality of matter, but blind people do not see it.

It would, of course, be foolish to deny that Trilling's failure to find sustenance in the American-Jewish community had external causes as well as internal ones. This was a community worm-eaten with liberalism, and Trilling recognized it as such: "Jewish religion is, I am sure, very liberal and intelligent and modern. Its function is to provide, chiefly for people of no strong religious impulse, a social and rational defense against the world's hostility. . . ." Jewish liberalism, like secular liberalism, suffered from a failure of imagination, an addiction to what Arnold had called "machinery," and an inability to cope with death. One had only to attend a Jewish festival, Trilling complained, "to have the sense of [modern Judaism's] deep inner uncertainty, its lack of grasp of life. . . ." To the extent that modern Judaism had made itself into a pale imitation of secular liberalism, another child of Enlightenment ideology (which many liberal Jews liked to fancy the child of Judaism), it left itself open to Trilling's criticism of the liberal imagination in general.[22]

The diminution of Judaism in American society was no more an occasion for celebration by Trilling than its desiccation within himself was an occasion for self-congratulation. Now, as it would be throughout his life, his relation to Judaism and the Jewish people was an honorable one; but he knew that more than honor is required for intellectual sustenance and spiritual life. "In what I might call my life as a citizen my being Jewish exists as a point of honor. . . . I can have no pride in seeing a long tradition, often great and heroic, reduced to this small status in me, for I give only a limited respect to points of honor: they are usually mortuary and monumental, they have being without desire. For me the point of honor consists in feeling that I would not, even if I could, deny or escape being Jewish."[23] Trilling also expressed his pained awareness of a certain "gracelessness" in his position, for (unlike some other contributors to this symposium) he was powerfully moved by the fact that millions of Jews in Europe were suffering unspeakable tortures for no other reason than that they were Jews, that they had inherited what he so minimized in his intellectual life. (It is important to remember that by February 1944 the truth about the terrible fate that had befallen the Jews of Europe, in every large Jewish community except the Hungarian one, was available in the newspapers to everyone wishing to find it out.)

By 1944 the disenchantment with current liberalism, already evident in the Arnold book (where Trilling's admiration for Arnold as "a Liberal tempered by experience, reflection, and renouncement"[24] is everywhere apparent), was becoming a central element in Trilling's criticism of literature and society. He had already grasped the paradox whereby the high priests of modern literature—Yeats, Eliot, Gide, Joyce, Proust, and Lawrence—were either actively hostile or coldly indifferent to the liberal ideas that were music to the inward ear of most of the critics who acted as expositors of the priestly writings to the reading public.[25] Even E. M. Forster, Trilling noted in his study of 1944, "for all his long commitment to the doctrines of liberalism . . . is at war with the liberal imagination. Surely if liberalism has a single desperate weakness, it is an inadequacy of imagination: liberalism is always being surprised."[26]

If we then ask what it was by which, in Trilling's view, liberalism was mainly surprised in the twentieth century, and especially in this year 1944, the answer is not far to seek. It brings us, moreover, at once to the truth—which may be called an open secret because it is surely visible to everyone, yet has been seen by almost no one[27]—that the single event in modern Jewish history that decisively influenced Lionel Trilling's thought was the Holocaust, the systematic destruction of the Jews of Europe by the National Socialist regime of Germany. In *The Liberal Imagination* (1950), a collection of essays published between 1940 and 1949, the unifying intention is to call into question, to "put under some degree of pressure the liberal ideas and assumptions of the present time. . . ."[28] The book is ultimately an attempt to confront liberal assumptions about the nature of man and his educability, about the pursuit of "happiness," about the moral character of high cultural achievement, and about "reality" itself, in the form of the Holocaust.

Forever hovering in the shadows, the subject comes up tangentially in "Reality in America" (where Trilling observes that liberal and progressive critics have willfully ignored Dreiser's "doctrinaire anti-Semitism") and in "The Sense of the Past" (where Trilling rejects the imputation to romanticism of guilt for Nazism), but it is central in "Art and Fortune." In this essay, Trilling links the modern artistic revulsion from and disgust with the human form, with history, with society, and with the state, to the Holocaust. More importantly, he argues that although the revelation of human depravity has been one of the chief enterprises of the human mind for at least four centuries, its discoveries have not been sufficiently conclusive, until now, to dislodge optimistic liberalism from its "strongly entrenched . . . belief in human and social goodness." The Holocaust has destroyed forever the liberal assumptions about human nature, about "reason and society and progress." It has demonstrated that "depravity" and not goodness is central in human nature. It has eliminated the margin of uncertainty that always existed between speculation about human depravity and "proof":

> Now everyone knows that Thackeray was wrong, Swift right. The world and the soul have split open of themselves and are all agape for our revolted inspection.

The simple eye of the camera shows us, at Belsen and Buchenwald, horrors that quite surpass Swift's powers, a vision of life turned back to its corrupted elements which is more disgusting than any that Shakespeare could contrive, a cannibalism more literal and fantastic than that which Montaigne ascribed to organized society. A characteristic activity of mind is therefore no longer needed.[29]

In view of such statements, it is difficult to share Alfred Kazin's opinion that Trilling never allowed the Holocaust to impinge on his belief in mind. "The abyss was at our feet," says Kazin, "because *we* believed in nothing so much as what Trilling called 'the life of the mind.' The life of the mind was of no use unless it addressed itself to the gas."[30] Contrary to what Kazin implies here and elsewhere in his portrait, this is precisely what Trilling did.

Trilling had a perfectly clear recognition that the murder of the Jews was the overwhelming and ultimate outrage of the Second World War, and he could be severe with books about the horror of the war, like C. V. Gheorgiu's *The Twenty-Fifth Hour,* that dealt "in so minimal and perverse a way with that extreme example of that horror, the fate of the Jews."[31] Yet it was not to the fate of the Jews in the aftermath of the Holocaust that Trilling applied the "lessons" of Auschwitz but to the ideological assumptions and visceral reactions of liberalism. Whenever, in his criticism, Trilling mocks the liberal tendency to be skeptical of literary characters who are entirely evil, or the liberal tendency to inculpate society while exculpating the criminal, or the liberal tendency to be "surprised" by the intrinsically incredible things that outrage "common sense," or the liberal fascination with the optimistic psychologies of Horney and Fromm and Sullivan, the reader can be confident that Trilling is mindful of the revelation of depravity that the Holocaust brought. This is especially clear when he writes of Dickens, the Victorian novelist most frequently chastised for "exaggeration" by simple-minded critics. By definition, a simple-minded critic cannot grasp complexity; and for Trilling nothing indicates Dickens's complex view of society better than his readiness to acknowledge the extreme and unexplainable character of madness and evil in the world. In his 1953 essay on *Little Dorrit,* Trilling observes that the character Blandois is "wholly wicked," and that his presence in the novel must "deprive us of the comfortable, philanthropic thought that prisons are nothing but instruments of injustice. Because Blandois exists, prisons are necessary." If the previous generation of readers refused to "believe" in Blandois, this was because they could not explain in what way his existence had been "caused" by an unjust or anomalous society. But in 1953 these evasions of common sense by optimistic liberalism are no longer permissible: "Events have required us to believe that there really are people who seem entirely wicked, and almost unaccountably so; the social causes of their badness lie so far back that they can scarcely be reached, and in any case causation pales into irrelevance before the effects of their actions; our effort to 'understand' them becomes a mere form of thought."[32] Lest there is any doubt that these coercive "events" refer to the Holocaust, one needs only to glance at a short piece of the previous year called "The Dickens of Our Day," in which Trilling also defends the "profundity and accuracy" of Dickens. "We who have seen Hitler, Goering, and Goebbels put on the stage of history . . . are in no position to suppose that Dickens ever exaggerated in the least the extravagance of madness, absurdity, and malevolence in the world. . . ."[33]

In a very different way, the effect of the Holocaust may be seen in the two most "Jewish" essays in the mature work of Lionel Trilling, "Wordsworth and the Rabbis" (1950) and "Isaac Babel" (1955). The former is one of the most unusual essays Trilling ever wrote—very personal, untypically loose in its definitions, highly strained, and brilliantly creative. Analysis of the essay must begin with a recognition of its time and place of presentation as a lecture. The occasion was the centenary of Wordsworth's death, commemorated at Princeton University in April 1950. Whatever it may have become since, the English department of Princeton was not in 1950 famous for its receptivity to Jewish persons or Jewish interests. Yet throughout the lecture, Trilling—one of the most civilized, indeed courtly, men in the academic profession—went out of his way to flaunt his Jewish background and identity, as if it had now become a point of honor for a Jew in whom, by his own admission, Judaism had shrunk to a very small status, to be as Jewish among the goyim as he had formerly been goyish among the Jews,[34] and to be Jewish in dealing with one of the great poets of an intensely Christian literature. "Wordsworth and the Rabbis" ought to make us question the accuracy of both Robert Alter's description of Trilling's career as "an achieved process of hyperac- culturation," and William Chace's absolute assertion that Trilling's Jewish- ness "figures only as a reality *against* which he defines himself, never *within* which he finds his definition."[35]

Trilling does not quarrel with the definition of Wordsworth as a Christian poet because "when we speak of a poet as being of a particular religion, we do not imply in him completeness or orthodoxy, or even explicitness of doctrine, but only that his secular utterance has the decisive mark of the religion upon it." Nevertheless, Trilling maintains that the reason for Wordsworth's current (1950) unacceptability is precisely "a Judaic qual- ity" that runs counter to the sensibility defined as "modern." The reason why Trilling himself, despite being infected by modernism, has responded warmly to Wordsworth is that he has long been intimate with the Mishnaic treatise called *Pirke Aboth* (Chapters of the Fathers). In a uniquely personal passage for one of his critical essays, Trilling recalls how his youthful acquaintance with the English translation of *Pirke Aboth* was really an evasion of his primary religious duties: prayer and Hebrew study. But he found The Wisdom of the Fathers "more attractive . . . than psalms, meditations, and supplications," despite the fact that *Pirke Aboth* recommended an alien way of life, different "from any life that I wanted to know." When he returned to this work he had known from youth he at once recognized that "between the Rabbis and Wordsworth an affinity existed."[36]

It is much to the point of Trilling's strategy and purpose in this lecture that the rabbis whose affinity to Wordsworth he is insisting on were Pharisees, the very group of Jews for whom nary a single good word has been said in all of English literature. The distance that Trilling has traveled as a Jew may be measured by the difference between the cautious way in which, in 1939, he indicated in a note that Arnold's "traditional" image of the Pharisees had been challenged by two (Christian) scholars, and the more assertive and even defiant manner in which he refers in 1950 to this Christian confirmation of what Jews, after all, have always known: "I shall assume that the long scholarly efforts of Mr. Herford as well as those of George Foot Moore, have by now made it generally known that the Pharisees were not in actual fact what tradition represents them to have been. They were anything but formalists, and of course they were not the hypocrites of popular conception."[37]

Despite apparent contradictions (such as the rabbinic hostility to nature and Wordsworth's to "study") there is, Trilling argues, "between the Law as the Rabbis understood it and Nature as Wordsworth understood it . . . a pregnant similarity." Torah for the rabbis and Nature for Wordsworth were surrogates of God, really divine objects "to which one can be in an intimate passionate relationship."[38] Not only the text of *Pirke Aboth* but even its authors are presented by Trilling as precursors and relatives of Wordsworth. He calls Hillel "a peculiarly Wordsworthian personality" because of his keen sense of the interplay between individuality and community. He links Akiba to Wordsworth by their (allegedly) similar recognition of the interplay between fate and free will.

Few readers will fail to sense an unseemly haste in these linkages and generalizations, even if they lack full awareness of the content and background of the rabbinic utterances. Far more persuasive and also (as the Arnoldian title Trilling later used for the essay, "Wordsworth and the Iron Time," illustrates) more crucial is the joining of Wordsworth and the rabbis on the basis of their antiheroism, their avoidance of the implication of moral struggle, whether against the enemy within or the enemy at the gates. Of the latter sort the Jews at least had intimate knowledge. Referring to Jewish suffering and the martyrdom of Rabbi Akiba and others after the Romans had destroyed the Second Temple, Trilling is struck by the absence of any mention of courage of or heroism or even of the enemy by these men who were admirably courageous and heroic in the face of a very tangible and brutal enemy. The scholars of *Pirke Aboth,* like Wordsworth's Leech-Gatherer, affirmed life through quietism. This, Trilling asserts, is the real reason why Wordsworth, and still more the rabbis, are out of favor with modern sensibility: they go "clearly against the militancy of spirit which in our culture is normally assumed."[39]

The image of the Jews that Trilling fashions from the *Pirke Aboth* is that of a people that suffers, yet refuses to seek value or self-definition in militant suffering. They are quite unlike the American Jews who in 1929 provoked the young Trilling to the snarling question: "Is a Jew a Jew without a pogrom in the middle distance?" They hardly fit the image of the "liberal and . . . modern" American Jews whom Trilling had spoken of derisively in 1944. In fact, the Jewish ethos is defined in this lecture of 1950 neither as a reaction to persecution nor as a pale imitation of modern liberal culture, but as a direct challenge to it: "The predilection for the powerful, the fierce, the assertive, the personally militant, is very strong in our culture. We find it in the liberal bourgeois admiration of the novels of Thomas Wolfe and Theodore Dreiser."[40]

Exactly where Lionel Trilling stands in this opposition between his Jewish-Wordsworthian self and his modern one is not wholly clear. He tends to use the pronouns "we" and "us" (a familiar Trillingesque mannerism) when referring to the moderns, even in passages where he appears to endorse the antithetical culture of Wordsworth and the rabbis. On the other hand, he insistently reminds the Princeton audience of his Jewish identity, and in the printed version of the lecture even adds a footnote intended to pay respect to "one of the long-suffering men who tried to teach me Hebrew."[41] What is certain is that he sees in *Pirke Aboth* and Wordsworth an antiheroic desire to avoid the tragic fate, and a respect for the quotidian existence, which stand as a mute judgment on "the failure to conceive the actuality of the life of common routine" that has been typical of modern literature since Tolstoi. When he finds a notable exception to this modern failure, such as Leopold Bloom in *Ulysses,* Trilling calls him "a Rabbinical character," not because he happens to be of Jewish birth, but because his nonmilitancy, his indifference to the idea of evil, and his "acceptance of cosmic contradiction" place him directly in the line of *Pirke Aboth.* In fact, in a much later (1968) essay on "James Joyce in His Letters," Trilling maintained, on the basis of a single remark in one of Joyce's letters, that for the Irish writer Jews "were exempt from the complexities of the moral life as it was sustained by Christians," Jewish good deeds being done out of instinct rather than moral will. In *Sincerity and Authenticity,* not merely the rabbis but the whole Jewish tradition going back to the Bible is removed from the historical stage and from every thought of struggle, dilemma, hard choice, and heroism.[42]

Nowhere in "Wordsworth and the Rabbis" does Trilling mention the Jewish people of the modern world or the fact that only a few short years earlier they had suffered the most terrible calamity of their long history. Yet the strain evident in the essay, its freedom of association bordering (for Trilling, at least) on license, and its dogged insistence on Judaizing Wordsworth are hardly to be explained except by Trilling's desire to respond, in the only way he saw open to him, to the Jewish calamity. To speak in 1950 of a Jewish suffering that was neither heroic nor tragic nor militant, to speak of a vanished Jewish life characterized by "acceptance of cosmic contradiction" (an old Eastern European Jewish quip, half-Hebrew, half-Yiddish, puts it thus:

אתה בהרתנו מכל העמים: וואָס האָסטו
געוואָלט פון דיין פאָלק ישראל?

"Thou hast chosen us from among all the nations; why did you have to pick on the Jews?"), was inevitably to conjure up an image not of Hillel and Akiba, but of the destroyed world of East European Jewry, the world of Trilling's fathers. Two years earlier he had written that "before what we now know the mind stops; the great psychological fact of our time which we all observe with baffled wonder and shame is that there is no possible way of responding to Belsen and Buchenwald. The activity of mind fails before the incommunicability of man's suffering."[43] The Wordsworth essay, brilliant yet flawed, shows that what Trilling really meant to say is not that there is no possible but that there is no adequate way of responding to the Holocaust.

In the essay of 1955 on Isaac Babel, the world of Eastern European Jewry, which had just been destroyed by violence, is present not by indirection but explicitly, as the embodiment of "the life beyond violence." The essay is built around what Trilling asserts to have been the conflict within Isaac Babel between the cossack ethos and the Jewish one. Babel had been, and represented himself in his stories as, a Jew in a cossack regiment; "and," Trilling remarks, "a Jew in a Cossack regiment was more than an anomaly, it was a joke, for between Cossack and Jew there existed not merely hatred but a polar opposition." The Eastern European Jew was, at least in his ideal character, the exact antithesis to the physical, mindless, and violent cossack. Trilling illustrates the opposition as it typically presented itself to a Jewish mind by recalling that "when a Jew of Eastern Europe wanted to say what we mean by 'a bull in a china shop,' he said 'a Cossack in a succah.' ''[44]

Trilling does not entirely accept Babel's picture of the Jews of Odessa as a collectivity of sensitive plants—unworldly, bodiless, intellectual, and passive. He briefly sketches the character of the Odessa Jews in the years after the succession of Nicholas II and emphasizes the fact that, despite official anti-Semitism and the Black Hundreds and organized pogroms, the Jewish community flourished and all its classes were marked by "a singular robustness and vitality, by a sense of the world, and of themselves in the world."[45] He notes that modern Hebrew poetry had its birth in Odessa with Bialik and Tchernikowski. Above all, he calls on his personal experience of the "Jovian" former chief rabbi of Odessa, Dr. Chaim Tchernowitz, as conclusive evidence that Babel's picture of the cringing, intellectual Jew is based not on the Jews of Odessa so much as on his memory of his father, the father who kneeled before a cossack captain who allowed a Russian mob to loot the Babel family store with impunity.

Nevertheless, Trilling sympathizes with Babel's resentment of the peculiarly "Jewish" handicaps that had been foisted on him by an accident of birth: an inability to swim ("the hydrophobia of my ancestors—Spanish rabbis and Frankfurt moneychangers—dragged me to the bottom"), ignorance of the natural world, and, most damaging of all, lack of the ability to kill his fellow man, "the simplest of proficiencies." Through a shrewd analysis of the *Red Cavalry* stories, Trilling shows that Babel took a view of the cossack much closer to that of the Russian intellectuals, who thought of cossacks as noble savages, than to that of the Jews, who thought them merely savages. He shows, too, how skeptical Babel was of Jewish claims to moral superiority based on the fact that for two thousand years the Jew had not stooped to weapons of violence. A Jew congratulating himself on having spurned that which was never available to him was like a starved man congratulating himself on his ability to fast. Linked by Babel (and apparently Trilling as well) with the morally ambiguous Jewish incapacity for violence is the distinctly negative Jewish trait of refusing to believe or acknowledge that one has enemies. In this matter, Trilling says, "we are not misled into supposing that Babel intends irony and a covert praise of his pacific soul; we know that in this epiphany of his refusal to accept enmity he means to speak adversely of himself in his Jewish character."[46]

Yet once Trilling has taken full account of Babel's attraction—so typical, in Trilling's view, of the intellectual—to cossack violence, he offers a moving exposition of Babel's equally powerful attraction to the Jewish life "beyond violence"—the life of suffering, the life of the spirit, and the life of unheroic endurance. Babel, according to Trilling, found his counter-image to cossack violence and grace in the Jews of Poland, who "move jerkily, in an uncontrolled and uncouth way; but whose capacity for suffering is full of a somber greatness." Trilling is quick to say that Babel could never have given his assent or allegiance, much less his soul, to the spiritual principle embodied by Polish Jewry. Indeed, a main reason why he responded to the spiritual life of Polish Jewry so powerfully was that, in Trilling's words, "it was a life coming to its end and having about it the terrible pathos of its death."[47] The essay's conclusion is an overwhelming stroke, which creates a frozen image of eternal tension in the Jewish intellectual who halts between two opinions. But if we stand back and examine it historically and dispassionately, it is a peculiar statement. Babel died in about 1941, and his writing, apart from a single play, had largely ceased by 1928; *Red Cavalry* was published in 1926 and *Odessa Tales,* in 1927. Unless defined in the narrowest sense of strict orthodoxy (and Trilling's interpretations surely do not require this), it is simply not true that the spiritual life of Polish Jewry was "coming to its end" decades before the Holocaust. The vibrancy of Polish-Jewish life between the two great wars is hardly a secret, and there are strong reminders of its multifarious richness in, for example, Celia Heller's book, *On the Edge of Destruction,* and the admirable YIVO film, *Image Before My Eyes.* Was Trilling again, as in the essay on Wordsworth and the rabbis, superimposing his image of the Holocaust on an earlier Jewish reality, succumbing to the (natural albeit mistaken) impulse to allow the Holocaust to cast its black shadow not only on the Jewish future but also the Jewish past? Was it also easier for him, as he claims it was easier for Babel, to respond powerfully to an image of what he thought was a dying Jewish culture than to a living one, such as he knew (though barely acknowledged) in the United States or might have known in Israel?

To recognize how much Trilling's thought was influenced, if in a troubling way, by the specter of the Holocaust, we need to recall what his criticism shows he values most highly, what moves him to eloquence and passion. Lionel Trilling gave his assent only to the idea of mind—mind that is sober, grave, infinitely patient, and untrammeled by the ties of community or of party. Because he believed that ultimately it was the only means by which men could communicate with each other, Trilling returned again and again to the defense of mind against the incursions of party, profession, and, especially in his later years, "culture." His critique of liberalism arose in large part from his recognition that for liberalism "it is always a little too late for mind, yet never too late for honest stupidity." Trilling interpreted Arnold's "disinterestedness" as being before all else an assertion of the primacy of mind over sect, party, and practical politics, an insistence that man "had his true being not as a member of this or that profession or class, but as . . . 'a man speaking to men.' " John Stuart Mill was an abiding presence in Trilling's work because the mental crisis of this saint of rationalism was a stark warning of how liberalism "inclines to constrict and make mechanical its conception of the nature of mind" by segregating it from the emotions, by excluding from the realm of mind "impulse and will, and desire and preference." His essay on "The Leavis-Snow Controversy" in 1962, one of the best Trilling ever wrote and surely the crucial one in defining the general theme of the collection called *Beyond Culture,* acknowledges "the fatigue and desiccation of spirit" that may result from "an allegiance to mind that excludes impulse and will, and desire and preference," yet finally champions the free play of mind against the impulse to compartmentalize and colonize it according to class and culture. The primacy of mind for Trilling may even be seen in the place we would least expect to find it—in his work on Freud, where he stresses, whenever possible, the rationalistic element of the interpreter of the night side of life. Trilling uses the Hasidic saying that "I learned the Torah from all the limbs of my teacher" to illustrate his belief that even antirationalists do not reject mind, but only mind as conceived by respectable society.[48]

But the Holocaust called into question the continued vitality, even the future existence, of what Trilling most valued. In the aftermath of the Holocaust Trilling had written (as noted above), "the activity of mind fails before the incommunicability of man's suffering," and *"before what we now know the mind stops"* (italics mine). When in his Jefferson lecture of 1972 Trilling undertook to evaluate the status of "Mind in the Modern World," he began with a comment on the little book that H. G. Wells had written out of despair and disillusionment over the Second World War. *Mind at the End of Its Tether,* says Trilling, was an unusual book in the postwar period. Despite "the dreadful suffering the war had entailed" and despite "the close approximation to success that had been made by the brutish antirational doctrine of Nazism," the dominant mood then was one of optimism and a continuing belief "that mind would play a beneficent part in human existence." But Wells, who had been among the century's most ardent expositors of the power of human reason to create "happiness," had come to see that "the power of mind which mankind required not only for the winning of felicity but even for survival was not to be counted on. Mind was at the end of its tether." From this high point of recognition of the insufficiency of "mind" as revealed by the Second World War, Trilling's lecture declines into a merely intelligent and rational canvassing of some of the modern attacks on mind, ranging from those launched by the political desperadoes of the academic world of the 1960s to the comfortably fashionable contemporary espousals of insanity as the only sane response to a mad society. He concludes by expressing disquietude about the future of mind, both because of the open attacks by its enemies and also because of "a falling off in mind's vital confidence in itself."[49] One is left with the sense that, having begun with Wells's clear recognition, which Trilling himself had already expressed, of the extent to which the Nazis had destroyed not only vast numbers of human beings and an entire culture but also the assumptions of Enlightenment rationalism, the lecturer chose to deal only with those perceptions of the crisis that expressed themselves in extreme, radical forms inviting still harsher criticism than they receive here. But the questions posed by Wells's repudiation of Enlightenment assumptions about the beneficent power of mind truly exercised remain unanswered.

Trilling had in many ways fashioned himself after Matthew Arnold; and in nothing was he more like Arnold than in his commitment to light and coherence. He had a special fondness for the letter of 1865 in which Arnold had written that "No one has a stronger and more abiding sense than I have of the 'daemonic' element—as Goethe called it—which underlies and encompasses our life; but I think, as Goethe thought, that the right thing is, while conscious of this element, and of all that there is inexplicable round one, to keep pushing on one's posts into the darkness, and to establish no past that is not perfectly in light and firm. One gains nothing on the darkness by being, like Shelley, as incoherent as the darkness itself."[50] More than most literary critics of his generation Trilling entered the darkness imaginatively. But he recognized the extent to which the Holocaust, as the epitome of moral disorder, threatened the coherence that all literary creation and even verbal discourse take for granted. In December 1972, despite the large body of Holocaust literature that had by then appeared, he reiterated his opinion of 1948: "I still think that Belsen and Buchenwald have not been truly responded to, never can be, to our cost."[51] Neither in his life nor, finally, in his criticism, would he agree to establish a "post" that was not "in light and firm." He could never have become what Jean Amery, who wrote brilliantly of the paralysis of intellect and of intellectuals when faced with Auschwitz, calls a Holocaust Jew, one for whom that event is the existential reference point. Neither would Trilling gaze long enough into the darkness to admit that his two chief values, mind and liberal culture, were not merely seriously compromised by the manner in which European civilization, by destroying the Jews, had destroyed itself; they were shown to be bankrupt.

We return, finally, to the question posed by the epigraph to this essay. How much of Lionel Trilling's temperament and intellect was shaped by his existence as a Jew? The answer is, not enough to serve as a key to the complex unity of his mind but more than has usually been supposed, and within that "more" are some things of crucial importance. Trilling, perhaps because of his fondness (dialectical rather than perverse) for being strongly "goyish" in addressing Jews, has not been the beneficiary of that beggarlike gratitude that the Jewish community generally shows to its renegade intellectuals who deign to notice, however negatively, its continued existence. The Trilling entry in the *Encyclopedia Judaica* tersely notes that "Trilling rarely showed interest in Jewish subjects." It should also note that his critique of modern liberalism, his sensitivity to the presence of radical evil in literary characters, his image of the unheroic, quotidian existence, his adjustment of the post-Enlightenment reverence for "mind," and his occasional quixotic rebellion against the Christian character of English literary study, grew out of his sense of himself as a Jew.

Lionel Trilling was so fine a critic that one would not readily wish him to have been other than he was—the most accomplished modern continuator of the moral tradition of Samuel Johnson and Matthew Arnold. And yet no Jew can fail to regret the loss of a figure like Trilling to Jewish life or the loss to Trilling caused by his detachment from the tree of life called Torah and from Israel, both the people and the land. For the latter he showed some interest and sympathy in his last years, although back in 1954 he had tacitly endorsed David Riesman's contemptuous view of American Zionism as a form of "Jewish separatism" that manifested the very American culture it "contrived to resist."[52] His name appeared in statements in the *New York Times* in support of Israel after the Yom Kippur (1973) war,[53] and not long before his death he expressed serious interest in serving as a Paley lecturer at the Hebrew University in Jerusalem.[54] But his written work showed no signs of attraction to a form of Jewish existence committed to life rather than redolent of death. Perhaps if it had, the writing of his last decade might have been better—even better—than it was: less convoluted, less mannered, and less concerned with shoring up long-cherished positions that had been seriously undermined, not so much by others as by himself.

Every admirer of Lionel Trilling has sensed that what he ultimately offers is more than a revision of the dominant liberalism of our day, more than a chastened commitment to mind, and more than a heightened awareness of literature as a criticism of life. What he gives us is a sense of yearning toward something beyond any of these; toward something conveyed in words like *will* and *faith* and *transcendence;* in phrases like *what life might be but is not,* or *the imagination of love,* or *the state of the soul in which the novel becomes possible,* or *the mystery of man's nature;*[55] all of them words and phrases that made his naturalistic and liberal readers uncomfortable. They were uncomfortable for good reason, because Trilling had charged that from "writers of the liberal democratic tradition" one never does or can get "the sense of largeness, of cogency, of the transcendence which largeness and cogency can give, the sense of being reached in our secret and primitive minds."[56] To the extent that Trilling makes his readers yearn toward these intangible things, we must believe that he yearned toward them himself. The Jewish reader touched by this yearning yet mindful of Trilling's inability or unwillingness to be inspirited by the miracle of Jewish rebirth in the aftermath of unprecedented disaster—an inability or unwillingness that came from too much refinement and intelligence, not from too little—may be reminded of Matthew Arnold's elegiac lament for Marcus Aurelius: "We see him wise, just, self-governed, tender . . . yet, with all this, agitated, stretching out his arms for something beyond,—*tendentemque manus ripae ulterioris amore.*"[57]

Notes

1. *Contemporary Jewish Record,* 7 (February 1944): 15.
2. Lionel Trilling, *Matthew Arnold* (New York: Meridian Books, 1955), p. 57; Arthur P. Stanley, *Life and Correspondence of Thomas Arnold, D. D.* (New York: Scribner, 1877), pp. 86, 93, 105.
3. Diana Trilling, "Lionel Trilling, A Jew at Columbia," *Commentary,* 66 (March 1979): 44. Trilling himself has written that "my appointment to an instructorship in Columbia College was pretty openly regarded as an experiment, and for some time my career in the College was conditioned by my being Jewish" (*The Last Decade: Essays and Reviews: 1965–75* [New York: Harcourt, Brace, 1979], p. 13).
4. Diana Trilling, "A Jew at Columbia," p. 46.
5. Irving Howe, *World of Our Fathers* (New York: Harcourt, Brace, Jovanovich, 1976), p. 412.
6. Cynthia Ozick, "Still Another Autobiography of an Assimilated Jew," *New York Times,* 28 December 1978.
7. Matthew Arnold, Preface to *Culture and Anarchy,* ed. J. Dover Wilson (Cambridge, 1960), pp. 29–30.
8. Trilling, *Matthew Arnold,* p. 385n.
9. Trilling, *The Last Decade,* pp. 11–12.
10. Ibid., pp. 12, 14–15. Elsewhere Trilling notes that Henry Adams is "hateful . . . in his anti-Jewish utterances" (*A Gathering of Fugitives* [Boston: Beacon Press, 1956], p. 117).
11. Lionel Trilling, "Chapter for a Fashionable Jewish Novel," *Menorah Journal,* 12 (June–July 1926): 279; idem, "Impediments," *Menorah Journal,* 11 (June 1925): 286; idem, "Art and Justice," *Menorah Journal,* 19 (June 1931): 472; idem, "What Price Jewry?" *Menorah Journal,* 13 (April 1927): 219; idem, "Genuine Writing," *Menorah Journal,* 19 (November–December 1930): 91.
12. Lionel Trilling, "The Changing Myth of the Jew," *Commentary,* 66 (August 1978): 33–34.
13. Trilling, *Matthew Arnold,* p. 233.
14. Lionel Trilling, *Beyond Culture* (New York: The Viking Press, 1968), p. 142.
15. Lionel Trilling, *Freud and the Crisis of Our Culture* (Boston: Beacon Press, 1955), p. 46.
16. Lionel Trilling, *Sincerity and Authenticity* (Cambridge: Harvard University

Press, 1972), p. 123. In a similar vein of absurdity is Trilling's explanation, on p. 20 of *Sincerity and Authenticity,* that Marx's reference to "the idiocy of village life" was not pejorative at all, because Marx "no doubt had in mind the primitive meaning of the word 'idiot,' which is . . . a private person."

17. See "Some Notes for an Autobiographical Lecture" in *The Last Decade,* p. 239.
18. Trilling, *Matthew Arnold,* p. 12.
19. Ibid., p. 324.
20. Lionel Trilling, Introduction to *The Portable Matthew Arnold* (New York: The Viking Press, 1949), p. 5.
21. *Contemporary Jewish Record,* 7 (February 1944): 16–17.
22. Ibid., p. 16.
23. Ibid., p. 15.
24. Arnold, Introduction to *Culture and Anarchy,* p. 41.
25. Trilling comments on this paradox in "The Meaning of a Literary Idea," an essay of 1949 reprinted in *The Liberal Imagination* (New York: Doubleday, 1957), pp. 291–92.
26. *E. M. Forster,* new ed. (London: Hogarth Press, 1967), p. 14.
27. Including William M. Chace, author of the otherwise excellent study, *Lionel Trilling: Criticism and Politics* (Stanford: Stanford University Press, 1980). Chase claims, p. 12, that "the Second World War . . . figures only distantly and cloudily in Trilling's writing."
28. Trilling, *The Liberal Imagination,* p. viii.
29. Ibid., pp. 255–56.
30. Alfred Kazin, *New York Jew* (New York: Alfred A. Knopf, 1978), p. 194.
31. Trilling, *A Gathering of Fugitives,* p. 80.
32. Lionel Trilling, *The Opposing Self* (New York: The Viking Press, 1955), pp. 56–57.
33. Trilling, *A Gathering of Fugitives,* p. 44.
34. Or still was, if we can credit Alfred Kazin's (self-flattering) depiction of the contrast between the two men: "For Trilling I would always be 'too Jewish'. . . . He would always defend himself from the things he had left behind" (*New York Jew,* pp. 46–47).
35. Robert Alter, *Defenses of the Imagination* (Philadelphia: Jewish Publication Society, 1977), p. 53; Chace, *Lionel Trilling,* p. 10.
36. Trilling, *The Opposing Self,* pp. 120, 124–25.
37. Ibid., p. 126.
38. Ibid., p. 127.
39. Ibid., p. 129.
40. Lionel Trilling, "Our Colonial Forefathers," *Menorah Journal,* 14 (February 1928): 217–220; idem, *The Opposing Self,* p. 133.
41. Trilling, *The Opposing Self,* p. 143.
42. Trilling, *The Last Decade,* p. 54; idem, *Sincerity and Authenticity,* pp. 85–86.
43. Trilling, *The Liberal Imagination,* p. 256.
44. Trilling, *Beyond Culture,* pp. 143, 120, 127.
45. Ibid., p. 130.
46. Ibid., pp. 133, 141, 142.
47. Ibid., pp. 143, 144.
48. Trilling, *The Liberal Imagination,* pp. xi, 16, 24, 38; idem, *Beyond Culture,* pp. 177, 184.

49. Trilling, *The Liberal Imagination,* p. 256; idem, *Mind in the Modern World* (New York: The Viking Press, 1972), pp. 4, 41.
50. Matthew Arnold, *Letters of Matthew Arnold,* ed. G. W. E. Russell, 2 vols. (New York: Macmillan, 1900), 1 : 289–90.
51. Letter to the author of this book.
52. Trilling, *A Gathering of Fugitives,* p. 99.
53. See, e.g., the letter in the *New York Times* for 26 October 1973, signed by Trilling, Irving Howe, Michael Harrington, Meyer Schapiro, Saul Bellow, and Alfred Kazin.
54. I am grateful to Professor Sholom J. Kahn of the Hebrew University for showing me his correspondence with Trilling on this matter. In the final letter, dated 25 June 1975, Trilling wrote that "We still hold on to the hope that we will have a piece of time which will be wholly our own and one of the first priorities of such autonomy as we may gain is a trip to Israel."
55. Trilling, *The Liberal Imagination,* pp. 88, 271, 292; idem, *The Opposing Self,* p. 49.
56. Trilling, *The Liberal Imagination,* p. 292.
57. "Stretching out his hands in longing for the farther shore." Arnold's source is Virgil's *Aeneid,* 6. 314.

3

Isaac Bashevis Singer
and
Jewish Utopianism

Isaac Bashevis Singer is that rarity among modern Jews, a literary intellectual who is not only hostile to leftism in all its forms, but who appears never even to have been seriously tempted by the siren call of leftist sloganeering and utopianism that has lured so many Jews to their destruction. In a world where youthful addiction to leftism was as common as the measles, and even Menachem Begin belonged for a time to the Hashomer Hatzair movement, Singer must have been a remarkable anomaly. In his autobiographical reflections he has pictured *Literarishe Bletter,* the Yiddish literary magazine in Warsaw for which he worked in the early twenties, as aflame with socialism. In *A Young Man in Search of Love,* he gives us an unsavory picture of a whole cadre of leftist bullies, from Isaac Deutscher to the Stalinist hacks of the Writers Club, who warned him that he would be hanged from the nearest lamppost on the day the revolution came to Poland. Even when he came to the United States, he felt surrounded by Jewish leftists. Arriving in New York in 1935, he was appalled to find the building that contained the offices of *Der Forverts* draped in red, and thought that he had by accident landed in the Kremlin instead of America. Simon Weber, now editor of *Der Forverts* (and formerly on the staff of the Yiddish Communist paper, *Freiheit*), recalls the shock his socialist sensibilities sustained on meeting Singer in 1939: "He was an arch-conservative even then—against Roosevelt, against social progress, especially against anything that sounded like communism or even socialism."[1] Weber speaks for that considerable segment of the Jewish world that even today regards voting for a Republican candidate as an irredeemable sin, but considers a past history of support for Stalin as a youthful sowing of wild oats and a sure sign of a generous nature.

Lionel Trilling, as we have already seen, found it ironical that the high priests of modern European literature—Yeats, Eliot, and Lawrence, among others—were either indifferent or actively hostile to the political liberalism of the vast majority of their readers, critics, and advocates. The paradox of Singer's relation both to what he has called "the Yiddish tradition . . . of sentimentality and of social justice" and to the varieties of liberalism and of leftism that inform the outlook of the magazines that now publish his stories and the critics who explicate them, is still sharper. This may help to explain why so little attention has been paid to the political outlook that pervades his work, though it is highly visible, contentiously expressed, and entirely unambiguous. Although a sizable distance separates the sophisticated confusion of *New Yorker* liberalism, the democratic socialism of Irving Howe, and the dogmatic leftism of the *New York Review of Books,* it is safe to say that all these promoters of Singer's literary reputation look with a mixture of irritation and contempt on his essentially conservative and pessimistic view that "no matter what people are going to do it will always be wrong and there will never be any justice in this world."[2] Whether the willingness of these "progressives" to celebrate the genius of so "reactionary" a character as Singer is a tribute to their large-minded tolerance or a reflection of their incapacity to take conservative ideas seriously is a question that need not be answered here. Certainly, the aggressively political remarks Singer has made in the numerous interviews he has given have generally been ignored as instances of the avuncular philistinism that characterizes his remarks on a whole range of subjects on which his interlocutors consider themselves infinitely more sophisticated than he. Singer, for his part, is resigned to, yet saddened by, the unwillingness of even his most astute admirers to be wooed by his work from their illusions of hope. To the author of this book Singer once remarked of Irving Howe that he was "a wonderful man, who has done much for Yiddish literature and for me. But he's not a youngster anymore, and still, still he carries on with this socialist *meshugas.*"

Singer is by no means the only Jewish writer who has taken a determined stand against socialism, but he is virtually alone in having done so without first being disillusioned. His first brush with communism came at the Warsaw Writers Club in the twenties. Essentially nonpolitical, the young Singer instinctively sought to avoid the tragic fate, to step aside from the conflict with the forces of reaction, even from the conflict with evil, and devote himself to imaginative literature. "I wanted to do what Jews had done for two thousand years—flee or hide somewhere until the danger passed." But this proved impossible in Poland, not only because totalitarian ideology precluded the essential secrecy of the imaginative life, but because the most aggresssive purveyors of this ideology were other Jews:

> My enemies were Jewish youths, fledgling writers who lauded the Russian revolution, already glorified Comrade Dzerzhinski, and demanded death for all rabbis, priests, bourgeois, Zionists, and even Socialists who didn't follow the Moscow line. I was shocked to see how bloodthirsty Jewish boys and girls had become. Two thousand years of exile, ghetto, and Torah hadn't created a biological Jew. All it took was a few pamphlets and speeches to erase everything the books of morals had tried to imbue in us throughout the generations.[3]

From his experience of the Warsaw Jewish Communists (including, as luck would have it, his mistress Runya) and from the physical torment he endured proofreading poetic propaganda, Singer drew abiding lessons. Primary among them was the revelation that the pseudoreligious desire to save "mankind" invariably leads to cruelty on a massive scale. This is because the worship of mankind is nothing other than idolatry, albeit anthropomorphic idolatry. Singer found that the personal relations of these Communist friends of the species were always little hells of hatred and discord, and that it could be very disillusioning to follow great reformers of abuses beyond the thresholds of their homes. He soon came to the conclusion that some strange paradox of human nature always led those doctrinally committed to the transformation of mankind to lace the treacle of humanitarianism with the acid of hatred of real human beings. Utopianism, Singer concluded early in life, was not love but hatred of mankind.

The writers of Jewish Warsaw had forgotten that, as Yeats wrote, "we make out of the quarrel with others, rhetoric, but of the quarrel with ourselves, poetry." For Singer, the essential quarrel of the Jew, as of the writer, was with himself rather than with external enemies, including the most destructive. "Was it the Yiddish writer's obligation to conduct an eternal dialogue with the anti-Semites?" No sooner had the Jew forgotten this central truth than he became a prey to the worship of idols: "In all the centuries that the gentiles had waged wars against each other the Ghetto Jew had waged a war with his inner enemy, with that power of Evil that roosts in every brain and constantly strives to lead it astray. The Emancipation had partially . . . put an end to this Jewish war. The Enlightened Jew had himself become a bit of the Evil Spirit . . . a master of specious theories, of perverse truths, of seductive utopias, of false remedies. Since the gentile world needed its idols, the modern Jew had emerged to provide new ones."[4]

Almost any of Singer's novels dealing with post-Emancipation Jewry will provide a sense of just what these idols are. Herman Broder, in *Enemies,* tries to explain to Masha the apparently lunatic persistence among Jews of fascination with socialist and revolutionary movements, in spite of the fact that Hitler's national socialism was the most thoroughgoing revolution the world had ever known, that Stalin's camps destroyed as many people as Hitler's, and that "in Moscow they had liquidated all the Jewish writers." This dogged, incurable attachment, says Herman, is a modern form of the old idolatry outlawed by Judaism. "The Gentile makes gods of stone and we of theories." In the autobiographical *Shosha,* Singer's alter ego Aaron Greidinger meets his former mistress Dora (Runya) and her fellow Communist Felhendler after their love for the Soviet "experiment" has been poisoned by some doses of imprisonment and torture. He is dismayed to find that although their Communist ardor now burns with a very subdued flame they have not penetrated to the source of their problem. They still "believe" in revolution, but have transferred their loyalties from Stalin in Trotsky. They have yet to grasp the first principles of the idol they serve, namely, that revolutions mean bloodshed and that devotion to mankind leads inevitably to terror.

Singer's imaginative vision of Jewish socialism and communism as a pseudoreligion links his novels of modern life like *The Manor* and *The Estate* or *The Family Moskat* with novels like *Satan in Goray* or *The Slave,* in which the false messianism of the seventeenth century plays a central role. The religious moralist who speaks the last words of *Satan in Goray* is explicit in his condemnation of all those who are no longer content to await the coming of the ever-tarrying Messiah, but seek through action to hasten his arrival: "LET NONE ATTEMPT TO FORCE THE LORD: TO END OUR PAIN WITHIN THE WORLD: THE MESSIAH WILL COME IN GOD'S OWN TIME. . . ." Singer's repeated returns to the subject of Sabbatai Zevi indicate his recognition of how deep-seated in Jewish sensibility is the idea of inevitable cataclysm in the transition from historical present to messianic future. But his stress on the calamities that followed in the wake of the delusion with Sabbatai Zevi lend force to his persistent identification of modern political revolutionaries as false messiahs. For Singer as for Aaron Greidinger of *Shosha,* all writing about false messiahs is writing about Hitler and Stalin as well. Aaron's second novel (like Singer's first) deals with Sabbatai Zevi and describes "with much detail the Jewish longing for redemption in an epoch that displayed similarities to our own. What Hitler threatened to do to the Jews, Bogdan Chmielnitsky had done some three hundred years earlier." Even the ignorant and unworldly Shosha can exclaim, on reading her beloved's fiction about the Jews of the seventeenth century: " 'Oh, Mommy, it's exactly like today!' " This incessant linkage of modern Jewish calamities with the disasters of three centuries earlier expresses Singer's conviction that the Jewish infatuation with leftist political movements and their promises of redemption is a delusion that gives every indication of being the most damaging to Jewish existence since the seventeenth-century delusion with Sabbatai Zevi.

The first major work by Singer in which the intensity of his dislike of leftist political movements makes itself felt is *The Family Moskat*. The devotion to "humanity" of the novel's Jewish revolutionaries slackens only in relation to the one people with whom they are organically, and should therefore be responsibly, related—the Jews themselves. It is significant that Singer gives an antileftist character named Lapidus some of the novel's classic utterances even though he appears in a single scene and has no role whatever in the action. Lapidus disturbs the smug humanitarianism of the circle of Jewish leftists gathered at Gina Genendel's by pointing out that they weep over every Ivan, every Slav, and every oppressed nation of the world, except the Jews. They are ready to spill their blood, or at least their ink, for the liberation of every people except their own because, in strict accord with socialist doctrine, they deny the existence of the Jews as a people (and thus undermine their right to exist in the modern world at all). Some deep-seated impulse of treachery leads the emancipated Jews depicted in Singer's novels to deny only to the people from which they have sprung those human rights that are indivisible from national rights. " 'We dance,' says Lapidus, 'at everybody's wedding but our own.' "

The reason why socialism, including Jewish socialism, tends to be anti-Semitic is, in Singer's view, to be found in its developmental ideology, its Darwinian moorings. In *The Manor* and its sequel and conclusion, *The Estate*, Singer presents Polish Jewry in the last third of the nineteenth century as torn between its traditional self-definition as a people chosen by God to receive the Law, and a whole slew of conflicting naturalist ideologies—"socialism and nationalism, Zionism and assimilationism, nihilism and anarchism"—that were united only by the conviction that the Judaism of the ghetto and the shtetl, the Judaism of a powerless people without a land, was doomed to extinction. Throughout the novel we meet characters put to a difficult choice between being religious and being animalistic. Singer presents the conflict between Judaism and naturalism as absolute, allowing no resting place in that halfway house called humanism. Calman Jacoby is no sooner lured away from the traditional life of piety than he finds himself wearing, instead of simple religious garb, "a fox-lined overcoat with little tails dangling from the inner seams." His new servant Antosia is "in some ways . . . like an animal" and as little embarrassed as an animal about inviting the married Calman to her bed. His gentile foil, Count Jampolski, is less finicky when similarly tempted:

"He made no secret of the fact that he was cohabiting with Antosia, and Felicia heard the maid on her way to him each night. In his old age her father had turned into an animal."

The conflict between naturalism and religion is pursued into the next generation, for whom Darwinism affords the license to obliterate all distinction between man and animal. Wallenberg, the time-serving Jewish convert to Catholicism, offers Ezriel Babad access to his library of secular books, particularly recommending " 'a recently published English book that is causing a furor in the world of science. Its theory seems to be that all life is a struggle for survival and that the strongest species will win out. . . .' " Naturalism is incompatible with Judaism because it is incompatible with religion itself. But it is also capable, in its Darwinian form, of development into anti-Semitism. The novel's pioneer in this direction is Alexander Zipkin, a vulgar medical student in whose mind naturalism, humanism, and anti-Semitism are inseparable. Since his mental operations are representative of those of the emancipated Jews both of Ezriel's generation and the one to follow, they merit detailed illustration:

> The conversation turned to religion. Zipkin said straight out that he was an atheist. People spoke of God, but where was He? Had anyone seen Him? Each race worshipped a different idol. Man, as Darwin had proved, was descended from the apes. He was just another animal: *homo sapiens*. Zipkin began discussing the doctrines of Marx, Lassalle, and Lavrov. The Polish Jew, he said . . . had outlived his role and become little more than a parasite. He wasn't productive, didn't speak the language of the country in which he lived, and sent his children to cheders. How long was the Jew going to wash himself in ritual baths and walk around in tzizis?

Engels called Marx "the Darwin of sociology" because "just as Darwin has discovered the law of organic developement, so Marx has discovered the law of human development in history."[5] The analogy between Darwin and Marx holds good in Singer's novels, where Darwin's nature and Marx's history speak with a single voice about the Jewish people: *they* are the chief impediment to the removal of inferior races and backward classes that biology and history "demand." The clear implication of labeling Jews parasites, unspoken by Zipkin but soon articulated by Ezriel's sister Mirale and her progressive friends, is that they should be "exterminated"—what else does one do with parasites?

Mirale is one among many illustrations in Singer's novels of the view that the driving force of secular idealism is the lust for blood. Claiming to derive her ethical precepts from other human beings rather than from divine revelation, she embodies the truth that in morals as in physics the stream cannot rise higher than its source. Her pious father recognizes no

"humanistic" middle ground between holiness and animalism: " 'A human being.' If one does not serve the Almighty, one is even less than an
animal. Animals kill only for food; murderers enjoy killing." For Ezriel, a
doctor, using terrorism to reform society is like summoning a butcher
when a surgeon is needed. But Mirale and the other budding terrorists
depicted by Singer do not merely offer pragmatic justifications for political
murder or take the "modern" view that violence is its own vindication of
the cause it serves. Rather, they love violence for its own sake as
something that fills a void in their souls. More than anything else, it is the
frenzied attraction to violence of these Jewish leftists that leads Ezriel to
rethink his assumptions about the superiority of "progressive" European
culture over stationary Jewish religion: " 'Why are they so bloodthirsty?'
Ezriel wondered. They were Jewish women, members of the race which
had sworn to uphold the Ten Commandments. . . . He recalled the winter
day in Jampol when Mirale had entered the study house to tell him that
Calman Jacoby had come to meet him. Now he spent his time cutting the
dead apart, and Mirale plotted to kill the living." This is Darwinian
evolution and Marxist development, indeed.

For centuries the Jews had not handled the weapons of violence, and so
the moral quandaries involved in using the sword or the gun had not
troubled them. Yet in Singer's novels of modern Jewish life, the question
of violence becomes central. Ezriel faces it not only in the bloodthirstiness
of his progressive sister but in the rebelliousness of his children. They too
have chosen to live outside the yoke of Torah, and to stoop to the gun; yet
their paths are divergent. Zina, the daughter, is a garden-variety Jewish
leftist who has embellished her aunt's straightforward socialist anti-Semitism with the rhetoric of anti-Zionism, a fury toward "this new nationalism
of the vicious Jewish capitalists." She too believes in the redemptive
power of violence and revolution. Indeed, Ezriel's discovery of her gun
and cartridges is a decisive moment in his own spiritual development. "It
was the first time in Ezriel's life that he had touched such an instrument of
destruction, and its weight astounded him. He didn't know how to handle
it. . . ." Like many a Singer hero, and indeed like most of Diaspora Jewry
through the centuries, he believes that the sword is for Esau, not for
Jacob.[6] His revulsion from the weapon is inseparable from his anger at
himself for having raised non-Jewish children.

That his own daughter should be tainted with the gentile religion of
violence at first seems to Ezriel a revelation of the true character of Jewish
identity, which is epitomized by powerlessness. "Jewish suffering had
produced a spiritually superior type. For two thousand years the Jew had
not been in power and had not carried a sword." But Singer does not allow
Ezriel to rest in this (characteristically Jewish) complacency, which has

already been called into question in *The Slave,* by Wanda, who is schooled
in the religion of the Bible not the ghetto, and by Jacob, who escapes from
captivity because he "heeded the advice of the Book of Aboth: 'If one
comes upon thee, to kill thee, rise first and kill him.' " The experience of
Ezriel's other child shows him that the Jews can no longer evade the
choice between the supposed virtue of powerlessness and their survival as
a people.

Joziek enters the life of the novel at the moment when he tells his father:
" 'I'm going to Palestine.' " Humiliated by an anti-Semitic insult at
school, and finding himself unable to respond with the potency either of
words or of force, he tells his father that he will no longer live as Jews have
lived for two thousand years. For Joziek, who attends a "modern" school,
the promises of the Enlightenment and assimilation have proved empty.
They have deprived him of that inner world and sense of chosenness that
had enabled the Jew to endure two thousand years of exile and persecution, but they have made of his residual Jewish identity a greater burden
than ever, for it must be borne without understanding the reason why. For
Joziek, as for his father, this question of violence has been decisive. He
will go to Palestine as a Zionist pioneer, not because he believes that there
he will be free of enemies but because he believes that there he will be
capable of striking back at them. When we next hear of Joziek, later in the
novel, he is called Uri Joseph, he is living in Palestine, and his photograph
shows him on a horse, carrying a rifle.

Since the horse and the gun were, in the eyes of Eastern European Jews,
the special property of the gentile, it might seem that Singer here depicts
Zionism as nothing but another form of assimilation. But Singer has too
deep a respect for the unpredictable vitality of Jewish life to assume that
there is some absolute law that decrees that as soon as the Jews have a
land of their own and acquire the instruments of statehood they inevitably
must become just like all the other nations. Singer has, to be sure, often
expressed the view that Yiddish literature remains more Jewish in content
than does modern Hebrew literature, and has deplored the tendency of the
younger Israeli writers to strive mightily to be "like the nations" even
though they write in Hebrew.[7] He has also linked Zionists with Bundists in
his acrid recollections of the political activists he knew in Poland: "Certainly I was very close to these people, and . . . you know, sometimes
when you see the cook, the food doesn't seem very appetizing." Nevertheless, "in the case of Zionism, I felt that whoever the cook was, the food
was wholesome."[8] Singer has "always believed" in Zionism as the most
important modern manifestation of the unspent creative energy of Judaism. For Joziek, Palestine is not merely a refuge from anti-Semitism, but
the only land in which the Jews can retain their traditional culture in an
increasingly secular world. "Joziek was not religious but he remained a

Jew. Now he even wrote in Hebrew and signed his letters Uri Joseph. He had married a Jewish girl. His children would be educated in Hebrew schools."

Singer's celebration of Zionism, however qualified, may help to explain his unquenchable fascination with the mystical messianism of seventeenth-century Sabbatianism, despite his stress on its disastrous effects. Gershom Scholem, the greatest scholar of Jewish mysticism, the biographer of Sabbatai Zevi and the historian of his movement, has stressed that "the desire for total liberation which played so tragic a role in the development of Sabbatian nihilism was by no means a purely self-destructive force; on the contrary, beneath the surface of lawlessness, antinomianism, and catastrophic negation, powerful constructive impulses were at work. . . . In our own times we owe much to the experience of Zionism for enabling us to detect in Sabbatianism's throes those gropings toward a healthier national existence which must have seemed like an undiluted nightmare to the peaceable Jewish bourgeois of the nineteenth century."[9] Precisely this groping toward a healthier national existence than existed in the shtetl and ghetto is stressed in *The Slave,* Singer's novel about seventeenth-century Polish Jewry in the aftermath of the Chmielnicki massacres. Jacob's decision, late in the story, to go to the Holy Land is, like that of hundreds who actually did go between 1696 and 1700, based on the gross delusion that Sabbatai Zevi is the Messiah and that the long-awaited redemption is at hand. But it also derives from a genuinely Jewish revulsion against the debased Judaism of the Exile. The book takes for granted, just as does Ezriel's son in *The Estate,* that Diaspora Jewry has crippled itself by its pacific ethos. "Stories he had heard of how the Jews had behaved during the massacres shamed him. Nobody had dared lift a hand against the butchers. . . . Though for generations Jewish blacksmiths had forged swords, it had never occurred to the Jews to meet their attackers with weapons. The Jews of Josefov, when Jacob had spoken of this, had shrugged their shoulders. The sword is for Esau, not for Jacob." But Jacob of the novel, long in exile from the Jewish community and therefore more immediately connected than his neighbors with the traditions of the Bible, knows that Jews did not always behave this way. At the very moment when he is being led away in chains because he has committed the "criminal" act of converting a Christian to Judaism, "Suddenly it occurred to Jacob that sometimes chains could be broken. Nowhere was it written that a man must consent to his own destruction." This revelation enables him to break his chains in Poland and also proves eminently useful in Eretz Yisrael where, we learn, "he dared defy armed Arabs or Turks."

Jacob's commitment of his destiny to the Sabbatian movement in the Land of Israel, although springing from delusion, turns out to be an unalloyed gift of heaven, bringing with it the blessing of a son who at age twenty is an instructor in a yeshiva. Although Jacob, when he returns to claim Wanda-Sarah's bones in Pilitz, curses the name and memory of Sabbatai Zevi, he does not doubt that in connecting himself with the historic Jewish community of Palestine, he has chosen life over death and borne witness to the continuing vitality of Judaism, even if expressed in hitherto unimagined forms. "Not even Sabbatai Zevi had come in vain. False birth pains sometimes precede the true." Despite all the brutality, destruction, and treachery he has witnessed and suffered, Jacob dies consoled by the knowledge, given him by his survival and rerooting in the Holy Land, that although "the leaves drop from the tree, . . . the branches remain; the trunk still has its roots."

I do not mean to suggest either that Jacob is a proto-Zionist or that Singer arbitrarily singles out Zionism as a good, true manifestation of messianism as distinct from all the bad, false ones—socialism, communism, and bundism, among others. What links Jacob with the Zionists of Singer's "modern" novels is a vision of rebuilding in the aftermath of degradation or catastrophe, a longing for Jewish national identity not merely as a refuge from persecution but as a return to the life-giving sap of a tree whose roots are buried but not dead. For Ezriel, Zionism shows that Judaism is vital and alive: "In the passage of two thousand years, hundreds of nations had become assimilated into other cultures. But the Jews still struggled to return to the land of their ancestors. This fact alone proved that the Old Testament contained divine truths." Singer does persistently single out Zionism from among other Jewish political movements that have also lost the old patience and therefore desire action in the concrete, historical realm rather than the endless deferment of hopes. Of the Zionists in *The Family Moskat,* we are told that "Everyone was against them—the orthodox Jews, the Socialist Bundists, the Communists. But they were not the kind to be frightened off. If the Messiah had not come riding on his ass by now, then it was time to take one's destiny into one's own hands."

That overtones of messianism cling to the Zionist enterprise, even despite its rejection of Jewish chosenness and its espousal of the ideal of "normalization," Singer would not deny; yet ultimately his stress is on the uniqueness of Zionism, not only as what Hannah Arendt once called "the only political answer Jews have ever found to antisemitism," but as a movement that, instead of making itself the instrument of a hypostatized history or nature, takes full responsibility for its actions. Here too Singer is at one with Scholem, who has written that "The greatness of the Zionist Movement has been that it was a movement that accepted historical responsibility, that undertook tasks and accepted responsibility for our actions, without any Messianic pretensions."[10]

In conclusion, we may say that although Singer is too deeply committed to the modern idea of the autonomy of the writer and the truth of the imagination to be a political novelist, political views have often informed and shaped his work. At the very outset of his career he decided to cut himself off from the Yiddish tradition of social idealism and identify himself with the Jewish tradition that says, "thou shalt not respect the person of the poor, nor favour the person of the mighty; but in righteousness shalt thou judge thy neighbour" (Lev. 19:15). He called into question many central assumptions of Yiddish writing, among them the idea that there is virtue in powerlessness, that socialism is a legitimate secularization of Jewish messianism, and that utopian idealism betokens love of mankind. He found the true analogy to the Jews' dogged devotion to socialism despite generations of socialist anti-Semitism in the continuing devotion of Sabbatai Zevi's followers to the false messiah long after he had converted to Islam; and in his novels of modern life he presents the Jewish infatuation with leftist political movements as the most permanent force of devastation in Jewish life since the seventeenth- and eighteenth-century delusion with Sabbatai Zevi. His retrospective view of modern Jewish history makes it perfectly plausible that the reduction of Israel to sandy wastes should today be a primary desideratum of international socialism. In Zionism and in Israel itself, Singer sees above all else evidence of the unpredictable vitality of Jewish life, rather than a messianic redemption from exile and a resurrection of the dead. For the Jewish world that Singer mourns may not be resurrected except in literature.

Notes

1. Quoted in Paul Kresh, *Isaac Bashevis Singer: The Magician of West Eighty-sixth Street* (New York: Dial Press, 1979), p. 190.
2. I. B. Singer and Irving Howe, "Yiddish Tradition vs. Jewish Tradition: A Dialogue," *Midstream,* 19 (June/July 1973): 35.
3. Isaac Bashevis Singer, *A Young Man in Search of Love* (New York: Doubleday, 1978), p. 96.
4. Ibid., pp. 109, 161.
5. Quoted in Jacques Barzun, *Darwin, Marx, Wagner* (New York: Doubleday, 1958), p. 169.
6. According to Rashi, the great French medieval interpreter of the Torah, Jacob on his deathbed chastises Simeon and Levi because, in taking up "weapons of violence," they have stolen "the blessing of Esau."
7. Isaac Bashevis Singer, "Yiddish, the Language of Exile," *Judaica Book News,* Spring/Summer 1976, p. 27.
8. Isaac Bashevis Singer, *Critical Views of Isaac Bashevis Singer,* ed. Irving Malin (New York: New York University Press, 1969), pp. 17–18.
9. Gershom Scholem, *The Messianic Idea in Judaism* (New York: Schocken Books, 1971), p. 84–85.
10. Gershom Scholem, "There is mystery in the world . . ." *Jerusalem Post Magazine,* 4 October 1974, p. 12.

4

Anatoly Shcharansky

On the ides of March 1977, Anatoly Shcharansky, while in the company of two friends and two Western correspondents, was seized by agents of the KGB, the Soviet secret police, and taken to Lefortovo Prison in Moscow to be investigated for "crimes against the State." Although the young mathematician and computer scientist had been active in the dissident movement on behalf of human rights as well as in the Jewish movement for the right to emigrate to Israel, no one doubted that he had been arrested and accused of treason as a Jewish leader. In his biography of Shcharansky,[1] Martin Gilbert points out that not a single non-Jewish member of the Helsinki Watch group to which Shcharansky belonged was interrogated in his case. The arrest, accusations, and trial were an attack on the Jewish activists and still more on the Jews of the Soviet Union. "Today," said Ida Nudel (subsequently exiled to Siberia for hanging a small banner displaying a Star of David from her balcony), "we . . . are accused of espionage, for the single reason that the accusation of killing Christian babies would sound ridiculous in this country of atheists." The Soviet leaders have lost their ancestors' belief in Christ, but not their ancestors' belief that the Jews killed him.

That such atavistic impulses could survive the revolution seems not to have occurred to the countless Jews in Russia who helped to bring it about. Chaim Weizmann recalled how "the arrogant Trotsky" sneered with contempt at any Jew moved by the fate of his own people, and how hundreds of thousands of young Jews in early-twentieth-century Russia were convinced revolutionaries "offering themselves for sacrifice as though seized by a fever." Even long after the bliss of the red dawn had faded, Soviet Jewish writers could offer sycophantic songs of praise to the Russian Pharaoh: "When I mention Stalin—I mean beauty,/I mean eternal happiness,/I mean nevermore to know,/Nevermore to know of pain." But even such verses could not save their author, Itzik Feffer, from being murdered in 1952 along with such Yiddish writers as Peretz Markish, David Bergelson, and David Hofstein. In his "Elegy for the Soviet Yiddish Writers," the late Chaim Grade imagined himself visited by the ghosts of Bergelson, who suffered eternally from regret precisely over "what we hoped for—the New Enlightened Man!" and *der Nistar,*[2] who, almost alone, had the prescience to warn his fellow Jews: "Children, beware, run away!"

But the surprise occasioned in the Yiddish writers by the ability of anti-Semitism to survive the revolution and even to flourish as a result of it would have been as nothing compared with the surprise, could they have lived to feel it, occasioned by the revival of Jewish life, Jewish identity, Jewish will, even Jewish religion, in the Soviet Union. If ever there was a valley of dry bones from which new life seemed unlikely to spring, it was Jewish life under bolshevism. Its enemies, like the Jewish Communist Izzi Charik, boasted that "We will trample and forget you,/Like rotted straw." Even its friends, like Isaac Babel in certain moods, could see no more in it than "the rotted Talmuds of my childhood . . . the dense melancholy of memories . . . a little of that pensioned-off God."

Once they had lost their illusions about the "New Enlightened Man," the Soviet Jewish writers could envision a generation of Jews eager to "run away" from socialism; and it was partly for his desire to run away, and to help other Jews run away, that Shcharansky was arrested, tried, and sentenced. But what made his offense and his courage to give offense all the greater—for what Jew in the Soviet Union does not want to run away?—was that he had something to run to, something for which he longed, something he preferred to socialism and to the Soviet Union. When, shortly after his arrest, Shcharansky's mother (who was not allowed to see him during the sixteen-month period that elapsed between his arrest and trial in July 1978), was asked to say something about her son, she pointed to a map of Israel and said: "Photograph the State of Israel and say, in the name of Anatoly, that his heart is there."

If for his mother and, now, for Jews generally, Shcharansky is a brand plucked out of the fire, part of a precious returned remnant barely saved from destruction, for his persecutors he represented a particularly brazen and articulate repudiation of Russia for Israel, of atheism for religious obscurantism, and of socialism for Zionism. Formally, Shcharansky was tried for treason (Article 64 of the Criminal Code) in collusion with the CIA,[3] and for anti-Soviet agitation and propaganda (Article 70). The prosecutor and his witnesses further alleged that "He studied Hebrew. . . . he did not participate in socially useful labour. . . . he was slovenly and morally unstable." But what the prosecution returned to repeatedly, almost obsessively, during the trial was that Shcharansky had, in preferring Israel, "denied our superiority." Russia, the prosecutor reiterated at various times during the trial, had a more democratic religious system than Israel (even Muhammad Ali had confirmed this), better doctors (especially psychiatrists), and, above all, better prison camps, whose edifying influence on their inmates had even won the praise of certain American criminologists. The public prosecutor's obsession with the rivalry between the USSR and Israel, a country that a cooler legal head might adroitly have dismissed as a poor thing but the Jews' own, seemed to express the Soviet belief that, as Radio Minsk put it, Judaism is "contrary to our Communist morality, the aims of our society, and the progress of modern life."[4]

Shcharansky, conducting his own defense in a trial that prohibited any reference by him to the testimony of witnesses or to the documents alleging espionage, addressed a hostile courtroom that included hecklers who showered him with such epithets as "spider" and "agent provocateur," and demanded that he be hanged. The only break in the solid wall of antipathy that he faced was his brother Leonid, sequestered in the back row. His address was informed by the conviction that, even when there are few or no witnesses, the truth must be told, the moral gesture must be made, because this is what justice requires, and the intrinsic value of justice, the power that it holds from the Maker of men and of things, remains forever the same, however much its extrinsic value may fluctuate. Eventually, of course, the story of Shcharansky's trial, like that of Alfred Dreyfus, reached the whole world. The Dreyfus trial, many claim, gave birth to the Zionist movement; the Shcharansky trial and its aftermath, many hope, will bring the rebirth of the Zionist movement.

The content of the address was Jewish history. People who had met Shcharansky in the early seventies were astounded by his spiritual hunger for a Judaism of which he had been largely ignorant. "He had no Jewish tradition behind him," reported one acquaintance. "Everything he reached, he reached by himself." It was this spiritual yearning, unsatisfied by secular Enlightenment and scientific socialism, rather than Soviet anti-Semitism, that drew Shcharansky toward the land, the people, and the God of Israel. But now, at his trial, he felt what it meant to enter a community of suffering, to be united with all the Jews of history who had resisted countless Hamans.

Shcharansky spoke of the Jewish exile, of the Zionist movement, of the large Jewish role in the Bolshevik Revolution, of Stalin's campaign against the Jews, of the emigration movement, of the Jewish determination not to disappear as a people, and of his pride in being a part of the modern Jewish renaissance. He told how he had declined the invitation of the authorities to betray the Jewish movement in exchange for a visa to Israel and reunion with his wife, Avital, who had been forced to leave him a day after their marriage in 1974, just before her emigration visa was to expire. His concluding words perfectly illustrate Cynthia Ozick's view that if Jews are content to blow through the narrow end of the shofar, that is, to speak as Jews instead of masquerading as "Mankind," they will be heard everywhere. Shcharansky's great distinction is that precisely by speaking as a Jew and not as an indiscriminate part of universal humanity he has become a universal symbol of freedom, dignity, and self-respect. And this is how he spoke:

> Five years ago I submitted my application for exit to Israel. Now I am further than ever from my dream. It would seem to be cause for regret. But it is absolutely otherwise. I am happy. I am happy that I lived honestly, in peace with my conscience. I never compromised my soul, even under the threat of death. . . . For more than 2000 years the Jewish people, my people, have been dispersed. But wherever they are, wherever Jews are found, each year they have repeated, "Next year in Jerusalem." Now, when I am further than ever from my people, from Avital, facing many arduous years of imprisonment, I say, turning to my people, my Avital: *Next year in Jerusalem!* And I turn to you, the court, who were required to confirm a predetermined sentence: to you I have nothing to say.

Neither the eloquence of his speech nor the greater eloquence of his silence could save Shcharansky from being found guilty as charged and sentenced to thirteen years of imprisonment. During the long years at Chistopol and Perm, years of isolation greater than other prisoners endured, of severe illness, of frequent solitary confinement, of hunger strikes to protest denial of visits and letters ("two letters a year in a good year") from his family, and of 403 days in punishment cells four meters square, Shcharansky continued to demonstrate, and was partly sustained by, those qualities that had distinguished his public career: courage, resilience, disinterested devotion to virtue, humor, and ironic wit. If the authorities placed him in an isolation cell to break his will, he sang aloud during his days there every Hebrew song he had ever memorized. If they told him it was futile to write letters of protest on behalf of mistreated fellow prisoners, he continued to do so because "the prisoner who writes such a letter may not save his neighbour in the next cell, but he saves his own soul." With mock nostalgia, he wrote to his mother of childhood days "when the priority of Russian serfs in science and technique was a favoured topic." With mock solemnity, he told her of his recent instruction in "the law [that] the use of humour is also undesirable." When his jailers prevented him from sending his mother a lock of his hair, he commended them for discouraging "superstition, prejudice and remnants of the past among certain undeveloped citizens." Even under the censor's watchful eye, Shcharansky's irony was (to use Lionel Trilling's valuable distinction) an irony of comprehension and engagement rather than of detachment. He thought of wit and humor as instruments of self-defense because they enabled him to prove to himself that "freedom can neither be given nor taken away, since man *is* freedom."

Yet it is clear from the evidence of Shcharansky's prison correspondence, abundantly supplied (along with many other previously unpublished documents) in Gilbert's indispensable biography, that even he could not have survived the nine years in prisons and labor camps without "outside help." Upon his release in February of 1986, he declared that "without religion I could not have withstood all that I suffered." He also stressed that by religion he did not mean something that could be subsumed under Jewish history or culture or Zionism, important as all these had been, and still were, to him. "I am a Jew. Our religion is not only part of our culture."

Shcharansky's Judaism had originated in what Proust used to call the indescribable bond of metaphor, the recognition that we stand where our ancestors stood because we were potentially present in their imaginations. He was captivated by the words: "In every generation a man should see himself as if he personally came out of Egypt." Six months after his bride had left for Israel, and he began to sense that their separation might be a long one, he wrote to Avital that seeing their life through the Bible could make things easier, and reminded her that "Jacob worked seven years for Rachel but in his eyes they were like a few days because of his love for her." During his imprisonment Shcharansky journeyed through time and space toward sympathetic identification with his Jewish forebears, from Dreyfus to Rabbi Akiva. Unlike his countrymen among the originators of Zionism who had sought to liberate themselves from the culture of the shtetl and ghetto to embrace the Enlightenment, modernity, and "normality," Shcharansky conceived of his future in Zion through images of the Jewish past. In one letter he even exhorted himself to go "forward, to the past!" But the weight and momentum of the collective experience of the Jewish people, its power to act as "gear wheels that move . . . our individual lives," could not be explained only in a historical dimension. That is why Shcharansky's quest for the past, a quest carried out in the intense loneliness of a Bolshevik prison, led him ultimately back to the ancient biblical promise (Deut. 5:3) that all Jews, including those not yet born, were present to receive the covenant at Sinai.

Shcharansky's cherished book in prison was the Book of Psalms. He was punished with 130 days in solitary confinement for a hunger strike protesting its confiscation. Upon his release from captivity on 10 February, he flung himself into the snow and refused to move until his guards restored the book they had again tried to confiscate. "I said I would not leave the country without the Psalms, which helped me so much." He had begun to study them in Hebrew after learning of his father's death in January 1980. At first they provided consolation ("a memorial stone in my heart") and a sense of unity with his family and with the Jews in Israel. But then they did more. The Psalms address those who, "encircled by mortal enemies," patiently await deliverance from "those who seek my life." Specifically, they refer to David, who, rescued from his enemies and from Saul, thanks the Lord who "brought me out to freedom." Shcharansky, too, was eventually brought out to freedom. But first he gained freedom from what Spinoza called human bondage, from the emotions that place man at the mercy of fortune. Shcharansky came to understand as fully as any man can hope to do why Spinoza urged that "no virtue can be conceived as prior to this virtue of endeavoring to preserve oneself." The freedom he gained through the Psalms was freedom "from the slave concealed deep within" each of us, and, in consequence, from fear of human beings and their instruments of oppression. At first he thought the psalmist's expression, "fear of the Lord," meant fear of God's retribution for transgressions. But once he recognized that this "fear" referred to man's awareness of the distance separating his will from God's essence, he acquired spiritual endurance and the saving knowledge that "fear of God is the one factor capable of conquering human fear." To achieve this conquest was to stand with those who stood at Sinai: "The counsel of the Lord is for those who fear Him;/to them He makes known his Covenant."

In September 1983, on the Jewish New Year, Shcharansky, having already been imprisoned for over six years, wrote that he faced the future "keeping the past in a knapsack, and I cross raging rivers and high mountains toward my present with Natalia." Now that Shcharansky has crossed those rivers and mountains, we know that what he carried in that knapsack to Israel was a Zionism leavened by suffering and permeated by religion, potentially a rich heritage for the children of Israel. And what will the children of Israel, in the Diaspora and in the land of Israel, now make of that heritage?

It is too soon to answer such a question or even to pose it precisely, especially since Shcharansky has not yet told his own story.[5] Who can say how many of the three hundred thousand people who came to pay tribute to Shcharansky when he visited New York in May 1986 reflected deeply on the implications of his story or on the fact that he tended to withhold his support from Jewish cultural and educational efforts in the Soviet Union that were not subservient to the goal of emigration to Israel? The story of how much Shcharansky suffered to achieve a goal that is within easy reach of every Western Jew may yet have great results in the Diaspora, but results that are incalculably diffusive and not readily visible.

It is in the land of Israel itself, where the remarkable story of Shcha-

ransky continues, that the issue of his heroic spirit may be more concentrated and visible; but this is by no means certain. No sooner had he
arrived in Zion than the vulgarity and parochialism of Israeli public
discourse on religion shamelessly exhibited themselves in a fusillade of
inane questions. Would Shcharansky wear a skullcap? Why didn't he kiss
the ground after his plane landed? Did he obey all 613 commandments?
How would he get on with his wife, who during their twelve years of
separation had become notoriously "Jewish" in the Holy Land? Would he
favor retention of the territories, or did his study of Arabic encourage
leftist hopes that he would join "Peace Now"? Shcharansky, having
wrestled with God as well as with the KGB, must have soon begun to feel
as Gulliver did when, after he had saved himself from drowning, the
Lilliputians demanded to know whether he broke his eggs at the little end
or the big one.

   Those who wish to pursue the Shcharansky saga beyond the confines of
Gilbert's book, which concludes with his arrival in Jerusalem and his
expression of the wish that "as many Jews as possible" will join him there,
will, for the time being, have to resort to the penultimate section of
Anatoly and Avital Shcharansky: The Journey Home, a book produced by
a team of *Jerusalem Post* reporters.[6] Although they admit, in their preface,
that "with two exceptions, those of us who worked on this book had never
been even slightly interested in Soviet Jewry," it is not the authors' past
lack of commitment but their present lack of sense and tact that requires an
apology. Their narrative of Shcharansky's reception in Israel exemplifies
the uneasiness he and his wife inspire in defensively secular Israelis. In
addition to asking, incessantly, the mindless questions mentioned above, it
presents the warm welcome given Shcharansky at Ben-Gurion Airport by
his wife's longtime supporters in the religious nationalist movement as a
sinister conspiracy to capture this hero of the "human rights" movement
for the alien ideology of "right-wing" Zionism espoused by his wife. (The
journalists' animosity toward Avital Shcharansky for her "acquired religi-
osity" and her "carping" for twelve years to gain her husband's release
mixes uneasily with their prurient inquisitiveness about her "self-denied
sensuality" and their gossip-columnists' allusions to her inferior cooking
and home-decorating skills.)

   If we are to believe the *Post* reporters, Shcharansky had barely entered
the airport when his old friends and supporters like the lawyer Irwin Cotler
and the journalist Robert Toth began busily telling everyone who would
listen that they feared Shcharansky's commitment to human rights would
be swallowed up by the Gush Emunim politics of his wife and the
"xenophobia" of the religious, whose pressure on him, according to an
unidentified leftist source, would be harder to resist than that of the KBG.
When one of the religious welcoming party admitted to the *Post*'s inquiring

reporter that he was ignorant of Shcharansky's efforts in Russia on behalf of persecuted Christians, the reporter quickly concluded that "Such ecumenicism would be frowned upon by these people." The only religious person at the airport who gets good marks from the *Post* team is the "religious politician" Avraham Burg, the Peace Now activist (apparently the only one at the airport) who was assigned by Prime Minister Peres to drive the Shcharanskys to Jerusalem. His particular merit is that, when he reached the entrance to Jerusalem, and admirers of the Shcharanskys who had gathered in front of what the journalists call "Merkaz Harav Yeshiva" tried to greet the couple, he "sped past without stopping."

The full name of the yeshiva in question is Merkaz Harav Kook. The name lopped off by the secularist zeal of the *Jerusalem Post* team is that of Rabbi Abraham Isaac Kook, first chief rabbi of Palestine after the British Mandate. Kook's special distinction among the formative thinkers of Zionism was his insistence that Jewish nationalism, however secular in outward appearance, is inwardly an expression of the religious impulse, that the national and religious elements in Judaism are an indivisible entity, and that it is "therefore pointless to wage a bitter and ill-conceived war against those who are loyal to only one aspect of the Jewish character." Kook addressed this admonition to the religiously Orthodox, many of whom are still greatly in need of such counsel. The lively interest taken in Kook's teachings today derives from the spreading recognition that his is the kind of voice required to still the noisy conflict of half-truths that threatens to sunder Israeli society. If the authors of this narrative had been more respectful of Kook and less of the egregious "speculation in the Israeli press about [Avital's] religious beliefs and [Anatoly's] secular views," they might have attained a glimpse of the promise that Shcharansky's story carries within itself for a fruitful compromise between "secular" and "religious" in the land of Israel. In his remarks to the National Press Club in Washington in May 1986, Shcharansky repudiated the label "secular Jew," declared that a "spiritual factor" was at work in everything happening to Soviet Jewry, and said that all the alleged conflicts between himself and his wife about religion "disappear the moment I stop reading the press." To one of his old friends from Moscow who, having already fallen prey to the bad intellectual habits of his new country, asked Shcharansky, "Have you become religious?" he replied: "I'm Jewish."

Notes

1. Martin Gilbert, *Shcharansky: Hero of Our Time* (New York: Viking Press, 1986).
2. "The Hidden One," pen name of Pinhas Kahanovich.

3. By "CIA" the Russians mean Western correspondents. Two of the fifty-one volumes of "evidence" consisted of clippings from the Western press.
4. The author of this book, interrogated by Soviet authorities in December 1976 for carrying Jewish books into the USSR, was told that "these Jewish craps [sic] subvert the Soviet way of life."
5. Publication of his memoir is planned for fall 1987.
6. The section on the Shcharanskys in Israel was composed by Abraham Rabinovich, Douglas Davis, Robert Rosenberg, and Louis Rapoport.

5

The Last Refuge of a Scoundrel: Gore Vidal's Anti-Jewish Patriotism

*Everything which another man would have
hidden, everything the publication of which would
have made another man hang himself, was matter
of gay and clamorous exultation to his weak and
diseased mind.*
—T. B. Macaulay on
James Boswell (1831)

A famous nineteenth-century thinker once wrote that "before learning to love, we must learn to hate." This theory of moral education proved music to the inward ear of the young Gore Vidal; he took it to heart and became so diligent a student in the preliminary course that he soon lost sight of the higher reaches of the curriculum towards which it was supposed to lead him. He has, during his long career, become a great, a prolific, a many-sided hater. Despite moderate success as, among other things, a novelist, a playwright, a scriptwriter, a pornographer, a politician, an essayist, a television celebrity, he has cultivated the sense of himself as a man driven by an angry mob of thick-skinned louts to utter the bitterest taunts he can invent.

In order to retaliate the injuries he imagines to have been inflicted on him as a writer, as a political radical, as a foe of the Judeo-Christian ethic and religion, as a homosexual, Vidal has "learned to hate" an extraordinary number of groups and individuals. He has learned to hate "the most tribal part of the United States," the south, whose inhabitants are bigots, "rednecks," and religious fanatics. He has learned to hate immigrants, especially if, like John Simon ("A Yugoslav with a proud if somewhat incoherent Serbian style [or is it Croatian?—in any case, English is his third language]") they are responsible for the degeneration of American prose. He has learned to hate psychiatrists, and to locate psychiatry "somewhere between astrology and phrenology on the scale of human gullibility, the cold-blooded desire to make money." He has learned to hate universities (surprisingly, since he never attended one), and especially English departments, "manned by the second-rate" and "increasing at a positively Malthusian rate." He has learned to hate believing Christians (whom he usually calls "Christers"), because they persecute minority groups, deprive women of equality by denying them abortions, and have "made a hell of Western man's life on earth" by forcing fornicators and adulterers, all "those not joined together by the Jewish/Christian God," to confine their activities to the seediest hotels. He has learned to hate the people of Pasadena, because they "hate the Jews, hate the Negroes, the poor, the foreign . . . really terrible people." He has learned to hate the Roman Catholic Church, because it has managed to shield its "$25-billion portfolio" in America from the IRS and because its idea of natural law prohibits homosexuality. He has learned to hate *The New York Times* because it is "homophobic" and has denied advertising space to the government of Egypt. He has learned to hate marriage and child-bearing, the mere contemplation of which causes him to have a faintish feeling such as might come over a sea-sick man upon hearing a call for pork-chops, although he "would favor an intelligent program of eugenics that would decide which genetic types should be continued and which allowed to die out . . . we do it regularly in agriculture and in the breeding of livestock." And so on, *ad nauseam*. But his long apprenticeship to hatred has so far prepared him for just one form of love, that of Narcissus: "I am mesmerized," he writes, "by the tributes to my beauty that keep cropping up in . . . memoirs."

In this cornucopia of rage and resentment, two hatreds stand out above the rest: America and the Jews. At some point relatively early in his career Vidal decided, for a variety of personal, sexual, aesthetic, and political reasons, that what he calls "the American Empire" was a kind of hell on earth ("we have created a hell and called it The American Way of Life"). Nevertheless, appropriately enough for someone who is, as the *Times Literary Supplement* once said of him, "of the Devil's party—and knows it," he has several times in his life aspired to leadership in this hell: in 1945 he told Anais Nin that one day he would become President of the United States; in 1960 he ran for Congress as the Democratic-Liberal candidate in New York's twenty-ninth district, and lost; starting in 1975, when he declared that the Presidency was the only thing he ever desired that he had failed to achieve, he began to issue "State of the Union" addresses to compete with those of the President. In 1982, he ran against Jerry Brown for Senator from California, taking as his slogan "get the government off our fronts," and, on his nonsexual platform, declaring both that America had been "at war with every nation on earth for 36 years" and that the only real threat to America was "the enemy within." Once again, he lost.

A character in one of Vidal's political novels (*Washington, D. C.,* 1967) asserts that "Politics is the only profession in which mediocrities can gain the world's attention through slander." Given the style in which Vidal has generally treated his opponents—in 1968 he gained the attention of about twelve million people by calling William Buckley a Nazi on television—he could only explain his defeats by imputing them to "a society . . . deeply and mindlessly homophobic." "I could have made it," he said in 1972, "if it hadn't been for this fag thing." Later he told the *Paris Review* that "I am proud to say that I am most disliked because for twenty-six years I have been in open rebellion against the heterosexual dictatorship in the United States."

To describe Vidal's anti-Americanism as the "philosophy" of somebody for whom *The New York Review of Books* and *The Nation* have served, in political matters, as a kind of *Women's Wear Daily,* does not adequately convey its virulence, especially since Vidal is himself a leading couturier of these journals. The America of Gore Vidal is aesthetically objectionable: it has a "proto-Op-art flag," and is "the land of the tin ear." America is intellectually contemptible: "Americans have no sense of the past, and indeed hate it"; the American majority's memory "is about four weeks at best"; "one must never underestimate the collective ignorance of that informed electorate for whom Thomas Jefferson had such high hopes." America is rife with religious persecution. Its Puritan founders left England "not because they were persecuted for their religious beliefs" but because they were forbidden to persecute others. Once they landed here, they created "the sort of quasi-theocratic society they had dreamed of . . . they formed that ugly polity whose descendants we are." The modern continuators of the Puritan persecutors are "Jews trying to censor the film of *Oliver Twist,*" "uneasy heterosexuals fearful of a homosexual take-over," and "redneck divines . . . joined by a group of New York Jewish publicists . . . to raise fag-baiting to a level undreamed of in Falls Church." "We must never underestimate the essential bigotry of the white majority in the United States."

Vidal's America is teetering on the edge of a Niagara of insanity. "You know, of course, that one out of every five people in the U.S. is mentally disturbed." America is "a nation that worships psychopaths." America is consumed by greed, a "nation of ongoing hustlers," a "corrupt society" in which every four years "the U. S. will be up for sale, and the richest man or family will buy it." (Vidal himself paid court to that rich family called the Kennedys during the early years of John F. Kennedy's administration, until he was banished—whether because of Bobby Kennedy's calling him "a hack writer" or proposing the slogan "Let's give Gore Vidal to the Vietcong" is still matter of debate—and took to deriding them as "The Holy Family.") In political organization, of course, the America of Vidal's febrile imagination is Gehenna and the pit of hell, a country whose "pretense of being a free or even civilized society" is a sick joke. In 1958 he wrote that "if ever there was a people ripe for dictatorship it is the American people today. Should a homegrown Hitler appear, whose voice . . . would be raised against him in derision?" By the 1980's Vidal's America, suffering the inevitable disasters that befall a "garrison state" or "armed camp," a country in which "there has never been a left wing," was bristling with countless Hitlers (among them Joseph Epstein, Robert Moses, Midge Decter) and "gas chambers" being designed for "blacks and faggots." (According to Vidal, *Commentary* believes that "all's right with America if you're not in a gas chamber, and making money.")

Given this somewhat gloomy view of the United States, it seems surprising that Vidal has chosen to spend part of every year here. His admirers and biographers disagree on whether to endorse his explanation that "despair" makes him "vacillate between living in Rome and raging in New York" or to suggest that the new Italian tax laws of 1976 forced him to spend less than six months of every year in the places he considered his true homes, Rome and Ravello. His readers in the *NYRB* and *Nation* and *Playboy,* eager for the author of *Myra Breckinridge* to stand in moral judgment on American life, should at least be grateful that he has not made good on any of the more extreme threats with which he has frightened them over the years. In 1972 he threatened to move to Ireland "for good"; in 1968, he solemnly warned: "For myself, should the war in Vietnam continue after the 1968 election, a change in nationality will be the only moral response." Not for the first time in his life, Vidal worked out a compromise with moral principles and kept his American citizenship. But he did not blush to reveal where his true loyalties lay. He saw nothing objectionable in the activities of Americans who supported the Vietcong against their own countrymen, and urged the U.S. to back Ho Chi Minh. In fact, ever since 1948, when his homosexual novel, *The City and the Pillar,* was, in his estimate, ignored by the American critics, he took as his touchstone for judging disputes between America and her adversaries, the slogan "the *other* country, right or wrong."

Vidal's hatred of America is, in its way, an impressive thing, but it has sometimes been forced to retreat in face of a still greater hatred: that of the Jews. Sooner or later, every great hater must participate in this most durable of all human hatreds; and Vidal did so sooner rather than later. From the start, his hostility towards Jews has been an idiosyncratic mixture of old-fashioned religious Jew-hatred and modern antisemitism. "Religious" may seem a peculiar adjective to describe anything said or done by so truculent a "Christer"-basher as Vidal, but there is no doubt that when occasion demands Vidal readily adopts the language of Christian anti-Jewish polemic (a language long abandoned by "advanced" Christians). All of what Cynthia Ozick calls the "calumny implicit in the term 'Old Testament' " is exploited in Vidal's every use of the term: "the Old Testament God of Vengeance"; "the Old Testament God at his most forbidding and cruel"; "the Old Testament's lurid . . . bloody tales." When the Hebrew Bible comes into view, Vidal's usual dislike of the Christian Gospels is replaced by the old triumphalist creed of usurpation of the dead, fossilized nation by the vibrant new dispensation; and he is fierce with any Jewish writer who seems to slight the New Testament (by not mentioning it, for example, or by failing to pay tribute to its more enlightened view of "Prostitution, that most useful of human institutions.")

Vidal is still old-fashioned in his Jew-hatred when he brands Judaism as "race-religion" and refers, obsessively, to virtually every Jew with whom he disagrees as "rabbi." Ever since Jesus said (in Matthew 23:8): "Be not ye called Rabbi!" the term has been available as an abusive epithet to Christian polemicists. Vidal, the most abusive of writers, freely spraying everybody to the right of the hammer and sickle with the epithet "fascist," considers "rabbi" his ultimate vituperation, his most crushing rebuke. The psychiatrist David Reuben, whose obsession with sexual matters greatly resembles Vidal's own except for his lack of enthusiasm for bisexuality and homosexuality, is a representative of "the rabbinical mind." When Vidal has exhausted his supply of venomous ingenuity against Reuben, he lapses into this—"Finally, realizing that at the deepest level, no rabbi can take this sort of blunt talk from a foreskinned dog . . . I suggest that he read that greatest of anti-Rabbis, Paul Goodman." Irving Howe, unlike Reuben a genuinely Jewish writer yet one as far from rabbinic ordination or anything else truly rabbinic as Reuben, is also for Vidal "Rabbi Irving Howe." When he enumerates the wicked foes of women's and gay liberation, they too turn out to be rabbis: "To deny giving expression to those [homosexual] desires may be pleasing to Moses and St. Paul and Freud, but these three rabbis are aberrant figures whose nomadic values are not those of the thousands of other tribes that live or have lived on this planet."

As will be readily evident from all of these onslaughts against "rabbis," what decisively differentiates Vidal's denunciation of Jews from "traditional" religious Jew-hatred is his conviction that the "Old Testament" is the source of the baneful idea that heterosexual acts are right, homosexual acts wrong. "Of all the tribes, significantly, the Jews alone were consistently opposed not only to homosexuality but to any acknowledgment of the male as an erotic figure." What is noteworthy in Vidal's frequent outbursts against the Hebrew Bible is not his inability to read (Was Potiphar's wife attracted to Joseph by his managerial abilities? Does Michal object to David "exposing himself before the eyes of his subjects' slavegirls" because of her attachment to royal decorum or because of sexual jealousy?) but rather his unchanging conviction that the diseases of the liver are of much greater import than the terrors of conscience. Unless somebody could prove that bisexuality and homosexuality are damaging to public health and society at large—which, of course, nobody possibly can—then, in sexual matters, argues Vidal, "it is impossible to say that some acts are 'right' and others 'wrong.' " Pornography is therefore a more trustworthy guide than all these "rabbis," for pornography "recognize[s] that the only sexual norm is that there is none." In fact, from the point of view of utility—and Vidal never misses a chance to buttress nihilism with infusions of a little Malthus and Bentham—homosexuality is infinitely to be preferred over the "rabbinical" injunction to increase and multiply. The world is overpopulated; the environment is threatened; the last thing we want is Hebraic philoprogenitiveness. Homosexuality is therefore not only not "wrong," it is, from the point of view of Vidal's felicific calculus, preferable to heterosexuality because it has the capacity to *reduce* the world's population. (In view of the fact that one and a half million Americans are now infected with the fatal AIDS virus, and medical authorities predict 50–100 million victims worldwide within the next two decades, this is one of the rare instances in which Vidal has understated the case for homosexuality and bisexuality.)

One reason why Vidal feels himself to be eternally besieged by the same "rabbinical" enemy in Moses and Freud and Irving Howe is that he is a firm believer in timeless racial categories. For this self-proclaimed "historian," nothing ever changes, and ideas are like baton-sticks handed from one century into the next. Sometimes Vidal's indifference to history appears in comic ways, as when he sallies forth against "Mr. J. G. Stephen" for his advocacy of state punishment of moral offenders in *Liberty, Equality, Fraternity* without the slighest awareness that his adversary (whose actual name was James Fitzjames Stephen, the brother of Leslie), published that book in 1873. But his quarrel with the eternal Jew resumes its characteristically humorless ugliness when, for example, Vidal has to deal with the apparent anomaly of a Jewish homosexual. "Driving through Wyoming, a Jewish friend of mine picked up a young cowhand and had sex with him." (Neither in Vidal's life nor in his novels do people ever "fall in love" or "make love"; they always "have sex"; and in one essay he berates Broadway playwrights for their obsession with "Love, Love,

Love.") So far, so good. But his friend, being Jewish, "was, as usual, guilt-ridden; so much so that the boy finally turned to his seducer and with a certain wonder said, 'You know, you guys from the East do this because you're sick and we do it because we're horny.' "

The "rabbis" of all times and places are enemies of women as well as of "bisexualists" and "homosexualists." "The hatred and fear of women that runs through the Old Testament (not to mention in the pages of our . . . Jewish novelists) suggests that the patriarchal principle [is] carefully built into the Jewish notion of God." (Not surprisingly, the only character in the great story of Judah and Tamar—chapter 38 of Genesis—who has caught Vidal's attention is Onan, mentioned at every opportunity. Tamar, the iron-willed heroine of the tale, whose abasement of Judah for flouting her rights is fully endorsed by the narrator of Genesis, has escaped his notice.) Nor is it only the Jewish novelists from whom the great liberator has come to free women; the Jewish critics too must be unmasked as oppressors of women. Vidal claimed to find in Irving Howe's moving tribute to his immigrant parents "sharing their years in trouble and affection . . . during the Depression" a revolting "hymn to tribal values." Howe, unwilling to accept the reduction of his own parents and millions like them to the mindless ideological categories of sexual politics, had asked: "Was my mother a drudge in subordination to the 'master group'? No more a drudge than my father who used to come home with hands and feet blistered from his job as a presser. Was she a 'sexual object'? I would never have thought to ask, but now, in the shadow of decades, I should like to think that at least sometimes she was." To which the humorless Vidal could only retort: "Now that woman is beginning to come alive, to see herself as the equal of man, Rabbi Howe is going to strike her down for impertinence."

Vidal has not been entirely unappreciative of the efforts made by certain determined and strong-willed Jews to put behind them the zealous hetero-sexuality and selfish fruitfulness advocated by their ancestors and by modern "rabbis." In 1979 Vidal told the aesthetes who read *Playboy Magazine* that Judaism is "an unusually ugly religion." It is therefore hardly to be wondered at that even the Jewish species of the human genus will occasionally rebel against it. We have already noticed his tribute to Paul Goodman for his "anti-Rabbinical" effusions. In a novel called *Kalki* (1978) he gives us a heroine named, before marriage, Theodora Hecht, who, despite the impediment of a "rabbinical grandfather," has become a bisexual, has had herself sterilized, and has written (badly, because with the aid of a Jewish ghostwriter) a tract called *Beyond Motherhood*. Here is how she describes that image of divine beauty that she put in place of the "unusually ugly religion" of her ancestors: "For the first time I found Hinduism attractive . . . and basic. I like the idea of depicting as god human genitalia. Christians had done that in the twelfth century. God the father was the penis, the son was the scrotum, the holy ghost was the ejaculation. Jews did not go in for that sort of thing. In the Old Testament sex was only for kings, and reproduction. There were no images. For us, there was nothing graven except . . . the word."

The wretched Jews—bereft of beauty, bereft of idols, bereft of images; left only with the word—and even this, according to Vidal, they have abused. He has long been resentful of Jewish writers in modern American literature because there are too many of them, because most know nothing about Gentiles, and because they pollute the language. In 1959 he complained that the current list of "OK" writers "consists of two Jews, two Negroes and a safe floating *goy* of the old American Establishment . . . only the poor old homosexualists are out." In 1973 he asked the readers of the *New York Review of Books* to commiserate with him because "kikes and niggers can no longer be shown as bad people; only commies and fags," and asserted that "few American-Jewish writers have been able to put themselves into gentile skins—much less foreskins." In 1974 he undertook, in the same journal, to impute the scant attention given the novels of Louis Auchincloss to a literary atmosphere allegedly dominated by Jews. "How can the doings of a banker who is white and gentile and rich be *relevant* when everyone knows that the only meaningful American experience is to be Jewish lower-middle-class and academic?" In 1984, when the novelist and critic Thomas Keneally gave Vidal's *Lincoln* a lukewarm review in the *New Republic,* he soon received a sweaty letter from the aggrieved author saying: "In tandem with *Commentary* . . . the Pravda of our Israeli Fifth Column . . . is *The New Republic* . . . You were doubtless picked up as a reviewer who had proven his Semitophilia; and so would give me a bad review."

The disproportionate number of Jews in this new literary establishment, so clearly in violation of the *numerus clausus,* their alleged tendency to promote other Jews to the exclusion of Gentiles, was made all the more galling by the inability of most of them to rise above the demotic style of immigrant rabble. Vidal, it should be remembered, fancies himself a "purist" in literary style. He agonizes publicly over such matters as "the use of the ugly verb 'shrill' " and the loss of "any distinction between 'nauseous' and 'nauseated.' " His essay on Susan Sontag not only derides her as a garden-variety "Jewish-American writer" pretending to be European, and dressing up her Jews as Gentiles. He also scolds her for indenting too many passages, over-using the word "new," confusing number, and having an ear "better attuned to the cadences of the lower orders than to those of the educated."

It is true that Vidal's own writing is replete with such offenses against syntax, logic, diction, and taste as the following: "Wilson's record of conversations and attitudes haunt a survivor." "Like most sex jokes, the origins of this pleasant exchange are obscure." "Of all my contemporaries I retain the greatest affection for Mailer as a force." "Nathan Voloshen was his principle [sic] contact." "I was startled to find how much I . . . used the colon in the forties." But it would be churlish to fuss over Vidal's failure to achieve the perfection of his own ideal if he did not keep insisting that "With each generation American prose grows worse, reflecting confused thinking, poor education, and the incomplete assimilation of immigrant English into the old language (see Henry James's remarks on the subject at Bryn Mawr, 1904)." *Jonathan Swift said of his satire that he always "spared a hump, or crooked nose,/Whose owners set not up for beaux."

So powerfully distressed was Vidal by the depredations that Jewish "immigrant" writers had visited upon the purity of the English tongue that they were capable of driving him even to what Samuel Johnson called the last refuge of the scoundrel: patriotism. In an essay in *The New York Review* in 1980, Vidal, Hesperidean dragon guarding the treasure of the wisdom of the west, argued that the only reason why Jewish writers such as Bellow, Malamud, and Roth *appear* to be dealing in ideas is that "they arrived post-James. Jewish writers over forty do—or did—comprise a new, not quite American class, more closely connected with ideological, argumentative Europe (and Talmudic studies) than with those of us whose ancestors killed Indians, pursued the white whale . . ." "Them" against "us": the ideology-ridden, contentious unassimilated immigrants, ranged against "us," gifted with minds so fine that no idea can violate them, with the rich blood of whale-hunters and Indian-killers coursing through our veins. No wonder that Irving Howe, in enumerating the characteristics of American Jewish prose style, referred to "a deliberate loosening of syntax, as if to mock those niceties of Correct English which Gore Vidal and other untainted Americans hold dear."

This dwelling upon the sullying of the old language by the new one used by the immigrants,** this fantastic insistence that three writers who very likely never turned a leaf of Talmud in their lives are Talmudists and therefore "not quite American," is a vivid reminder that antisemitism has

---

*As usual, Vidal has trouble with dates. Henry James's "The Question of Our Speech" was delivered at Bryn Mawr, at Commencement, in 1905.

**Flannery O'Connor catches this feeling very well in her story called *The Displaced Person:* "She saw the Polish words, dirty and all-knowing and unreformed, flinging mud on the clean English words until everything was equally dirty." Of course, O'Connor was describing not a regular contributor to *The Nation* and *New York Review of Books* but a nativist southern white called Mrs. Shortley.

for centuries been obsessed with the impure, even subhuman nature of the Jews' language. Luther insisted that the language of the thief is the language of the Jews. He referred to Yiddish, which Vidal likes to spell yiddish, as an "adventurous mix" and charged that no other language had been so massacred by the Jews as German. Another German language purist, writing in 1700, said: "The Jews have dealt with no language as 'sinfully,' as one says, as with our German language. They have given it a totally foreign intonation and pronunciation." Eventually, by dint of centuries-long perseverance, the German Jews succeeded in purging themselves of this linguistic sign of corruption that they had brought from the East and praying only in German; but it availed them nothing. In 1933 the Nazi regime gave as its reason for burning books written by Jews *in German* that the Jews' language was not to be considered German: "A man can change his language," said Hitler, "without any trouble—that is, he can use another language; but in his new language he will express the old ideas; his inner nature is not changed."

Vidal's sense that the Jews' "Talmudic" discourse unfitted them to be fully American did not, however, dispose him to think well of their desire to reestablish their national life in the reconstituted homeland in Palestine. In 1963 he travelled to Egypt, hoping to interview Nasser for *Look* magazine, but having to settle for an interview with M. H. Heikal, the editor of *Al Ahram,* and also of "The Philosophy of Revolution, Nasser's *Mein Kampf,*" which Vidal found "a rather touching work reminiscent . . . of Pirandello." Heikal told Vidal that Arabs were "the only people *never* to persecute Jews," and he was greatly impressed by the "accuracy" of the information.* After ducking and nodding in response to similar nonsense, Vidal volunteered to present to the American public "Egypt's case against Israel, just as Egypt would like it presented. Partly out of a sense of mischief (we hear altogether too much of the other side) and partly out of a sense of justice, I thought that the Arab case *should* be given attention in the American press." The American press, he charged, had disregarded the Arab case in its "usual news columns," and refused to sell advertising space to the Egyptians. Here again, the machinations of the Jews had the power to rouse not only Vidal's sleeping sense of justice, but his dormant patriotism: "We must persevere in landing that [Arab] account. It will be a big one some day."

Although most of Vidal's fulminations against Jews fit into the large patterns described above, there are also, throughout his work, many

---

*From the middle of the twelfth century, Jews *en masse* fled northward from the harsh treatment of the Moslem Almohades ("Proclaimers of the Unity of Allah") who had invaded Spain from North Africa. According to the account of Rabbi (yes, a *real* rabbi) Abraham ibn Daud, some Jews, in desperation, turned to the Christians "and sold themselves to help them flee from the lands of Ishmael, while others fled naked and barefoot."

instances of a kind of hit-and-run petulance, weird non-sequiturs expressive of resentments that escape logical categories. In the midst of a nagging essay about the need to modify the law in order to accommodate homosexuality (Vidal combines the liberal craving for forbidden fruit with the liberal craving for legality) he declared that "It is, of course, exhilarating to determine to what degree Hannah Arendt was responsible for Hitler." In the midst of a polemic against "The Hacks of Academe," he castigates Leslie Fiedler for doing exactly what, according to Vidal's own lights, a student of homosexual tendencies in American culture ought to do: that is, exclude Jewish authors. "As far as I know, Fiedler has yet to finger an American-Jewish author as a would-be reveler in . . . Sodom-America, but then that hedge of burning bushes no doubt keeps pure the American Jewish writer/person." Objecting to remarks by art critic Hilton Kramer in favor of the family and against proselytizing for homosexuality, Vidal identifies him as "a Catskill hotel called the Hilton Kramer" and is so pleased with himself for having thought of this very small joke that he repeats it four times in the next four sentences (e.g. "the hotel disapproves of Wills and me because we are not Jewish") in a kind of impotent dry rage that can never satisfy itself.

These blank cartridges were fired against Hilton Kramer in an essay called "Sex is Politics" (*Playboy,* 1979) that demonstrates not only a new level of hysteria but a new "ideological" element in Vidal's war against the Jewish zealots of heterosexuality. Although he had long lamented "the continuing heterosexual dictatorship that has so perfectly perverted . . . just about every male in the country" (*NYRB,* 1974) he now decided to single out, for special attention among these perverters of American manhood—and special menace—the Jews. Side by side with Vidal's usual nostrums for American society, fewer families, fewer children, limitation of parenthood to those deemed eugenically worthy of it, were allegations of a sinister new alliance between "militant Jews" and "militant Christers," a declaration that "Jewish tolerance has never really extended to homosexuality" and an insistence that "fag-baiting by American Jewish journalists has always been . . . antigoyim." The "irrational rage that [Alfred] Kazin and his kind feel towards homosexualists," the remark of Joseph Epstein in *Harper's* that if he had the power to do so, he "would wish homosexuality off the face of this earth,"* moved Vidal to issue a stern warning. No Jew should dare to speak about any minority in this way

---

*From so unscrupulous a polemicist as Vidal, a reader would never guess the actual context and tenor of what Epstein wrote in 1970, which was: "If I had the power to do so, I would wish homosexuality off the face of this earth. I would do so because I think that it brings infinitely more pain than pleasure to those who are forced to live with it; because I think there is no resolution for this pain in our lifetime, only, for the overwhelming majority of homosexuals, more pain and various degrees of exacerbating adjustment. . . ."

because "in a Christer-dominated society . . . a pogrom is never *not* a possibility."

Two years later, writing in *The Nation,* Vidal decided to temper this threat with the offer of a second chance to the zealously heterosexual Jews. In an article originally entitled "*Some* Jews and *the* Gays," later reprinted as "Pink Triangle and Yellow Star," he proposed an alliance between Jews and homosexuals, two of the three "despised" American minorities. (Blacks constitute the third, but on that front Vidal prefers to insist that blacks have many a "good reason for replacing Jerusalem with Mecca.") "Unfortunately, most Jews refuse to see any similarity between their special situation and that of the same-sexers." He grants some differences between the two groups, but contends that "there is no difference in the degree of hatred felt by the Christian majority for Christ-killers and Sodomites." (The alleged hatred of American Christians for Jews as "Christ-killers" is constantly alluded to in Vidal's work, and has been as constantly refuted by every public-opinion survey. The most recent one, reported in *The New York Times* on January 8, 1987, indicates that "90 percent [of White Protestants of conservative religious views] disagree with the statement that 'Christians are justified in holding negative attitudes towards Jews since the Jews killed Christ.' ") His clinching argument, however, is that Jews and "homosexualists" share a common history in that both groups were singled out for destruction by Hitler: "In the German concentration camps, Jews wore yellow stars while homosexualists wore pink triangles. I was present when Christopher Isherwood tried to make this point to a young Jewish movie producer. 'After all,' said Isherwood, 'Hitler killed six hundred thousand homosexuals.' The young man was not impressed. 'But Hitler killed six *million* Jews,' he said sternly. 'What are you?' asked Isherwood. 'In real estate?' "

Vidal, like Oscar Wilde, believes that the one duty we owe to history is to re-write it. There is no evidence that the Nazi regime pursued a policy of systematically murdering homosexuals, except for SS and police who engaged in sexual relations with other men. The outlandish figure of 600,000 murdered homosexuals was invented for the very same reason that the figure of 600,000 homeless civilians was invented by anti-Israel propagandists during the war in Lebanon: it begins with a six and is conducive to licentious equations with the six million murdered Jews. Richard Plant, in his judicious and compassionate recent study, *The Pink Triangle,* estimates that "somewhere between 5,000 and 15,000 homosexuals perished behind barbed-wire fences" between 1933 and 1945. Hitler's second in command from 1919 to 1934 was the openly homosexual Ernst Röhm, head of the SA; Hitler ignored every report of Röhm's homosexual activities and insisted that an SA officer's "private life cannot be an object of scrutiny." The most fanatical campaigner against homosexuals was Röhm's rival, Himmler, and even he believed in the policy of trying to "cure" homosexuals by ordering them to visit bordellos in the camps. In general, the Nazi policy was to put homosexuals in labor camps, where their terrible sufferings were supposed to "straighten them out" and, in the words of Rudolf Hoess, bring them "salvation through work." This was not a policy worthy of the Nobel Peace Prize, but nevertheless distinctly different from the policy of murdering every single member of a particular community, a policy followed only with the Jews. Many homosexuals died in camps as a result of hard labor and sadistic punishments; the same was true of communists, socialists, Jehovah's Witnesses, and also common criminals. But so far Vidal has not proposed a Jewish alliance with any of these groups.

Vidal also maintains that homosexuality and Judaism are natural allies because "homosexuality is only important when made so by irrational opponents. In this, as in so much else, the Jewish situation is precisely the same." In this, as in so much else, Vidal is talking nonsense. Although it is difficult to believe that someone who can hardly write three consecutive sentences on any subject without introducing homosexuality into the discussion is truly convinced that homosexuality is given importance only by external hostility, it is easy to believe that a mind like Vidal's has attached itself to the vulgar thesis of Jean-Paul Sartre and Georges Friedmann, which claims that antisemitism itself creates Jewish consciousness. The real question, as noted elsewhere in this book, is not how the hostility of "irrational opponents" created Jewish consciousness but, on the contrary, how the Jews, unlike other nations, remained loyal to their god—to God—*despite* persecution.

But it is not these desperate stratagems for equating homosexuals and Jews that drive Vidal to attach special guilt and responsibility to the Jews. He does, after all, mention in passing that blacks and Chicanos and rednecks also inflict misery on "same-sexers." Why, then, does he single out the Jews for blame and threat? The answer is that the Jews have suffered. Not only must they not be allowed to monopolize all that beautiful suffering which other groups would like, *ex post facto,* to share, but they must behave particularly well to other suffering minorities precisely because they have suffered so much and so long. We are all familiar with this line of "argument," usually exploited by apologists for Palestinian Arab irredentism: How can Jews, of all people, etc., etc.? Conor O'Brien pointed out several years ago the mad corollary implicit in this argument, namely, that if Jews have a duty to behave particularly well because Jews have suffered so much persecution, "it seems to follow that the descendants of those who have not been persecuted do not have a special duty to behave particularly well . . . and the descendants of the persecutors could be excused for behaviour which would be hard to excuse in other people and which would be quite inexcusable in the descendants of the persecuted." Given his descent from "ancestors [who] killed Indians," and his own behavior towards Jews, one can see the powerful appeal of this corollary to Gore Vidal. It is, however, O'Brien adds, a corollary that flows from an argument easily recognizable as antisemitic because it is applied to no other people, such as the Irish, who have undergone sustained persecution.

No sooner has Vidal adopted this favored formula of post-1967 anti-semitism than he glides into the related one: that the Jews are themselves the new Nazis. Midge Decter's remarks about gays practicing discrimination in certain professions are none other than "Hitler's original line about the Jews," which led to the "final solution." Joseph Epstein, over at *Harper's Magazine,* aspires to do what Hitler did "or tried to do" in Germany. Vidal presses upon the Jews a hard choice: either come into "the same gas chambers as the blacks and the faggots" or reveal yourselves, as Midge Decter and Norman Podhoretz have already done, to be "so many Max Naumanns (Naumann was a German Jew who embraced Nazism)."

Thus Vidal in 1981 in *The Nation.* But the culminating point of his derangement, the *annus mirabilis* of his development as an antisemite, was yet to come. In March of 1986 he published in the 120th anniversary issue of *The Nation* a splenetic piece called "The Empire Lovers Strike Back," the most violent and incendiary of all his attacks on the Jews to date. The essay appeared to have been provoked by two short pieces, one in the *New York Post* by Norman Podhoretz, the other in *Contentions* by Midge Decter, criticizing Vidal's familiar depiction of the United States as a predatory country founded and sustained by theft, brutality, religious fanaticism, and mass murder. But Vidal also claimed that he was further provoked by a remark Podhoretz made to him twenty-five years earlier to the effect that he, Podhoretz, wasn't much interested in the Civil War, on which subject Vidal was trying to write a play. So great was the offense given by this (alleged) remark that, after twenty-five years of deliberation, Vidal now decided to strike as hard as he could to even the score. In his previous engagements with Podhoretz and Decter, to say nothing of Epstein, Kazin, Howe, Moses, and Freud, the score had usually been sexual and literary: now it had become a question of patriotism. No sooner did Vidal hear this remark than he "realized . . . that [Podhoretz] was not planning to become an 'assimilated American,' . . . but rather, his first loyalty would always be to Israel." Despite this instantaneous illumination, he harbored the secret of Podhoretz's treachery for a quarter of a century. Now, out of patriotic fervor, he felt obliged to inform his fellow-patriots who read *The Nation* that Podhoretz and other Jews who don't evince sufficient curiosity about "what the *goyim* were up to before Ellis Island" thereby prove that they have no interest in becoming "assimilated Americans" (unlike Vidal, who lives abroad, *they* could not become Americans simply by virtue of being born here) but instead would be "Israeli fifth columnists"* whose "first loyalty would always be to Israel."

Vidal "explained" the defense of American interests by Podhoretz and Decter as a sham used to frighten the American people "into spending enormous sums for 'defense,' which also means the support of Israel in its never-ending wars against just about everyone"; American Zionists dupe their fellow-Americans, or rather "real" Americans into believing that they need to defend themselves against Russia only "in order to get Treasury money for Israel (last year $3 billion)."** The only genuine element in their apologias for America, he contended, was their recognition of a profound kinship between two criminal regimes: "in the Middle East another predatory people is busy stealing other people's land in the name of an alien theocracy. She [Decter] is a propagandist for these predators (paid for?), and that is what this nonsense is all about."

The Vidalian theme that Jews are not Americans, adumbrated earlier in his literary essays, is here drawn out into extreme and radical form. "Of course I like my country," retorts Vidal to Decter's criticisms of his harangues against that "American Empire" which for decades he had been likening to Nazi Germany. "I'm its current biographer. But now that we're really leveling with each other, I've got to tell you I don't much like your country, which is Israel." Since Jews are guests in America, they ought to remember that "tact . . . require[s] a certain forbearance when it comes to the politics of the host country," and Jews who support Israel should register with the Justice Department as agents of a foreign power. Neither were Vidal's exquisite sartorial and linguistic sensitivities in abeyance in

---

*Expression coined by Spanish General Emilio Mola in 1936 to mean "subversives acting in support of an invader."

**This appeal to selfish interest has proved more persuasive to readers of *The Nation* than to Americans generally, 65% of whom believe Israel to be a reliable ally and strategic asset of the United States—and for good reason. The figure of $3 billion is, by Vidalian standards of accuracy, correct; but it is misleading. $1.8 billion was for military aid, $1.2 billion for economic aid; but in 1985 Israel paid the U.S. $1.1 billion, leaving a net balance of $1.9 billion. Compared to the $1.8 billion military aid to Israel, the U.S. has so far contributed $130 billion in the support of Western Europe through NATO, and $30 billion for the security of Japan, Korea, and the Far East. 340,000 American troops are stationed with NATO—30,000 troops in the Far East. If the U.S. had to use its own military forces to protect its interests in the Middle East instead of relying on Israel's, military analysts estimate it would have to spend $150 billion a year.

"The Empire Lovers Strike Back." He accused Podhoretz of wearing "our flag" (elsewhere, remember, derided by Vidal as "proto-Op-art") "like a designer kaftan" and announced that Vidal's Concordance to the Yiddish language shows that "the one yiddish [sic] word that has gained universal acceptance in this country is *chutzpah*."

Vidal concluded with a call for the destruction of the state of Israel, a polite call, to be sure, since it was couched in the soothing (to *Nation* readers) language of egalitarian nihilism: "the time has come for the United States to stop all aid not only to Israel but to Jordan, Egypt and the rest of the Arab world." Since Israel receives aid and buys arms only from the United States, while her adversaries receive arms and money from dozens of countries, this is a proposal for driving Israel into the sea.

Vidal's replies to the (few) letters of protest that *The Nation* received were devoted mainly to upholding his reputation as the "alley fighter" (as his acolytes are wont to name him) of Grub Street: he urged one critic to get "psychiatric attention," another to "join the Israeli Army." But he also, despite his insistence in earlier years that Jews and homosexuals are similar in all important respects and "in the same boat" as "despised minorities," now blamed the Jews themselves for arousing "the essential anti-Semitism of the American people," a strategy of explanation he has not yet tried out for the alleged anti-homosexualism of the American people.

The accusation of dual loyalty or, in Vidal's essay, of outright treachery against Jews has long been a commonplace of western Jew-haters too "enlightened" and too far removed from a cohesively Christian society to accuse Jews of drinking the blood of innocent Christian children or desecrating the host or menacing public health. Dr. Thomas Arnold, the historian of Rome and headmaster of Rugby, explaining his opposition (in the 1820's) to admitting Jews to universities or to citizenship, said that England was the land of Englishmen, and that Jews, as "lodgers," could have no more than honorary citizenship and no share at all in government. He denounced "that low Jacobinical notion of citizenship, that a man acquires a right to it by the accident of his being littered *inter quatuor maria*." In *Sodome et Gomorrhe*, surely a favorite text of Vidal's, Proust has M. de Guermantes explain just how Swann failed to become an "assimilated" Frenchman: "It is true that Swann is a Jew. But, until to-day . . . I have always been foolish enough to believe that a Jew can be a Frenchman, that is to say, an honourable Jew, a man of the world . . . He forces me to admit that I have been mistaken, since he has taken the side of this Dreyfus . . . against a society that had adopted him, had treated him as one of ourselves." It was the Dreyfus Affair, called by Hannah Arendt the dress-rehearsal for the Nazi movement, that gave impetus to the Zionist movement, not Zionism that gave birth to the Dreyfus Affair.

Antisemites are discriminating in their accusations of dual loyalty; they reserve them exclusively for Jews. Does anyone recall patriotic Gore Vidal rebuking Greek Americans for their prolonged, resolute opposition to Jimmy Carter's attempt to lift the ill-conceived embargo on the supply of arms to Turkey that had been imposed in 1975, an opposition pursued with—to quote one liberal journal's analysis—"a degree of single-mindedness and outspokenness never equalled and rarely even approached by the Jews"? Does anyone recall patriotic Gore Vidal suggesting that American citizens of Irish origin were treacherous in exercising their right, as free citizens of a free country, to oppose congressional efforts to extradite IRA terrorists or to cut off American arms shipments to the IRA? No, it is only the Jews who have the power to rouse his slumbering patriotic fervor.

In another of his replies to a letter of protest sent to *The Nation* Vidal challenged a Jewish interlocutor: "Question: What happens if the national interest of Israel is exactly opposite that of the United States? Under which flag does the Israeli-American serve?" This is surely a peculiar question to come even from someone so inclined to the gross, the blatant, and the flagrant, as Vidal. For it immediately invited the counter-question: what is the distance between the *potentiality* of what American Jews might do in a hypothetical dispute between Israel and America, and the *actuality* of what Gore Vidal did do during the war between North Vietnam and America? It is also surprising that someone who keeps parading himself as the "biographer" of America speculates about what Jews might do in a future conflict of interests without any reference whatever to what they did do in a past conflict, known as the Second World War. It is now well-established that President Roosevelt's record with respect to the Jews of Europe was shameful. In relation to its size, America did very little to accept refugees; it also refused to take action to save Jews, such as bombing the rail lines leading to Auschwitz or promising immunity from bombing to the Hungarians if, in 1944, they would disregard Eichmann's command to send the Jews to their deaths. American Jewish organizations, faced with the choice between "interfering with the war effort" by publicly opposing the Roosevelt administration, and adhering to the slogan of "rescue through victory," chose the latter course, although they knew by the end of 1942 that very few Jews would remain to be rescued after "victory." According to Vidal's rules of behavior for post-Ellis Island Americans, the American Jews behaved admirably; whether they behaved honorably is another question.*

What has befallen Vidal as a result of his open espousal of Jew-hatred of

---

*A recent public opinion poll among those American fundamentalist Christians whom Vidal holds in such contempt shows that 27 percent of them share his view that "Jews are more loyal to Israel than to the United States," but that 49 percent of this minority consider this a favorable attribute.

the crudest kind? If his equation between the situation of Jews and homosexuals were accurate, he would be in very hot water right now. No attack on the latter group is nowadays allowed to pass with impunity. In spring 1986, for example, a student at Yale made fun of the university's "Gay and Lesbian Awareness Days" by posting fliers announcing "Bestiality Awareness Days." For this defamation, he was found guilty by a disciplinary committee of having violated Yale's rule against "harassment, intimidation, coercion or assault" and suspended from the university for two years.** But antisemitism does, after all, seem to be a different matter from anti-homosexuality. "If they think they can do me any harm by calling me an anti-Semite," Vidal told Richard Grenier as long ago as 1980, "they're wrong . . . There are a lot more anti-Semites in America than people who like Jews." There is not much evidence to support Vidal's sanguine low-mindedness, but the reactions to his screed do show that there are a lot more liars, fools, cowards, sycophants, and moral nonentities in American intellectual life than we would wish to believe. Journalists such as Tom Wicker *(New York Times)* and Edwin Yoder *(Washington Post),* who have persuaded themselves that nobody is antisemitic who does not explicitly advocate or carry out the mass murder of Jews, saw nothing objectionable in the article. Although Roger Wilkins of the leftist Institute for Policy Studies prides himself, as one critic put it, on the ability to "spot 'racism' at a distance of twenty miles," not one of his Argus eyes could see anything at all in Vidal's article that could be construed as an attack on American Jews or Jews generally or even the state of Israel. Another of *The Nation's* resident experts on racism, Alexander Cockburn, hastened to assure its readers that "the Nazis approved of Zionism."* Arthur Hertzberg, as if trying to prove to Vidal that not every rabbi is a nasty piece of work, expressed himself "delighted" that Vidal had said (actually, he hadn't) "complimentary things about Peace Now," and only regretted that Vidal's "personal quarrel" with Podhoretz and Decter had not been conducted in private. Several journalists, among them Rod MacLeish and Jody Powell, declared their neutrality as between antisemitism and objection to it, eager to flaunt a tolerance so capacious that it extends to fanatical intolerance.

There were also, to be sure, some sharp attacks on Vidal, from the right

---

**The suspension was subsequently lifted.
*That Nazi named Adolf Hitler expressed in *Mein Kampf* what every scholar knows to be the typical Nazi estimate of Zionism: "While the Zionists try to make the rest of the world believe that the national consciousness of the Jew finds its satisfaction in the creation of a Palestinian state, the Jews again slyly dupe the dumb *Goyim*. It doesn't even enter their heads to build up a Jewish state in Palestine for the purpose of living there; all they want is a central organization for their international world swindle. . . ."

and (less numerous, though often more cogent) from the left. But, on the whole, Vidal has proved to his own satisfaction, not for the first time, that he can indulge his base appetites with impunity. The gravel walks of his villas are still being rolled, the royalties from his books continue to be paid, the *New York Review of Books* continues to feature his name as "a major force in world literature and thought" in its ads soliciting new subscribers, the Library of America still carries his name (and his Italian address) on its letterhead; and Victor Navasky, editor of *The Nation,* has pronounced that Vidal's article was not only "judicious and scholarly" but also very good fun, in fact "irony," thereby indicating that he bore a large share of responsibility for Vidal's conviction that America is "the land of the tin ear."

Commentators in the *Dartmouth Review* and the *National Review* (which described *The Nation* as "the cesspool of opinion journalism") actually suggested that it was precisely Vidal's avowed "homosexualism" (to use his preferred term) that gave him immunity. "For homosexuals," wrote Jeffrey Hart, "it seems there are no cultural constraints. They can violate the most powerful rhetorical taboos and . . . not be discredited." In fact, however, antisemites of all sexual and most political preferences have been able to express Jew-hatred with impunity since 1967. In 1973, Vidal himself "wondered how the Jewess-baiter [whom he had met at Fred Dupee's home] could hold a job of importance . . . anywhere." By now he must know.

The resurgence after 1967 of old forms of slander against Jews can be readily traced in some of the outpourings of Vidal's colleagues in the journals for which he has regularly written, *The Nation* and *The New York Review of Books*. I. F. Stone has for twenty years been assaulting Israel from his nationally distributed column, from the pages of *The New York Review of Books,* from between the covers of many books, and from lecture platforms throughout the country; all the while alleging that the Jews were suppressing his pro-Arab views, and that "it is only rarely that we dissidents . . . can enjoy a fleeting voice in the American press." The accusation that Jews control the press can also be found in the poisonous basilisk exhalations of *The Nation's* bold Philistine warrior against Israel, Alexander Cockburn. In August 1982, when Israel was being battered from pillar to post by virtually the entire press, Cockburn complained that "the cowardice of almost all American reporting on Israel has long been a source of wonderment," and that for thirty-four years it had been impossible to find in American newspapers or television reports "any indication that Israel might have behaved in a manner other than beneficial . . . to humanity at large." As if to confirm Yehuda Bauer's insistence that "nothing has changed in the modern world about antisemitism but the language," Cockburn explained the "wonder" thus: "It was plain that the U. S. press was—by and large—obediently catering to Zionist fantasies." A year and a half later, this fiercely independent and disobedient journalist was "suspended indefinitely" by the *Village Voice* for taking a $10,000 fee from the Institute for Arab Studies, whose board chairman was a member of the PLO Executive Council. At this point, Cockburn was snatched up by that lover of ironies, Victor Navasky, to write for *The Nation*.

Important segments of American political culture have also shown themselves in recent years full of charity, forgiveness, and "understanding" of political demagogues who trade in antisemitism. At its last national convention the Democratic Party could not bring itself to pass a resolution condemning antisemitism lest it offend the supporters of Jesse Jackson (Vidal is one of them), whose long record of Jew-baiting in print and speech had charitably been overlooked until he committed a slip of the tongue in referring to New York as "Hymietown." Jackson, for his part, will not repudiate the racist hoodlum Louis Farrakhan. And why should he, when Farrakhan, after condemning Judaism as a "dirty religion" and expressing his usual theories about sinister Jewish domination of American society, is warmly applauded by members of the National Press Club in Washington (1984) and specially commended by Mary McGrory of the *Washington Post* as a person of quality? Avid observer of the American scene that she is, it somehow never occurred to Miss McGrory that someone who had often vilified Jews and advocated the destruction of Israel before crowds who punctuate his harangues with cries of "Sieg Heil!" might be suspected of wanting to inflame anti-Jewish tendencies. And so, exactly like the numerous apologists for Vidal, she ridiculed the idea that Farrakhan was antisemitic, arguing that "His remarks were anti-Zionist rather than anti-Semitic."

Is this large readiness to forgive the expression of raw Jew-hatred and political antisemitism a sign of bountiful hearts trying, as well as mere human beings can, to imitate that "Old Testament" God who is addressed by Jonah as "gracious . . . compassionate, long suffering, and abundant in mercy"? Or is it, in its forgetfulness of the past, pitilessness towards the murdered Jews of Europe, and recklessness of the future, more aptly judged by the sentence from those rabbis whom Vidal hates without knowing them?—"Whoever is merciful to the wicked will end by being indifferent to the innocent."

Part II
ISSUES

6

Stealing the Holocaust

Martin Buber: Man wird sie stehlen.
Interlocutor: Sie Meinen, wie Jeschu von
Nazareth?
Martin Buber: Der Prozess ist bereits in vollem
Gange.

From 1933–45 the National Socialist regime of Germany carried out policies of discrimination, oppression, and murder that resulted in the destruction of around 5.8 million European Jews. The Jews held a unique position in the Nazi world because they alone, among all the peoples subject to German rule, had been marked for total destruction—not for anything they had done or failed to do, but because they had been born of three Jewish grandparents.[1] Their guilt lay exclusively in having been born. Although only Jews could be guilty of being Jewish, the centrality of the Jews in the mental and political universe of the Nazis established a universal principle that involved every single person in German-ruled Europe: in order to be granted the fundamental human right, the right to live, one had to prove that he was *not* a Jew.

The anti-Jewish policies of the Nazis, which ultimately resulted in the loss to world Jewry of one-third of its population, were the direct result of the ideology of anti-Semitism. This would hardly seem worth mentioning were it not for the fact that several highly influential modern thinkers have alleged that anti-Semitism is one of the greatest pieces of good fortune to have befallen the Jewish people. The Jean-Paul Sartre–Georges Friedmann version of this thesis holds that anti-Semitism produced Jewish consciousness, Jewish persistence, and the perseverance of Jewish existence. This perverse theory fails to explain why other peoples in the ancient Near East who suffered banishment and persecution interpreted their misfortunes as proof of the inefficacy of their national god and prudently surrendered their religious practices, while the Jews, faced in exile by the same persecution, kept theirs. Unless Georges Friedmann had run into a Jebusite, a

Girgashite, or a Hittite in the streets of Paris, he ought to have been asking what inner impulse kept the Jews loyal to their god and destiny *despite* persecution instead of assuming that they did so *because* of it. The second version of the thesis that anti-Semitism has sustained Jewish peoplehood is that the state of Israel came into existence as the result of the Holocaust and the ensuing bad conscience of the West. The most recent version of this may be found in the allegation of the *Washington Post*'s Pulitzer Prize-winning reporter Loren Jenkins, who imputes the "culture of violence" in Lebanon to "Western guilt over the murder and torment of the Jewish people." Of course, nothing could be further from the truth. The Jewish communities annihilated by the Nazis were the most Zionistic in the world, and, as Hillel Halkin has remarked, they could have done far more for the Zionist cause as live immigrants to Palestine than they were ever able to do as dead martyrs used to prick the conscience of the West. The British, who then ruled Palestine, were so unimpressed with "the murder and torment of the Jewish people" that they continued, for several years after it ended in 1945, to prevent Jewish immigration and to strangle the state. It was not anti-Semitism, but the Jews themselves, who broke open the gates of Palestine for the survivors of the Holocaust.

The term *Holocaust* began to be used in English sometime between 1957 and 1959, in order to express the then widespread feeling that what had happened to the Jews during the Second World War was unprecedented, as indeed it was. It has often been pointed out that the Nazis also killed, through starvation and brutality, not less than two and a half million Soviet prisoners of war, and murdered many thousands of the Polish intelligentsia during the first year of occupation of Poland and tens of thousands of other Poles as real or alleged resistors. They also destroyed whole Polish villages, massacred the Czech intelligentsia, and destroyed thousands of Russian and Ukrainian peasants during German occupation of those areas. But, as Yehuda Bauer has pointed out, the purpose of these policies was to denationalize the Eastern European nations and to absorb into the Germanic race those people who were what the Nazis thought of as "Nordic," to murder the intelligentsia and destroy all cultural life, and to turn the rest of the people into a mass of slave laborers in the international Nazi regime. This is what we mean by the term "genocide," hardly a policy meriting the Nobel Peace Prize and yet distinctly different from the planned murder of every one of the members of a community. Bauer demonstrates that, contrary to legend, there never was a Nazi policy to apply the measures used against the Jews to other national communities.[2] Thus the term *Holocaust* came into use to describe the uniquely terrible fate that had befallen the Jews of Europe: They had become the first, though not necessarily the last, people to be singled out for complete physical annihilation.

The uniqueness of Jewish suffering and of the Jewish catastrophe during the Second World War had no sooner been defined than it was called into question, by Jews as well as by Christians. The fact and the idea of suffering are central in Christianity, whose ethical values are based on the idea of a community of suffering. Many Christians also believe that, as Mary Ann Evans (later known as George Eliot) wrote in 1848, "Everything specifically Jewish is of a low grade." Yet here was a Jewish claim to a specific suffering that was of the "highest," the most distinguished, grade imaginable. Among the Jews, too, large numbers of "universalists" kicked resolutely against the notion of a distinctively Jewish catastrophe. They believed that the enormity of the Holocaust could only be recognized by the world at large if it were "universalized," if its victims were recast as "human beings" rather than as Jews. This is not the place to discuss either the self-abasement or the mental poverty inherent in such efforts. Cynthia Ozick has remarked, with characteristic shrewdness, that universalism is the ultimate Jewish parochialism. The supposed distinction between being human and being Jewish is one that has plagued Jewish existence at least since the time it was formulated in Y. L. Gordon's assimilationist slogan: "Be a man outside and a Jew at home." The German Nazis may be said to have brought this distinction to its full flowering by decreeing that the Jews were not human at all, so that in order to be granted the fundamental right, the right to live, you had, under Nazi rule, to prove that you were *not* a Jew.

One of the earliest and—because it became the occasion of a sensational lawsuit—still most notorious attempts to steal from the Jewish victims of the Holocaust precisely that for which they were victimized, was the 1955 dramatization of *The Diary of Anne Frank* by Francis and Albert Hackett. Bruno Bettelheim, in *The Informed Heart,* probably goes too far in charging that Anne Frank's story itself gained wide acclaim because "it denies implicitly that Auschwitz ever existed. If all men are good, there never was an Auschwitz." What is certain is that the play, written under the guidance of Lillian Hellman, expunged all of Anne's references to her hopes for survival in a Jewish homeland, and changed Anne's particular allusions to her Jewish identity and Jewish hopes to a blurred, amorphous universalism. One example should suffice to illustrate the general pattern. In the *Diary* Anne writes:

> Who has made us Jews different from all other people? Who has allowed us to suffer so terribly up till now? . . . If we bear all this suffering and if there are still Jews left, when it is over, then Jews, instead of being doomed, will be held up as

an example. . . . We can never become just Netherlanders, or just English, or just representatives of any other country for that matter, we will always remain Jews. . . .

In the stage version, this is reduced to the following piece of imbecility:

We are not the only people that've had to suffer . . . sometimes one race, sometimes another.[3]

This distortion may have helped at the box office, and thereby have made Anne Frank's name known around the world. But for every lie, a price must eventually be paid (though not, it must be added, always by the liars). In the 1970s the International Youth Center at the Anne Frank house in Amsterdam was for a time used as a PLO information center, where Anne's suffering was made prelude to what was called "the Auschwitz" of the Arab refugee camps. With this obscene travesty, the wheel comes full circle: the young girl who suffered, and who knew that she suffered, because she was a Jew, is first misrepresented as a universalist embodiment of the indiscriminate suffering of "sometimes one race, sometimes another," and then appropriated by a vast propaganda machine as the symbol of the very organization that in Article 20 of its 1968 constitution denies the existence of Jewish peoplehood, in Article 22 labels Zionism "Fascist and Nazi," and publicly commits itself "to liquidate the Zionist entity politically, economically, militarily, culturally, and ideologically."

Cut free from her Jewish moorings, improperly understood by her own people, Anne Frank has become available for appropriation by those who have a sounder appreciation of the worth of moral capital, and know how to lay claim to sovereignty over it when the question of sovereignty has been left open. The PLO is not the only organization that has sought to annex Anne for its own purposes. Some organs of the Catholic church in Latin America have begun to suggest the suitability of Anne Frank for sainthood in the Roman church. Educational publications of the church in Argentina began in 1975 subtly to link Anne's fate with that of Catholic martyrs over the centuries, without bothering to mention either that she was Jewish or that the death she suffered was part of a vast process of destruction aimed directly at Jews.[4] This was perhaps a merely parochial phenomenon of the church's missionary effort among Jews in Argentina. Yet who can be sure, now that Pope John Paul II has celebrated a mass at Auschwitz, and Carmelite nuns have established a convent just outside the death camp, that even this ultimate Jewish abattoir may not be in process of becoming a Christian holy place? "Sie werden es von uns wieder stehlen," Martin Buber had predicted.

The process that I call stealing the Holocaust began with small acts of (usually innocent) distortion. Who does not recall the inflamed rhetoric of the American civil rights movement of the 1960s, with its references to the curtailment of free-lunch programs in Harlem as genocide, or its casual descriptions of Watts as a concentration camp and of the ordinary black neighborhood anywhere as a ghetto? Not all of the orators who used this language could have been unmindful of its flagrant dishonesty, could have been wholly ignorant of the fact that no place in New York or Los Angeles or Chicago in 1960 was even remotely like Buchenwald in 1938 or Warsaw in 1942 or Auschwitz in 1944. But why fuss about precision of language or intellectual delicacy when the exigencies of radical politics make it convenient to reduce Jews from the status of human beings to that of metaphors for other people's sufferings? The only problem was that the people who were incessantly told that they were the new Jews, that they lived in ghettos and concentration camps, and that they were victims of genocide, began to look around to see who the Nazis were in this situation. And, not surprisingly, they chose for this role the Jews themselves, that is, the white people whom they saw and dealt with and received help from most frequently. In the 1960s it became routine for black demagogues in New York to charge Jewish teachers with the "cultural genocide" of their black pupils. As if by some law of physics or conservation of energy, the instant that another group becomes "the Jews," the Jews themselves become the Nazis.

But all this was an amateurish rehearsal for what was to come. The most determined, sustained, and dangerous attempt to steal the Holocaust was begun by the Soviet Union and the Arab world after the 1967 Middle East war, and is now one of the most lethal weapons deployed against the land of Israel and the people Israel. After the Six-Day War, cartoons were published depicting Moshe Dayan as Field Marshal Rommel, with swastikas on his uniform. These cartoons appeared not only in the Soviet Union and the Arab countries but in the journals of American civil-rights organizations like that of the ironically named Student Non-Violent Coordinating Committee. Before the Six-Day War, when the Straits of Tiran were closed and Arab armies were advancing toward her borders and Nasser and Shukairy were promising to turn the Mediterranean red with Jewish blood, Israel was the recipient of a good deal of cheap sympathy. But after the war Israel discovered that the price she would have to pay for winning a war that, if lost, would have meant her destruction, was the nearly universal loss of the sympathy the Jews had been collecting since 1945 when discovery of the Holocaust became general. All those statesmen and journalists whose eloquence had for twenty-two years gushed forth on the subject of the dead Jews and of their vanished civilization now fulminated with rage and resentment against a people and a state that preferred life to death and even to the rhapsodic eulogies that might be bestowed on dead Jewish martyrs and the glory that was Israel.[5]

Since 1967 this rage and resentment against the Jews for refusing to be passive victims have expressed themselves mainly in the depiction of Israelis as Nazis and Palestinian Arabs as Jews. In the 1970s UNESCO condemned Israel's archaeological digs in Jerusalem as "crimes against culture," a charge intended, as Norman Podhoretz pointed out, "to conjure up the burning of books by the Nazis."[6] The Soviet ambassador to the UN accused Israelis of "racial genocide," and the Committee on the Inalienable Rights of the Palestinian People (which in UN parlance means only Arabs, never Jews) compared the "sealing of a part of the city of Nablus" with the creation of "the ghettos and concentration camps erected by the Hitlerites in several cities of Europe." The members of this UN committee had learned their techniques from the sloganeers of the American civil-rights movement who spoke of Harlem as if it were Auschwitz.

The triumphant stroke in the campaign to steal the Holocaust from the Jews by inverting the roles of the victim and the predator was the Soviet-inspired "Zionism is racism" UN resolution of 1975. For nearly a century, the word *racism* was in Europe virtually synonymous with anti-Semitism, with Jew-hatred. For the Soviets to have foisted on the United Nations a resolution that says that Israel, the last coherent center of the historic Jewish civilization destroyed by the Nazis, is itself the sole inheritor of Nazism, was to have made the public memory of the Holocaust into a potent instrument for the destruction of the Jewish people. For Jew-haters everywhere this monstrous inversion has been meat and drink, a seminal idea whose fruitfulness burgeons in new forms every day. The student bodies in twelve British universities were inspired by it to pass "Zionism-Racism" resolutions that were used to ban Jewish student organizations. At Bristol University, for example, a Reform rabbi who was scheduled to speak on "Jewish Ethics" was prevented from doing so because it was suspected he would utter "Zionist," that is, "racist" sentiments. Fidel Castro, in speeches before the Third World conference in Havana and at the United Nations in 1979, described Israelis as the Nazis of our time, monsters who had driven the modern Jews (otherwise known as Arabs) off their land, committed genocide, and so forth. Vanessa Redgrave, a PLO activist, went out of her way to portray a Jewish victim of—as it were—the "original" Holocaust in order to drive home the intended equation of the Jewish victims of Hitler with the Palestinian Arab victims of the Israelis. And in a "debate" with Fania Fenelon, the survivor whom she portrayed, she claimed that she could hardly be an anti-Semite because the Palestinians are "Semites." (This vulgar retort, which appears about once a week in papers like *Le Monde,* plays on the ignorance of those who have forgotten that the word anti-Semitism was created as a euphemism for Jew-hatred, and that anti-Semites hate Jews, not Semites.)

Stealing the Holocaust became central in the ideology of the most militant and aggressive of anti-Israeli groups, particularly the American Friends Service Committee. This wealthiest and most politically active corporate component of the Religious Society of Friends, better known as Quakers, has consistently, since 1967, sought to portray Israelis as the new Nazis and Palestinian Arabs as their "Jewish" victims. In November 1976 its New England branch announced: "Now Israelis are making Jews out of Palestinians. In the Palestinians I recognize my Jews." This was the theme repeated ad nauseam by speakers at the Friends' February 1977 conference on "New Imperatives for Israeli-Palestinian Peace" in Washington, D. C. The executive secretary of the AFSC, Louis Schneider, told the audience of his thoughts on a 1976 visit to Israel that coincided with the Jews' observance of the thirty-fourth anniversary of the Warsaw Ghetto uprising: "It was deeply saddening to have been in Israel during the season when Jews were celebrating one of their own struggles from tyranny . . . and the Arab minority in Israel were heard voicing their own aspirations for freedom during their demonstrations against Israeli control." This implied equation of Israelis in Judea with Nazis in Warsaw set the tone for the whole meeting and was made explicit by many subsequent orators, including I. F. Stone and an Arab American who said—to thunderous applause—that Israel had created a Palestinian Auschwitz at Tel Zaatar. The PLO representative who, in laying his wreath at the Warsaw Ghetto commemoration of 1983, said that "the Palestinian people are the victims of the new Nazism," had gone to school with the American Friends Service Committee. For these people, as for the Russians and Arabs in the UN, the disgusting practice of riding on the coattails of the Jewish experience of discrimination, exile, oppression, and murder, has become more than a means of collecting sympathy and expressing hatred; it has acquired the stature of a moral idea.

Anti-Israeli journalists soon developed a standard formula for exploiting the Holocaust. A few examples from the late 1970s through 1980 should suffice to identify the pattern. Nick Thimmesch, the *Los Angeles Times* Syndicate's tireless journalistic warrior against Israel, declared on 6 October 1977, that Menachem Begin's statements about the right of Jews to live in Judea were "the language of Hitler." The *Christian Science Monitor* began a four-part series (June 1979) on "The Struggle for Palestine" by referring to the Palestinian Arabs as "the Jews of the Arab world." It further asserted that they are living in "Diaspora," that they long for restoration to Jerusalem, and, indeed, that they are the latest Zionists. Doug Marlette, syndicated by the Knight News Service, reported (21 October 1979) how the eyes of Palestinian Arab refugees always looked out at him from under the photos in Yad Vashem of Jewish children being marched into gas chambers. Jonathan Randal disclosed to readers of the *Washington Post* (5 March 1980) that Palestinian Arabs were living "in diaspora" or else in Lebanese camps that were replicas of Dachau and Auschwitz. Five days later the novelist John Updike not only endorsed the view that "the Palestinians are Jews" but had the colossal gall to ask the readers of the *New Yorker* (10 March 1980) to join him in bemoaning the "fact" that this is "a perspective seldom found in American newspapers." Is it possible that Updike reads no American newspapers except the *Jewish Week?*

Whatever misgivings Updike may have had about the ability of Western journalists to make Jews into metaphors should finally have been laid to rest by their treatment of the war in Lebanon. The propaganda battle against Israel began with the invention of the figure of six hundred thousand homeless civilians by the Palestinian Red Crescent Society, which happens to be headed by Yasser Arafat's brother. The figure, a patent absurdity on the face of it for an area whose entire population is under five hundred thousand, was irresistibly attractive to anti-Israeli journalists for the same reason that it was invented in the first place: it began with a six and facilitated the licentious equation of six hundred thousand Palestinian Arabs with the six million Jews. That is why it continued to be used (for example, by Robert Fisk in the *Times* of London, and Jessica Savitch on NBC) long after it had become "clear to anyone who has traveled in southern Lebanon . . . that the original figures . . . were extreme exaggerations" (David Shipler, *New York Times* Service, 15 July). Steven Benson, the openly anti-Semitic cartoonist of the Phoenix *Arizona Republic,* published a whole series of pictures showing goose-stepping Israelis in German helmets guarding cattle cars and patrolling concentration camps; and his cartoonist colleague Oliphant—predictably—showed West Beirut as the Warsaw ghetto, with the PLO as the besieged Jews and the Israelis as the Nazi beasts. (Just which Jewish resistance leader of 1943 set the precedent for Arafat's daily baby-kissing for U.S. television cameras was not indicated by Oliphant or Alexander Cockburn [in the *Wall Street Journal*] or any of the other discoverers of Warsaw in Beirut.) Peter Taylor, reporting in the *Sunday Telegraph* on the mass rally in Tel Aviv to demonstrate support for the operation in Lebanon, found that "the towering, shrine-like podium at the rally, supporting rank after rank of sombre worthies and topped on high by an arrogant parade of flags, inevitably involved images of another place and another time" (25 July 1982). William Pfaff *(International Herald Tribune)* declared that "Hitler's work goes on," done by "the Jews themselves." John Chancellor, musing autobiographically on the bombing of 2 August, confessed that he "kept thinking yesterday of the bombing of Madrid during the Spanish Civil War." Since Chancellor was about twelve years old when Madrid was bombed by the Junkers 52s of Hitler's Luftwaffe in 1936, one may venture to guess that it was not memory that brought forth this analogy so much as a keen awareness that the short and ready way to prominence in that Goshen of mediocrity called broadcast journalism is the equation of Israelis with Nazis and Palestinian Arabs with Jews. Israel's aging enfant terrible, Yeshayahu Leibowitz, whose claim on public attention had previously rested on his relentless insistence that Ben-Gurion hated Judaism more than any man he had ever known, became an instant celebrity in the European press by coining the epithet "Judeo-Nazi" to describe Israel's actions in Lebanon. The English writer of spy stories, John Le Carré, held forth in the *Observer* (13 June 1982, with characteristically bad diction) about how "Begin and his generals . . . are . . . inflicting upon another people the disgraceful criteria once inflicted upon themselves," and in his novel about Israelis and Arabs of the following year gave tacit approval only to those Israelis who pilloried most of their countrymen as Nazis.

The campaign of calculated distortion begun by the Russians in 1967 had by June 1982 become so successful that every half-educated Israel-hater was soon repeating the formula with the regularity of a steam engine. The situation quickly reached the point where Conor Cruise O'Brien proposed making this vilification a kind of litmus paper for the detection of anti-Semitism: "If your interlocutor can't keep Hitler out of the conversation, . . . feverishly turning Jews into Nazis and Arabs into Jews—why then, I think, you may well be talking to an anti-Jewist" *(Jerusalem Post,* 6 July 1982). In reaction to the frequent regurgitation of this formula in the news media and by PLO spokesmen, some people must have begun to wonder whether a movement that can conceive of itself only as a mirror image of its Jewish enemy is a "nation" or an antination, whose whole meaning and existence derive from its desire to destroy a living nation.

Ordinarily, in surveying so dismal a spectacle, one can take comfort from the fact that, as Orwell liked to say, there are some ideas so stupid that only intellectuals can believe them. But the allegation that Israelis were doing to Palestinian Arabs what Nazis had done to Jews was in the summer of 1982 being voiced by prominent and often powerful politicians: Olof Palme, Andreas Papandreous, Bruno Kreisky, and Francois Mitterand. Even the usually sober and cautious George Shultz was infected by the plague of Holocaust analogizing in the aftermath of Sabra and Shatilla, though he stopped short of equating Israelis with Nazis and suggested only that they resembled the nations of the world that stood idly by and did nothing while the Jews were being murdered by Hitler. For him the Israelis were not yet the Nazis, but the Palestinian Arabs certainly had become the Jews. Statesmen, as Shakespeare showed in *Julius Caesar,* are just as likely as other people to get their thoughts entangled in metaphors, and to act fatally on the strength of them.

That is why it is necessary to adhere sternly to the simple but indispensable truth that, as Cynthia Ozick has written, "Jews are no metaphors— not for poets, not for novelists, not for theologians, not for murderers, and never for anti-semites."[8] The blurring of the crime that was the Holocaust is, of course, not always political and not always a weapon used against Jews or Israel. It often seems characteristic of nothing more than the intellectual vulgarity and lack of distinction that are besetting sins of our culture. That it is omnipresent, no one can doubt. A feminist rally is likely to feature placards that read "Pornography is to Women what Nazism is to Jews!"; a spokesman for gays is apt to compare their psychological and social confinement to cars, bars, restrooms, and theaters with the concentration of Jews in World War II; the protestors at an antinuclear rally will paint "U.S.S. Auschwitz" on the nearest Trident submarine; and a novel by William Styron will contain a little lecture on the parochial interpretation that has been put on the Holocaust by Jews who view it as their tragedy rather than an instance of that enslavement that has afflicted many peoples in the past and will continue to do so in the future. None of these travesties is politically motivated; but all of them express a deep-seated wish to transform the Nazi murder of the Jewish people, a crime of terrifying clarity and distinctness, into a blurred, amorphous agony, an indeterminate part of man's general inhumanity to man. To the extent that they succeed, they subserve the malignant designs of those who wish finally to release the nations of the West from whatever slight burden of guilt they may still bear for what they allowed or helped Hitler to do to the Jews of Europe, and so remove whatever impediments of conscience stand in the way of the anti-Israeli juggernaut. In the present political climate, whoever makes of the murdered Jews of Auschwitz and all the other killing centers metaphors for all humanity degrades rather than exalts them, and renders easier the dirty work of those who would make them the representatives not of humanity in general but of their polar opposites—the enemies of the Jews in particular. Those who deprive the dead Jews of their deaths are of necessity in collusion with those who seek to deprive the living Jews of their lives.

Notes

1. Yehuda Bauer, *The Holocaust in Historical Perspective* (Seattle: University of Washington Press, 1978), p. 32.
2. Ibid., p. 35.
3. See Benno W. Varon, "The Haunting of Meyer Levin," *Midstream,* 22 (August/September 1976): 20.
4. See the article on this controversy by Nissim Elnecave, "Por que la Iglesia esta especulando con los martires Judios para sanctificarlos como Catolicos?" *La Luz,* 20 July 1979, pp. 12–15.
5. See, on this subject, Cynthia Ozick's "All the World Wants the Jews Dead," *Esquire Magazine,* 82 (November 1974).
6. Norman Podhoretz, "The Abandonment of Israel," *Commentary,* 62 (July 1976): 26.
7. For information on the AFSC campaign against Israel, I am indebted to Marvin Maurer, "Quakers in Politics," *Midstream,* 23 (November 1977): 36–44, and H. David Kirk, *The Friendly Perversion* (New York: Americans for a Safe Israel, 1979).
8. Cynthia Ozick, "A Liberal's Auschwitz," in *The Pushcart Prize: Best of the Small Presses,* ed. Bill Henderson (Yonkers, N.Y.: Pushcart Book Press, 1975), p. 127.

7

The Attack on Holocaust Studies

The subject of the Holocaust has become a seething cauldron of controversy. Not a year passes without a new, spectacular, and usually obscene attempt to deny the actuality or distort the history or pervert the meaning of the event; and nearly every denial, distortion, and perversion subserves the campaign to delegitimize the state of Israel.

In 1982, for example, readers of the *Jewish Chronicle* and *Jerusalem Post*[1] witnessed the spectacle of George Steiner defending his play about Adolf Hitler (*The Portage to San Cristobal of A. H.*, originally a novella) against Martin Gilbert's cogent criticism of its gross historical inaccuracies and licentious equations of Nazism with both Torah and Zionism. The latter are concentrated in Hitler's final monologue. As to why the monologue goes unanswered, Steiner offered several explanations. One was that he did not wish to descend to the level of "didactic Shavian debate" but, rather, aspired to the sublime detachment of Milton from his brilliant Satan or Dostoevsky from his Grand Inquisitor, and hoped to keep faith with the literary principles of Henry James and Jean-Paul Sartre, who liked to speak of a sacred pact that prohibited the writer from assuming any moral responsibility toward his reader.

This is the merest nonsense. If Blake and Shelley believed (mistakenly) that Milton was of Satan's party, it was certainly not because of any reservations Milton felt about confuting the devil. Satan's great speeches and moments are largely confined to the first two books of *Paradise Lost,* after which he not only declines in stature, but is "answered" by several thousand lines of angelic verse. The real problem is not just that Steiner's loyalty to a minor literary tradition (one without value for Jane Austen, Thackeray, or Dickens, among others) is much greater than his loyalty to the Jewish people, but the horrifying fact that, as he admits in a rare moment of candor, he is "not sure that A. H. can be answered." That is to say that Steiner cannot, for all his erudition, give the lie to any of the following assumptions and assertions of his play's hero: the Nazi idea of the master race chosen (by itself) to impose its law on inferior races is identical to the Jewish (and Christian) idea of a people chosen by God to receive His law; the Nazi idea is also like the Zionist idea (even though the Zionists explicitly rejected chosenness for "normality"); the state of Israel was created because of the Holocaust (and not in spite of the murder of millions of the most Zionistic Jews in the world); and Israel's sense of its beleaguered condition grows out of its birth in the Holocaust (and not out of brooding over such minor annoyances as sixty-five years of Arab terrorism and five major wars).

That every one of these malicious slanders converged perfectly with the major themes of PLO propaganda, and that his novella and play appeared at a time when Europe was being swept by a tidal wave of "literature" and films restoring heroic status to Hitler, when Israel was consistently represented by its enemies in the UN and the press as an inheritor of Nazism, when Jewish intellectuals at British and American universities, where the PLO was the most popular liberal idolatry, were hastening to distance themselves from Israel—all this was a mysterious accident that Steiner could not explain but by reference to his creative daemon.

Grotesque performances of this kind almost make one wish that the famous doctrine of "silence" regarding the Holocaust had been observed rather than written about so abundantly. But to be silent now in the face of such monstrosities is an unaffordable luxury; it is futile to hope that the Pandora's box of trouble that has been opened by discussion of the Holocaust can now be closed. All of the scholarly resources and survivors' testimonies that can be employed in the disinterested pursuit of the truth about the Holocaust will not be more than adequate to ward off the calculated distortions and incitement of ugly passions that now permeate the anti-Zionist revisionist campaign.

That is why the current attack on Holocaust studies by large segments of the American-Jewish scholarly and rabbinic establishment is cause for dismay and alarm. The disparagement of Holocaust studies and the depiction of the majority of its practitioners as unscholarly, trivial, and mercenary, have become smelly little orthodoxies of the Jewish studies establishment. In recent years I have had occasion to interview many candidates for teaching positions in modern Jewish history at my university. Most were writing dissertations at eastern universities that train Jewish historians. To the mere mention of the word "Holocaust," nearly all responded with a supercilious sneer, a small, stale joke ("there's no business like *shoah* business"), and a smug formula about the Holocaust and anti-Semitism being parts of gentile, not Jewish, history. One young woman, a student of one of the more aggressive polemicists against

Holocaust studies, bristled when one of my colleagues asked her (as a specialist in French-Jewish history) for her opinion of André Schwarz-Bart's novel, *Le Dernier des Justes*. "I read a few chapters," snarled this heretofore amiable and sweet-tempered historian, "and threw it down. I hate this wallowing in suffering and I'm not studying *Leidensgeschichte*." "Perhaps," I asked, "Piotr Rawicz's *Le Sang du Ciel* was more to your liking?" She had never heard of it. Several other candidates, obviously aping their professors, denied that any published history of the Holocaust (including the work of Hilberg, Dawidowicz, and Bauer) merited the name of historical scholarship, that is, achieved the level of cool, dispassionate observation of fact in which they were being trained. Is there a link, I asked myself, between the claim of budding Jewish historians that there is no history of the Holocaust and the neo-Nazi claim that there was no Holocaust?

Numerous broadsides against what is variously described as "the centrality of the Holocaust," "the Holocaust industry," "Holocaust Zionism," and "Holocaust Judaism" have appeared in most Jewish and several secular journals. They have been written by such prominent figures as Jacob Neusner *(Reconstructionist, Moment, Forum,* and *National Review),* Robert Alter *(Commentary),* Arnold Jacob Wolf *(National Jewish Monthly),* Arthur Hertzberg *(Midstream),* and Paula Hyman *(New York Times).* Few would wish to quarrel with some of the abstract propositions put forward in these articles: Judaism is more than the Holocaust; Torah is a tree of life, not a necrophilic rummaging among the dead; and the Holocaust is an event, not an academic discipline, and should be studied in the context of Jewish history.

But far more than this is alleged by the critics of Holocaust studies. The Association for Jewish Studies, the professional organization of Judaica scholars in North America, complained in 1980[2] about the large amounts of money going to Holocaust scholars and asserted, in its newsletter, that they include "an inordinate share of quasi-academic hucksters." Robert Alter, in *Commentary,*[3] claimed to see a cause-and-effect relationship in the fact that during a period (1979–80) when three books on the literature of the Holocaust had been published, no book in English was published on modern Yiddish or Hebrew literature, and no critical biography of Sholom Aleichem was under way. Resentment of the fact that more American students enroll in courses on the Holocaust than on Haskalah is a constant theme of the critics of Holocaust studies, who like to imply that the choice symbolizes a moral preference for Josef Goebbels (though not Abba Kovner) over Judah Leib Gordon.

In June 1981, Professor Arnold Band, editor of the *Association for Jewish Studies Newsletter,* who has never complained about examples of pedestrian work in French-Jewish history, of maudlin sentimentalism in American-Jewish history, of trendy opportunism in writing about Jewish women, or of Mishnaic exegesis that never rises above the level of paraphrase, returned to the attack on Holocaust studies. After commenting on the scandal of the neo-Nazi *Journal of Historical Review,* whose purpose is to demonstrate that the Holocaust never happened, he implied that the absence of severe scholarly standards in the area of Holocaust studies might be partly to blame for the journal's existence.[4] He did not indicate what blame attached to the Organization of American Historians—one of those scholarly organizations whose disinterestedness the Association for Jewish Studies reveres—for selling its membership list to these neo-Nazis so that they could distribute their journal in the most effective way.

Petty jealousy over funding of and attention to Holocaust studies, and this over-refined finickiness about their level of scholarship, reveal more than the special susceptibility of Judaica scholars to violations of the tenth commandment, or the fundamental insecurity of the AJS about the legitimacy of Jewish studies in the eyes of the academy at large. They reveal a sneaking awareness of the fact that the Holocaust is the tragic inheritance of the whole Jewish people, not the private property of scholars. No one can doubt that survivors and other nonspecialists who fail to meet the AJS's published requirements for commenting on the subject ("Yiddish, Hebrew, German, and one Slavic language, preferrably [sic] Polish") will abuse the standards that scholarship has established for itself. These people are not, after all, professors of Judaica. The trouble with such professors is that they are blind in one eye; they see profoundly in one direction but miss everything else. The collective mind of American Jewry lacks profundity, but (for this very reason) sees more of the surface of Jewish life than does the AJS. It understands that the Holocaust is the only past American Jews now have, just as Israel is the only basis of their future.

The true center of this controversy is a struggle for the soul of American Jewry. We can see this clearly by turning to the critic of greatest generalizing power who has sought to tear American Jews loose from their attachment to the Holocaust and to Israel: Jacob Neusner. On March 8 1987, which by a fortuitous coincidence came a few days after an American Jew named Jonathan Pollard had been sentenced to life imprisonment for spying for Israel, Neusner published an article in the *Washington Post* designed to show the absurdity of American Jews' attaching themselves to Israel when they are already walking the gold-paved streets of Eldorado: "If ever there was a Promised Land, Jewish Americans are living in it."

Neusner, a professor of Judaic Studies at Brown University in Rhode Island, praised the cohesiveness, the security, the prosperity, the philoprogenitiveness, the "authentically Jewish voice" of the American Jewish community, and also the liberal, tolerant American polity that has integrated Jews so thoroughly into its mainstream that "no fewer than seven U. S. senators—7 percent of the Senate from only 2 percent of the population—are Jewish." This triumphant dithyramb was amplified by a grotesque travesty of the Zionist argument, summarized by Neusner as "tell [ing] American Jews that . . . we are all going to die in gas chambers, singing Christmas carols" and should therefore "feel . . . guilty about living in the United States."

Neusner did not scruple to cite, in support of his contention that Jewish life not only flourishes mightily in the United States but will continue to do so into the distant future, the Pollyana school of "revisionist" special-pleading sociologist–demographers who claim that Jewish intermarriage with gentiles actually adds to, instead of depleting, Jewish numbers. He blithely ignored the fact that the methods and claims of these cheerful demographers have been seriously, indeed fatally, called into question not only by their Israeli colleagues but by the director of the Population Studies Center at Neusner's own university.[5] In any case, the crucial consideration in American Jewish demography is fertility; and there is nearly universal agreement that American Jews have averaged lower fertility than non-Jews for over a century, a pattern which, if it continues in the future, will cause Jewish fertility to fall far below replacement levels. Failure to produce offspring, and failure to keep within the community the few children you do produce, are not usually taken (especially in a markedly aging population group) as overwhelming evidence of a people's will to live.

Boasting (confidently) that Jewish Americans are more secure than Israelis will ever be, Neusner argued that whereas "the American dream has come true" for American Jews, Zionism has not only failed to provide physical security for Israeli citizens, it has failed to become a spiritual center for the Jewish people. Israeli scholarship is "pretty dull" in general, according to Neusner, and in Judaic Studies is "provincial, erudite, unimaginative and unproductive." Except for Buber and Scholem (exempted from the general curse, it would seem, because both are dead and neither was in Neusner's own academic speciality), "not a single" Israeli thinker or scholar "has won any audience outside of Israel. No historians, no philosophers in Judaic studies have a hearing overseas. Israeli scholarship boasts no social scientist working on Jewish materials in a way that interests anyone but Jews." Jacob Katz, Jacob Talmon, Shlomo Avineri, Yehuda Bauer, S. N. Eisenstadt—all have labored in vain, or at any rate have failed to catch the collective ear of Providence, Rhode Island.

Confident that most readers of the *Washington Post;* trained by such contentious Israel-bashers as Jonathan Randall, Loren Jenkins, and Edward Cody to view Israel as a breeding ground of fanaticism, oppression, and brutality, would be unlikely to balk at such relatively minor criticisms as the allegation that the Jewish state has virtually no art or poetry or music or scholarship worthy the name, Neusner offered straw to the Egyptians in a battery of rhetorical questions: "Today, in all the Jewish world, who, as a matter of Jewish sentiment, reads an Israeli book, or looks at an Israeli painting, or goes to an Israeli play, or listens to Israeli music?" Without waiting for a reply—after all, even a few readers of the *Post* might have been able to reply to such gross, flagrant, blatant misrepresentations with: "Agnon, Hazaz, Appelfeld, Shahar, Oz, Shabtai, and Yehoshua in fiction; Amichai, Kovner, and Pagis in poetry; Ben-Haim in music, and . . ." Neusner rushed ahead to produce the (to him) indisputable evidence that Jews in search of a genuinely Jewish life choose America over Israel. "World Jewry has voted with its feet. . . . More Israelis live in the United States than in Jerusalem." This novel explanation of *yeridah* (emigration from Israel) should prove music to the inward ear of many a Hebrew-speaking taxi-driver or seller of unkosher meat in Manhattan.

American Jews are both worse and better than Neusner makes them appear. If they are disproportionately represented in such worthy endeavors as art, learning, and the Senate, they are also disproportionately represented in Wall Street crime, in frenzied and fraudulent religious cults, in the tawdriest and most meretricious aspects of "show business," in leftist propaganda and agitation of the most mindless, brutal character, and in support of terrorist organizations, including the Jew-killing organization called the PLO.

It is true that Jews who gather themselves together in pursuit of these unwholesome activities have satisfied the requirement of "propinquity," one of the criteria by which the sanguine sociological surveyors Neusner invokes measure "Jewish cohesiveness" in America.[6] But one may be permitted to wonder whether Jews' proximity to other Jews while, let us say, campaigning for unlimited abortion or knitting babyclothes for unwed mothers in Nicaragua, is evidence of the "distinctive" culture they have developed and of the great future in store for Jews in Neusner's "promised land" or of their continuing unease in this new Zion.

Although he referred repeatedly in these two articles to the "strong evidence of Jews' communal cohesiveness," Neusner gave little hint of wherein it consists, apart from a passing allusion to "synagogues and all sorts of Jewish organizations." But it is hardly a secret that American Jewry, like French or Brazilian Jewry, is held together today not by study of Torah, not by synagogue attendance, not by Jewish Studies programs, but precisely by its devotion to that from which Neusner would like to tear it asunder; namely, the state of Israel. To millions of American Jews Israel provides, precisely as Zionism claimed a Jewish state would, a center of national feeling; a model of courage, resilience, and faith; and a lodging for the organized memory of Jewish national consciousness. The Auschwitz survivor who traveled from America in April of this year to be present when Chaim Herzog, Israeli's president, officially visited West Germany, spoke for tens of thousands besides herself when she said that "only when the state of Israel was established could I feel that our martyrs had been redeemed, and that I could again hold my head high."

Although Neusner blames Israel for not being "light to the Gentiles or even bright for most Jews," the imagination of American Jews is fired by the obligation to support Israel, whether through collecting money, mobilizing politicians, or influencing public opinion; and even many who do none of these things nourish (and are nourished by) a sweet, secret hope for the peace of Jerusalem. Without Israel, much of blossoming American Jewish life, from the collection of funds for local Jewish institutions (more than half of which are raised ostensibly "for Israel") to the enrollment of students and employment of faculty in Jewish Studies programs across the land would find itself fatally cut off from the root and bole of the tree that has given it sustenance. No better example of the dependence of American Jewish life upon Israel need be adduced than the fact that the Reform branch of American Judaism, once militantly anti-Zionist, is now firmly (some would say exclusively) based in Zionism.

I well remember how a lay leader of this movement, having come to address my (orthodox) congregation on the subject of the international Jewish fraternal organization of which he was soon to become American president, stood next to me during the Ma'ariv (evening) service holding the siddur (prayer-book) upside down. Nothing could induce this fine fellow to take the time to learn the Hebrew alphabet, but for Israel he was willing to (and indeed did) sacrifice his health and professional career.

Ironically, nobody has offered more eloquent testimony to American Jewry's spiritual entanglement with Israel than Jacob Neusner himself, though he has chosen not to share this interesting piece of information with the readers of the *Washington Post*.

In many articles and a book derived from them, Neusner has deplored the fact that American Jewish life is based upon a myth of Holocaust and heroism that is suitable for Israelis but has no relevance to American Jews and serves only to instill in them a sense of "dislocation" in a place where they ought to live (as he does) "without apology or guilt." (Like the perfect liberal he aspires to be, Neusner has no objection to evasion of moral responsibility, but a powerful aversion to the guilt that evasion might produce.) "Ours," he once wrote, "is a mythic situation in which we talk about what other people go through, but then we find ourselves unable to explain the world in which we live." He has for many years accused American Jews of living a kind of charade because they have made the murder of European Jews and the heroism of Israelis into components of their "civil religion." For his part, Neusner does not brood about "someone else's death in Europe and someone else's rebirth in the Land" but attends to such "real" problems as the health of his colleagues, the illness of a friend's child, his obligations towards his family.[7]

Most American Jews have failed to achieve the guiltless disconnection from the fate of Israel that Neusner recommends for their psychic health. That is why they responded to the sentencing of Jonathan Pollard not by proclaiming their unswerving allegiance to the "real promised land" of America, and not by fretting over accusations of dual loyalty, but by worrying about, and trying to stem, the political damage that the case may do to the state of Israel. Most American Jews do not daily congratulate themselves on their superior virtue for having chosen to linger in a place where they live (at present) more comfortably and securely than their Israeli cousins, who pay the highest taxes in the world, who serve in the army from 18 to 55, and who have been embroiled for 40 years in a war of independence that has already cost them more than 16,000 lives.

This little matter of life and death seems never to have crossed Neusner's field of vision when he cast his cold, critical eye upon Israel. In an untypically gentle (albeit typically condescending) movement of his essays he allows that Israel has "wonderful hotels, great scenery, first rate tours," and that he "cannot imagine anything more beautiful than the Sabbath in Jerusalem." Did it never occur to him that those hotels were built and that Sabbath made possible by the blood of the men and women whose graves stretch endlessly over the brilliantly landscaped military cemetery on Mt. Herzl in Jerusalem, the largest, the most beautiful, and the most terrible "great tourist scene" in Israel? Those men and women have died, and many times their number have been maimed, and countless thousands of families have been shattered, in order to establish and preserve a free and independent Jewish state, the only state in which Jews are likely in future to preserve a culture and inner world of their own, the only state certain to receive Jews in flight from Russia or Ethiopia or . . . who knows where? But now comes Professor Neusner to tell these Israelis that this was not enough to justify their sacrifice in the eyes of American Jewry: they ought also to have been producing more poems and paintings and concertos capable of "recharging our Jewish batteries."

The most ignorant American Jew, looking at these graves on Mt. Herzl, in some of which lie mute, inglorious Agnons, will understand better than Neusner has, the meaning for the Jewish people of its re-rooting in (as it were, the "original") Zion: "Spilt blood," wrote the Israeli poet Amichai, "isn't roots of trees,/But it's the closest to them/That man has."

In one uncharacteristic surge of modesty, Neusner admits that not he but "God alone knows the future." Yet surely his confidence that America is the "real Promised Land" ought to be qualified by some awareness of Jewish and American history as much as by the (grudging) admission that he is not divine. The oldest Jewish communities of just fifty years ago—in Germany, in Poland, in Yemen, in Iraq—are today no more; and one reason why so few of the Jews of Europe survived Hitler's war against them is that the "real Promised Land" of America shut its gates to Jews in their hour of greatest need. Perhaps that is why the majority of American Jews continue to believe, as their ancestors did, in the interconnectedness of all Jewish life, continue to believe that their life in Exile depends precisely upon "myths" about other Jews. The Haggadah commands that every Jew view himself as having gone forth from Egypt. Jewish folk identity in Eastern Europe was preserved by what Maurice Samuel described as "an ingenious charade, which governed their religious life, which in turn interpenetrated their secular life. They pretended they were still living in their ancient homeland."[8] Modern poetry about the Holocaust is entirely traditional in its insistence that all Israel was present in the death camps because every Jew was potentially present at Mount Sinai.

Neusner has forgotten that the value of a myth depends not on its demonstrability as fact, but on the attitudes it creates and the actions it engenders. The heart is commonly reached not through the understanding but through the imagination. Neusner himself recognizes this when he says: "where my heart is—there must be the story of who I am." But his heart is very amply contained in Providence, Rhode Island, while the heart of American Jewry reaches back to Auschwitz and forward to Jerusalem. That is why his effort to impose upon American Jews a seemingly logical, domestic myth—building Jerusalem in America's green and pleasant land—is doomed to failure.

Notes

1. See *Jerusalem Post Magazine,* 2 April 1982, pp. 8–10.
2. *Association for Jewish Studies Newsletter,* 27 (October 1980): 1.
3. "Deformations of the Holocaust," *Commentary,* 71 (February 1981): 45–54.
4. *Association for Jewish Studies Newsletter,* 29 (June 1981): 1.
5. See Steven M. Cohen and Calvin Goldscheider, "Jews, More or Less," *Moment,* 9 (September 1984): 41–46; S. DellaPergola, "Patterns of American Jewish Fertility," *Demography,* 17 (1980): 261–73; Sidney Goldstein, "Ameri-

can Jewish Demography: Inconsistencies that Challenge, in *Jerusalem Letter/ Viewpoints:* Jerusalem Center for Public Affairs, 16 October 1986.
6. See Calvin Goldscheider, *Jewish Continuity and Change* (Bloomington: Indiana University Press, 1986).
7. "Beyond Catastrophe, before Redemption," *Reconstructionist,* 46 (April 1980): 8–11.
8. *In Praise of Yiddish* (New York: Cowles, 1971), p. 7.

8

The Journalists' War Against Israel

In *The Doctor's Dilemma,* George Bernard Shaw devotes an unusually full stage direction to the introduction of "a cheerful, affable young man who is disabled for ordinary business pursuits by a congenital erroneousness which renders him incapable of describing accurately anything he sees, or understanding and reporting accurately anything he hears. As the only employment in which these defects do not matter is journalism . . . he has perforce become a journalist." The contemptuous view of journalists that is characteristic of almost every important imaginative writer since Smollett who has described them[1] is likely to be confirmed by a survey of reporting and editorializing on the Arab-Israeli conflict during the past decade, from about 1976–86.

My own interest, in this subject was first aroused in 1972 by the ABC-TV commentator who, minutes after the Israeli Olympic athletes had been murdered by the PLO at the Munich Olympic games, said that his overriding concern of the moment was not for the dead Israelis—theirs, after all, was blood under the bridge—but for what might result from the well-known Israeli propensity to exact an eye for an eye and a tooth for a tooth. After that shock, I began to observe the professional communicators who cover events of, or linked to, the Arab-Israeli conflict more closely and systematically. Gradually, I discovered that there are certain well-established patterns of tendentious reporting and commentary, a large body of shared clichés repeated again and again. Yet nothing has inured me to the surprise that accompanies each fresh outrage perpetrated by the more imaginative innovators among the journalists. I was surprised in 1974 by the receptivity (discussed below) of many prominent journalists to General George Brown's allegation that Jews control America. I was surprised in April 1984 when the *Washington Post,* as if taking its cue from ABC's treatment of the Munich massacre, supplied the following caption under the picture of an Israeli woman slumped in the seat of a bus she had been riding when she was killed by a PLO bomb: "A woman was one of three persons killed yesterday when a bomb exploded on an Israeli bus in the latest incident of a growing wave of violence that was expected to raise fears about retaliation against Arabs." I was surprised, in August of the same year, when the racist agitator Louis Farrakhan, after expressing (albeit in cruder language) General Brown's theories about Jewish domination, was wildly applauded by the members of the National Press Club, and specially commended by Mary McGrory of the *Washington Post* for his impressive physique, good tailoring, and bright disposition. She, of course, ridiculed the idea that he was anti-Semitic. "His remarks," she explained to readers who might be so benighted as to suppose that admiration for Hitler's achievement with respect to the Jews or advocacy of the destruction of the state of Israel suggested a lack of charity in the Jewish direction, "were anti-Zionist rather than anti-Semitic."

The main purpose of this essay is to describe and analyze the dominant patterns of bias, misreporting, and selective moralizing that have obtained during the past decade. But ultimately I would like to propose that "surprise" in the face of journalistic hostility to Israel is no longer excusable, and that the task of demonstrating again and again that bias and duplicity and occasionally even depravity characterize reporting and editorializing on the Middle East conflict has been finished.

Readers following its reporting of the war in Lebanon must have been somewhat taken aback to see in the *Times* of London on 26 July 1982 a large headline that read: "Spanish media fail test of truth." Although it was encouraging to learn that the *Times* admitted the relevance of such a test to the press, it was disheartening to discover that the story from Madrid was devoted to deploring what was alleged to be "a biased, anti-British account of the Falklands conflict." Old-fashioned lovers of truth had begun to have the distinct feeling that they were getting from the *Times* a biased, anti-Israeli account of the Lebanon conflict. A typical despatch from Christopher Walker in Jerusalem (29 June) opened thus: "On the eve of the last Jewish Sabbath the bull-like figure of Mr. Ariel Sharon . . . appeared on television." Mr. Walker, suddenly solicitous of the sanctity of the Sabbath, might in fairness have proceeded to tell his readers what the weasellike figure of Yasser Arafat was doing during the fast of Ramadan, but he did not. On 10 July, a photograph of a wounded Lebanese girl being carried to a first-aid post in Sidon bore the caption, "The grim face of war that the Israeli censors would prefer the outside world not to see." On 16 July, the *Times* received from the wire services a photograph showing left-wing gunmen guarding a crossing point between East and West Beirut with a caption clearly stating that the wrecked buildings in the picture "were destroyed during the 1975–76 civil war." Even the *Guardian,* whose venom toward Israel often infected the very headlines over its letters to the editor, printed the caption intact. But the *Times* (as it admitted in an unobtrusive correction printed four days later) omitted the sentence that accurately described the devastation pictured. In this piece of deception, the *Times* was following a pattern already established by the television journalists, who showed impressive pictures of devastation in Tyre, Sidon, Damour, and southern Beirut, but "preferred the outside world not to know" that a war had been raging in these places for seven years. When the nonstory of Arafat's alleged readiness (in the midst of war) to accept Israel's right to exist was given out by a group of anti-Israeli U.S. congressmen, the *Times* made the nonstory its front-page lead under the lying headline, "Arafat signs pledge to recognize Israel." Robert Fisk, Walker's colleague and ally in Beirut, referring to Congressman Mc-Closkey's announcement that "Arafat accepts all UN resolutions relevant to the Palestinian question," called the event (or nonevent) "a dramatic— indeed an historic—breakthrough." Not a shade of skepticism fell over Fisk's effervescence, except for his skepticism about Israel, which "claimed that Congressman McCloskey was renowned for his anti-Israel stand and had on various occasions attempted to delay American aid to Israel," a claim Fisk apparently had no possible way of checking. But what he was certain about was that the paper brandished by McCloskey "showed that Mr. Arafat accepted not only Resolution 242 but also Resolution 338." That Arafat did not specifically recognize UN Resolution 242 or 338, neither of which refers to the Palestinians or to the Palestinian question at all; that he said nothing about Israel's right to exist; that the totality of UN resolutions dealing with "Palestine" is a contradictory hodgepodge that includes condemnations of Zionism as the greatest evil ever visited upon this planet; that this transparent farce has been performed, under the direction of gullible or unscrupulous journalists, a hundred times in the past decade—none of this was mentioned by Robert Fisk for the benefit of those readers of the *Times* who think the "test of truth" is as relevant in London as in Madrid.

The scandalous disregard for truth that characterized much of the reporting of the war in Lebanon, especially when the reporting emanated from Beirut, called to mind (and for many confirmed) the allegations made in February 1982 by Zeev Chafetz, then director of Israel's Government Press Office. Chafetz charged that substantial segments of the Western news media—among them the *New York Times, Washington Post,* the BBC, and ABC-TV—follow a double standard in reporting and commentary on the Arab-Israeli conflict because they fear and respect Arab terror, but take for granted and abuse the freedom allowed them in Israel's open society. He explicitly argued that terror prevents critical reporting on the PLO and Syria, and that ABC's attack (in the program "20/20") on Israel had a causal, not accidental, connection with the murder in Beirut in July 1981 of an ABC reporter. Chafetz also claimed that five U.S. journalists had been held in 1981 for nearly twenty-four hours by Palestinian Arab terrorists without the incident being reported in their newspapers for over nine months.[2]

Replies to these charges were remarkably feeble. The *New York Times,* in a rare display of modesty, indicated that what happened to its own reporters was not necessarily newsworthy (although it requires little effort to imagine the indignation that would burst forth from Anthony Lewis and James Reston if any *Times* reporters suffered similar abuse in Israel). The *Washington Post,* after two weeks of pondering Mr. Chafetz's charges, admitted that its Beirut correspondent, Jonathan Randal, had indeed been arrested, but did not think the incident merited being reported.

Neither ABC-TV nor Jonathan Randal (as I shall make clear later) is a newcomer to PLO apologetics. But both are only parts of a larger tendency, one not explainable by the coercion of PLO terrorism, to flout normal standards of truthfulness in reporting and rationality in editorializing on Israel. What coercion was at work on CBS's Dan Rather and Diane Sawyer when they glibly suggested, after Sadat's assassination in 1981, that he had been killed because of Israel's famous intransigence on the "Palestinian" question? Did anyone hold a gun to the head of Ed Bradley or his program producer when, on a Sunday night CBS News report (2 October 1976), he read an item about Jerusalem against a pictorial background of a map that prominently displayed the label "Mandelbaum Gate" as the dividing point between Jewish and Arab Jerusalem—this nearly ten years after the division had ended and the gate had been dismantled?[3] *Time* magazine, not among the offenders mentioned by Chafetz, has carried on a virtual war against Israel for years, a war whose strategy was first analyzed by Rael Jean Isaac in the *New Republic* (18 October 1980). *Time* consistently pursued the line, virtually out of *1984,* that "Sadat started his peace campaign by going to war" (27 March, 1978). After Begin's election in May 1977, *Time* invited its readers to ponder the significance of the fact that "Begin (Rhymes with Fagin)" and, in August 1981, prior to Begin's 1981 visit to Washington, called on the United States to "interfere in Israeli internal politics," presumably to install a regime satisfactory to the board of Time-Life, Inc.

Eventually, *Time* was fatally tempted by its anti-Israeli zeal into running afoul of American libel law. In 1985, the magazine was found guilty, in a U.S. federal court, of "defamation" and "falsity" in a story that alleged that Ariel Sharon had discussed with Lebanese Christian leaders the need to take revenge for the assassination of Bashir Gemayel just before the Falangist massacre in the Sabra and Shatilla refugee camps in Lebanon. The lengthy, highly publicized trial revealed conclusively that *Time* had no basis whatever for its story, which had been concocted by one of its Israeli reporters, David Halevy. The judge who presided over the case, Abraham Sofaer, politely indicated after the trial his view that Halevy was an inveterate liar. Renata Adler, in her penetrating study of the case, stressed that Halevy showed not only "a breathtaking disregard for what was and what was not 'exact' or 'accurate' or 'true,' " but "a genuine inability to tell the difference"—in which respect, however, he was only the epitome of his colleagues. "What was true and false also seemed, at times, a matter of almost complete indifference to them. Above all, the journalists, as witnesses, looked like people whose mind it had never crossed to be ashamed."[4]

Large numbers of these unshameable people, especially those who work for *Time,* the *Washington Post,* and the *Christian Science Monitor,* have for years unceasingly reported so much "inflexibility," nastiness, fanaticism, and brutality in Israel that many of their impressionable readers must marvel at the prodigious energy that enables so tiny a people to commit so many Brobdingnagian misdeeds. Israel has become the moral gymnasium for the journalists of the world, a place in which they do moral calisthenics designed to revitalize muscles that have grown flabby from disuse during their assignments in other countries. No terrorist (or what *Time* calls "political prisoner") can be imprisoned and interrogated, no bedouin can be asked to pen his goats, and no chassid can cast a stone at a Sabbath violator without screaming headlines reporting the incident. Chaim Herzog once noted that the *Times* of London (27 October 1980) could not find space on its front page for the Iraq-Iran war, or the Afghanistan war, or the murder of 450 people in the Jamaican elections, but for only one foreign "affair"—the stone-throwing incident between religious and secular Israelis on the road to Ramot. Ayatollah Khomeini, returning from Paris to head a massive revolution in Teheran, found himself relegated to page three of the *New York Times* on a day when the establishment of a new settlement at Shiloh in Samaria received a four-column, front-page headline. I can well believe the claim of an Israeli representative of the Cable News Network who boasted to me that Israel was the second major "producer" of news in the world.

In the event that nothing of note is happening in Israel, journalists may resort to the invention of news. In late 1975 staff members of National Public Radio accompanied Daniel Berrigan and other anti-Israeli diehards on a kind of propaganda raid on the Israeli Embassy in Washington, where they assailed the officials at the door with the standard harangues, deliv-

ered with that special zest that arises only from the proximity of microphones. A more spectacular example of the self-invented scoop was
conceived by Barbara Walters (22 September 1977). Harry Reasoner began
that evening's ABC News report by announcing that Arafat, in an interview with Walters, had proclaimed his readiness to recognize Israel.
Viewers who waited through the program for the great scoop discovered
that Arafat had not said anything of the kind, had not, indeed, even
mentioned Israel, much less her right to exist. Walters grandly announced
that Arafat had accepted Resolution 242. What Arafat actually said in the
interview was that he would like a "new resolution," that is, that he did
not accept 242. Also, of course, he expressed his willingness to establish
another "independent Palestinian state." As to whether Arafat recognized
Israel's right to exist as a sovereign, independent state, Barbara Walters
never thought to ask.

Ironically, one of the most prized formulas of Israel's journalistic
enemies is precisely the allegation that no negative criticism of Israel ever
appears in the American press because it is directly controlled or indirectly
coerced by Jews fanatically devoted to their brethren in the ancestral
homeland. When the former chairman of the Joint Chiefs of Staff, General
George Brown, charged in 1974 during prime time on CBS that Jews
control the whole country through banks and newspapers, Eric Sevareid
did more than offer qualified endorsement of the accusation. He also
presented himself, on CBS, as a brave knight hurling himself into the path
of the Jewish juggernaut because—so he alleged—one could not say that
Brown was even half right "in this country without the roof falling in on
the sayer. . . ." If the roof fell in on Sevareid, it must have done so very
gently, for three years later (6 October 1977) millions heard him express
outrage that Israel, because of her Jewish supporters in the U.S., should
control U.S. foreign policy. He seemed equally uncrushed and vigorous on
6 January, 1979, when millions saw him on prime-time television bemoaning Israel's commitment to aggression, aggrandizement, and the consump-
tion of American tax dollars.

One of the most persistent purveyors of the anti-Semitic fiction that
"Jews control the press" is Nick Thimmesch of the *Los Angeles Times*
Syndicate. In October 1977 he used his column to charge that the American-Jewish lobby had "shut off free speech" and frightened anti-Israeli
journalists into silence. When Thimmesch was publicly challenged (see
Seattle Times, 14 October 1977) to square his allegation with the fact that
not only he but Georgie Anne Geyer, Rowland Evans and Robert Novak,
Nicholas von Hoffman, Anthony Lewis, Howard K. Smith, and a small
army of others had managed to flout the Jewish terror, and was invited to
name one or two television commentators who spoke *for* Israel in the way

that these spoke *against* her, he declined to reply publicly.[5] But in February 1979 he returned to the attack. Arabs, he complained, were being "stereotyped" on television as "oil-rich sheiks" and "terrorists," and the likely reason for this distortion of the truth was that many of the offending programs "are written by Jews." Verifiable factual assertions are not Thimmesch's strong card, but he has offered one identifiable example of a journalist who, because he has dared to criticize Israel, "finds it difficult to speak his mind in the United States." And who is this courageous voice, all but "snuffed out" by the Jewish lords of the press? None other than I. F. Stone, who for two decades proclaimed from a nationally distributed column, from the pages of the *New York Review of Books* (whose Middle East "expert" he used to be), from between the covers of many books, and from lecture platforms in every state of the union, that "the Jews" suppressed his pro-Arab views, and that "it is only rarely that we dissidents . . . can enjoy a fleeting voice in the American press."[6]

The slander that "Jews control the press" is so entirely at variance with all empirical evidence that it serves as a useful symbol of the derangement of the anti-Semitic mind. Christopher Sykes, a historian sharply critical of "Zionist propaganda," once observed that supporters of the Arab cause in the 1930s and 1940s invariably bewailed the control of the British press by Jews despite the fact that "the Arabs enjoyed the unstinted support of Lord Northcliffe, the first Lord Rothmere, and later of Lord Beaverbrook," the press barons who owned virtually the whole British press. The Arabs therefore had "an overwhelming propaganda advantage, such as was never enjoyed by the Jews, during the whole Mandate period."[7] Whoever may own the American press (Jews are believed to own about 3 percent of it, and supporters of Israel would be happy if they owned less), there can be little doubt as to who owns its sympathies.

Closely related to the ritualized accusation that Jews "snuff out" voices critical of Israel is what may be called the journalistic version of the preemptive strike against Israel and American Jewry. Among its skilled practitioners are Thimmesch, Sevareid, Stone, Mike Royko of the Chicago *Sun-Times,* and James Reston. Perhaps its classic instance came in the spring of 1978 when the *Washington Post* and *New York Times* expressed indignation at the "frenzy" (*Post*) and "scurrilousness" (*Times*) of American Jews who were allegedly defaming Zbigniew Brzezinski, President Carter's national security advisor, as anti-Semitic. Neither newspaper could be bothered to name the frenzied and scurrilous Jews who had made the accusation. But when William Safire traced the story to its source he found that Brzezinski himself had told journalists that "some people" were calling him an anti-Semite. Brzezinski correctly assumed that the journalists would quickly identify the collective culprit and administer the desired scolding. Typically, the masters of the preemptive strike will refer vaguely (and always without a single verifiable instance) to a vast Jewish "organized . . . campaign" (Royko, Chicago *Sun-Times,* 1 December 1980) to label as anti-Semitic anyone who criticizes any Israeli policy. Having warned in advance that the "friends of Israel" (Reston's sly periphrasis for Jews) will subject them to "a torrent of abuse" and call them anti-Semitic, they feel free to launch not so much into a criticism of some particular Israeli policy as into the charge that Jews control the press, the publishing houses, and even the lecture circuit. And why should anybody be called anti-Semitic merely for saying that?

The centrality of I. F. Stone in the formulation of the accusation that Jews control the press and enjoy "unchallenged hold on our government" (Thimmesch) is a reminder that a crucial role in the news media attack on Israel is played by Jews and Israelis themselves. Indeed, the one issue in this controversy on which the friends and enemies of Israel are likely to agree is that there are "too many Jews" in the news media. Jewish journalists like I. F. Stone, Norman Cousins, and Anthony Lewis have made it their special duty to uphold the pristine purity of the original Zionist ideal now so badly blurred, tarnished, and smeared by the actions of the real, live Zionists. Indeed, despite the fact that their other activities as Jews have been tactfully concealed from public view, these journalists offer themselves as defenders of the glory that was Judaism against the depredations visited on it by modern Israel, a country full of people who have forsaken their noble heritage for that of Esau by stooping to weapons of violence. Norman Cousins (March 1978) charged that the Israeli bombing of PLO bases in Lebanon "disfigures the Jewish character" and does harm to "the position of the Jewish people in history." Air raids on terrorist bases are, of course, a dirty business because the PLO always tries to locate these bases amid schools, apartments, and hospitals. But how could a liberal Jewish journalist writing from the physical and spiritual fleshpots of New York or Washington be expected to see that the "cleaner" an antiterrorist raid is for Cousins or Lewis, the dirtier and deadlier it is for the soldiers on the ground? At the height of the war in Lebanon, the shrewd George Will invited "persons making fine moral calibrations about Israel's conduct and fretting that Israel is 'losing its soul' " to recognize that "the PLO is hiding behind the babies that Arafat is kissing for U.S. television cameras" (*Newsweek,* 2 August, 1982).

If these defenders of "prophetic" Judaism deplore the fact that live Zionists are less truly Jewish (and Zionist) than their dead ancestors who never stooped to the gun, still other Jewish critics of Israel deplore the primitive fanaticism of Israel's religious minority. Stephen Rosenfeld, in a typical diatribe (January 1979), snarls at Jews who settle in Judea as wild "fanatics" who prevent "Palestinian" nationhood and thereby render peace impossible. Bob Simon, covering the 1981 election campaign in Israel, was visibly pained by the fact that "traditional" European Jewish ideas—socialism, for example—were losing their hold over Israelis and being replaced by "Sephardic" (i.e., Oriental) populism and—incongruous as this might seem for Jews—religious intensity. A non-Jewish (and far uglier) version of this line may be found in the columns of Georgie Anne Geyer. In one tirade (17 June 1981) she deplored the brutal, amoral, and warmongering character of Israel's "Sephardic" population and fretted greatly over the danger that Jews might lose their historical reputation for being "liberal-minded, and dovish."

What Franz Kafka called "display Jews" are snatched up with alacrity by the news media as guest columnists, not so much for what they have to say as for their ability to validate the claim that "not all Jews support Israel's position on the PLO." The division of opinion on this matter among American Jews may be ninety to ten in support of Israel, but the news media are not in the business of proportional representation. When Milton Viorst arranged an evening in shul with PLO spokesmen visiting Washington, D.C., and some Jews in the audience failed to treat them with the deference they receive from journalists, the *Los Angeles Times* Syndicate was quick to seek out and disseminate Viorst's high-minded reflections on the imperfect devotion of American Jews to free speech. When Arthur Hertzberg let it be known that his version of the Zionist idea conflicted with present Israeli policy, the *New York Review of Books,* a relentless critic of the Jewish state for many years, invited him to attack Israel's government in its pages.

More extreme figures, especially Israelis of the far left, play a major role as witnesses for the prosecution in the case against Israel. In April 1982 Anthony Lewis wrote a column about books allegedly banned by the Israeli military government in Judea and Samaria. The story, which turned out to be a tissue of lies, was attributed by Lewis to two Israeli sources, Ory Bernstein and Amos Elon. The latter "authority" on Israeli affairs assured those who were shocked by Lewis's story that "It's all part of the preparations for a fascist regime! Soon we'll have it all, concentration camps as well as the burning of the books."[8] Usually these Israelis receive only scant identification, and Americans and Europeans are unlikely to be aware of their marginal status in Israeli political life. Uri Avnery, editor of the semipornographic weekly *Ha'olam Hazeh,* used to appear with sufficient frequency on the major television networks for Americans to think of him as a prominent representative of a major party in the Knesset. His interview with "friendly and soft-spoken" Yasser Arafat during the war in Lebanon (17 July 1982), an interview so lacking in critical acumen, so permeated by oily sycophancy, so empty of all substance that the ordinary junior high school newspaper would have been embarrassed to print it, made Avnery an international celebrity in the news media.

In the seventies, the tendentious coverage of Middle East affairs on "All Things Considered" caused sufficient consternation in the American-Jewish community to prompt National Public Radio head Frank Mankiewicz to order (in 1978) a detailed internal investigation. The report, although conceived by its author, Steven Emerson, as an apologia for those who had commissioned it, did condemn the "politically tainted rhetoric" of NPR's south Lebanon reporter Tim Llewellyn and did "strongly recommend" that in future interviews concerning the Middle East, "each personality be properly identified so that the listener knows what he is getting." In its unregenerate days the program typically introduced people like Felicia Langer, a well-known pro-Communist and the favored lawyer of terrorists caught in Israel, as "an Israeli lawyer" who just happened to have strong opinions about the wickedness of her government and country. Israel Shahak, viewed by most Israelis as a harmless eccentric working with the Maoist Matzpen party, is cited constantly by anti-Israeli journalists as "an Israeli professor" who has been torn from his test tubes by the moral compulsion to reveal his country's abominations to the world. But perhaps only Thimmesch had the temerity to describe this matinee idol of the PLO lecture circuit, who has been investigated for treason, as a man whose "Israeli patriotism is unquestioned." It hardly needs to be added that the very same journalists who use Jewish witnesses against Israel will disqualify those who support Israel on any particular issue just because they are Jewish. Geyer, who probably spent more ingenuity than any other American journalist in distorting the truth about allegations of Israeli torture in the Sami Esmail case, rejected out of hand (in her column of 15 June 1978) the detailed refutation of the Esmail propaganda campaign that had appeared in the *New York Times* because it had been written by two Jews.

One reason why Shahak, Langer, Lea Tsemel and other Israeli leftists have struck such a responsive chord in anti-Israeli journalists is that they persistently reiterate the Soviet-inspired formula that Israelis are Nazis who oppress the real "Jews," otherwise known as Arabs. (In fairness to Shahak, it should be noted that he has not reserved this slander for Jews. In October 1979 he wrote a lengthy defense of Stalin, and concluded by calling Soviet dissidents like Vladimir Bukovsky "Nazis.") The transformation of Arabs into Jews and of Israelis into Nazis, originally a Soviet invention and later elaborated by Arab speakers in the United Nations, is now freely used by anti-Israeli militants of every political persuasion. Its pattern is so fixed that it seems to come out of a textbook for courses in yellow journalism.

Shortly after the Lebanese war began, the British Communist newspaper *Morning Star* published an editorial headed "Stop the Genocide" (11 June). Screaming headlines and generous and sympathetic coverage were accorded to every outburst by Olof Palme, Andreas Papandreou, and Bruno Kreisky, who alleged that Israelis were doing to Palestinians what Nazis had done to Jews. Nicholas von Hoffman, writing from America for the *Spectator,* likened Israelis in Lebanon to Nazis in Lidice, and expressed the belief that as a result of his efforts and those of like-minded journalists, "Americans are coming to see the Israeli Government as pounding the Star of David into a swastika." Neither von Hoffman nor the other journalistic crusaders against neo-Nazism thought it worthwhile to comment on the prominence of Nazi flags and mementos in the captured PLO headquarters in Lebanon. The formula became so fixed and easy to learn that it could be exported to places that had never seen Jews or Nazis, like Kuala Lumpur, where the *New Straits Times* prognosticated that "Just as Adolf Hitler's diabolical plan for a 'Final Solution to the Jewish Problem' failed to drive the Jews out of Europe, so will fail Israel's savage efforts to uproot the Palestinians" (29 June).

Obsession with the problem of "uprooted" Palestinian Arab refugees among journalists, few of whom have taken any notice of the ten million refugees displaced by the Russians after World War II or have shed tears for the Vietnamese and Cambodian refugees, people truly without a home, without hope, and without help, reflects the obsession with Israel as the major source of global conflict. The old religious idea that Jerusalem is the navel of the universe survives in a perverted form in the modern journalistic commonplace that nearly every conflict in the world stems from Israel's "failure" to solve the "Palestinian problem." The most prominent exponent of this view is former Undersecretary of State George Ball, a frequent guest columnist in the *New York Times* (and many other papers), a man distinctly available to every radio and television program desirous of an "expert" on the Middle East who can be counted on to blame Israel not just for every dispute with its neighbors, but for every problem in the Middle East and Asia (the Russians in Afghanistan, Iraq in Iran, Iranians invading an American embassy, Pakistanis burning an American embassy, and so on). Abba Eban thought he detected a "messianic symptom" when "George Ball recently appeared on a television program in New York for six minutes without blaming Israel for whatever he was talking about" (*Jerusalem Post,* International Edition, 26 October–1 November 1980). But Eban spoke prematurely. On 1 February of the same year newspapers across the country carried a column by Ball asserting that "our shattered embassies" in Iran and Pakistan as well as the Russian invasion of Afghanistan were the result of Israel's stony intransigence. He also laid America's defense and energy problems at the door of Israel. He expressed confidence that the United States could get strategic air bases in Saudi Arabia and the other Arab sheikdoms if it pressured Israel into conceding whatever the Arabs wanted. He implied, too, that if Prince Fahd did not have to spend his days and nights fretting over Jewish control of Jerusalem, and if Arafat were able to realize his ideals in a little state of his own, cheap and abundant oil would flow to Americans in a torrential stream.

The war in Lebanon was for Ball proof that, as he told the readers of the *New York Times* on 28 July 1982, the U.S. had "entrusted the shaping of . . . foreign policy to Israel." How else to explain American leaders' failure to understand that "no one should expect the Palestine Liberation Organization to give up its commitment to Israel's destruction . . ."? That such ravings could be published in apparently sober and serious newspapers is a gruesome indication of the extent to which traditional anti-Semitic ideology is now tolerated by our professional communicators in the press, radio, and television. When the war between Iran and Iraq began, it was not merely each of the combatants that blamed "Jews and Zionists" for directing the hand of the other; *Time* magazine was quick to discover a "reliable source" (unnamed) in the State Department who said that the Iran-Iraq war had begun (and presumably continues year after year) because of Israel's failure to solve the omnipresent "Palestinian problem."

George Ball is a Washington diplomat turned journalist. But other American journalists who fancy themselves State Department functionaries also consider it their patriotic duty to blame Israel for most global and domestic afflictions, no matter how remote from the Arab-Israeli dispute, and to allege that Israel is a huge millstone around the American neck. This is particularly true of the numerous media sympathizers with Saudi Arabia, like Nick Thimmesch, Otis Pike (a politician turned journalist), Strobe Talbott (*Time*), and Joseph Harsch. Harsch likes to carry the struggle against Israel all the way back to 1948, with the obvious intention of implying it was a mistake to have admitted her into the family of nations in the first place. He argues that Israel is the single foreign country in which American interests have been defined not by the wise experts of the State Department but by "a lobby of pro-Israel activists too powerful to be defied by our government" (*Christian Science Monitor*, 18 June 1981). It was only because of "the need for Jewish support in the elections" of 1948 that "politics won out over long-range national interest" and continued to do so for every minute of the succeeding thirty-three years. Translated from the language of anti-Semitic obsession, Harsch's contention is simply that U.S. interests in what the *Monitor* likes to call Palestine have been defined not by the dispassionate judgment of trained specialists but by the popular will of the American people, expressed through their elected officials. Like all elitist ideologues, Harsch cannot abide the fact that the United States is ultimately ruled by its people and not by its bureaucratic experts, those arrogant specialists who (as the British historian G. M. Young used to say) know so much about so little that they can neither be contradicted nor are worth contradicting.

The increase in anti-Semitic violence around the world in recent years cannot be separated from the vast network of apologists for it that exists in the news media. The PLO, like other anti-Semitic organizations before it (including a few notorious governments), holds that every Jew is guilty of the crime of having been born and is therefore a legitimate target for poison, bullets, and bombs. Every Jew is an enemy, whether he is an infant asleep in Nahariya, a child attending an Aguda camp in Brussels, a worshiper at a synagogue in Paris, Vienna, Rome, or Istanbul, or any man, woman, or child who happens to be in any Israeli bus or street or market where a PLO bomb explodes. The distinction between this kind of killing and the guerrilla attack on military targets that results in innocent casualties is simple and obvious; yet it is consistently blurred by the news media in dealing with Israel.

But unwillingness to condemn terror is the least of the offenses committed by journalistic warriors against Israel. Arab terrorists have capitalized mightily on the modern belief that the more a group that claims to be oppressed employs bestiality and murder to "express" its grievances, the more credible are its claims. Far from damaging the PLO cause, the long series of massacres—the killing of the Olympic athletes, the shooting of thirteen mothers and babies at Kiryat Shemona, the slaughter of twenty schoolchildren at Maalot, the butchery of the women of Kibbutz Shamir, the bloodbath at Lod Airport, and hundreds of other barbarities—has established its legitimacy in the eyes of the news media (to say nothing of governments, more of which recognize the PLO than recognize Israel). Typical reactions to the latest PLO or PFLP massacre of Jews (or Christians who visit Israel, or Moslems who consort with Jews, or anyone at all who travels on an airplane) include a *Christian Science Monitor* editorial citing the incident as compelling evidence of the urgent need to solve "the Palestinian problem," a Barbara Walters sermon (for example, in March 1978) to Ezer Weizman exhorting Israel to "turn the other cheek," and a torrential outpouring of journalistic explanations of the psychological pressures and political imperatives that force Palestinian Arabs to commit murder.

One spectacular example of the standard pattern will have to suffice. In February 1978 an ABC-TV program called "Hostage" examined the terrorist use of hostages to achieve political ends. The stars of the show were, of course, Palestinian Arabs and their supporters, although much attention was given to the Moluccan terrorists in Holland. Throughout the program the narrator took it for granted that in any terrorist outrage it is not the victim—the mutilated child or the murdered mother—but the terrorist himself who is the injured party and whose grievances require immediate healing. In November of the same year ABC-TV's Frank Reynolds justified what struck many viewers as an hour-long commercial for violence entitled "Terror in the Promised Land" with the astonishing remark that the "Palestinians" had been forced to kill people because no one would "listen" to them, and "to refuse to listen is to strengthen their argument that violence is their only recourse." Needless to say, those viewers whose memories had not atrophied in the preceding eight months understood just the opposite to be the case; the more they are "listened" to, the more clearly do terrorists recognize the profitability of murder. For in between their two prime-time shows on ABC the Arab terrorists found time to commit some of their most spectacular outrages, including the murder in March of thirty-five men, women, and children, and the wounding of seventy others, on the coastal road near Haifa.

In September 1986, just after Palestinian Arabs had butchered Pan-Am passengers in Karachi and Jews worshiping in Istanbul, Bill Moyers of CBS, another advocate of the "listening" theory of terrorism, said that what was needed was a massive effort to discover, with respect to the killers, "Who are these young men? What's happening out there to rouse their fury?" Since, as Moyers surely knows, no national or ethnic group claiming victimization has ever received more publicity, has ever been "listened to" more than the Palestinian Arabs, his real meaning was, as the *New Republic* shrewdly noted, "not that we pay insufficient attention to the wishes of these murderers, but that we are insufficiently cooperative in helping them realize them" (29 September 1986). Since the primary wish of the murderers is to destroy Israel and the Jews who inhabit it and also the Jews who do not inhabit it, how exactly does Moyers propose to abate their "fury"?

Probably no opinion comes so close to being universal in the news media as the view that terrorist violence always proves the righteousness of a cause, and that everyone is guilty of a terrorist crime except the person who happens to commit it. When, in September 1981, Bruno Kreisky blamed the PLO murder of Jews at Vienna's main synagogue on "the state of Israel," he could be confident that he spoke the language of moral "explanation" habitually used by his journalistic interlocutors. In April of the same year, for example, Georgie Anne Geyer had implicitly endorsed the May 1980 murder of five Jewish Bible students and the wounding of seventeen others by Arab terrorists in Hebron. She considered the terrorists the injured party because offense had been given to the deep-seated prejudice that Hebron Arabs are known to have against Jews living in their midst, a prejudice similar to that which promotes violence against blacks who "invade" white neighborhoods.[9] As the Israeli poet Abba Kovner once wrote, when the guilt of the persecutors and murderers of Jews is at issue, "there is always someone more guilty—(the victim)/(the victim)."

The powerful bond of sympathy between many journalists and Arab terrorists, long evident in expressions of admiration for the terrorists (see, for example, Edward Cody, *Washington Post,* 7 July 1982 on the organizer of the 1978 coastal road massacre) and in tortured apologetics for their barbaric deeds, turned, in a spectacular incident of May 1986, into active collusion and criminal complicity. The "NBC Nightly News" for 5 May broadcast a three-and-a-half minute interview with Mohammed Abbas, then under indictment in the U.S. as the organizer of the hijacking of the Achille Lauro and the murderer of the American-Jewish passenger, Leon Klinghoffer. NBC's spokesmen admitted, indeed boasted, that the network had agreed to keep the terrorist's whereabouts secret in exchange for his granting them an exclusive interview. Lawrence Grossman, president of NBC News, justified the arrangement by claiming, predictably, that he had been acting on behalf of the public's right to know and "understand" the views of "all leaders." But no amount of justification could conceal the fact that this act of complicity with terrorism was the existential realization of journalistic ideas about terror that had long ago infected the profession.

More pervasive and certainly more insidious in its influence on public opinion than apologias for terrorism and outright attacks on Israel, is the tendentious and charged language used in news reports of the Middle East conflict. Traditionally, Americans expect that their newspapers (unlike the British and Western European press) will clearly distinguish news reporting from editorial opinion; and so they tend to assume that whatever is in print on the news pages is disinterested observation and reporting. Yet in nearly every instance in which the two parties to the Arab-Israeli conflict use different terms to label a place or group or event, the press adheres to the Arab usage. A few examples will serve to suggest the pattern:

Arab Usage	*Israeli Usage*	*News Media Usage*
Occupied territories	Administered or disputed territories	Occupied territories
PLO guerrillas	PLO terrorists	PLO guerrillas
West Bank	Judea and Samaria	West Bank
Syrian peacekeeping forces	Syrian occupying army	Syrian peacekeeping forces
Palestinians	Palestinian Arabs	Palestinians

In a related category are certain fixed epithets, applied with a mechanical illogic and unsuitableness far exceeding anything found in the *Iliad*. Thus the epithet "moderate" has been affixed to Saudi Arabia so consistently that many Americans and Europeans might well come to think it is a geographical term. This is the same Saudi Arabia that consistently advocates "jihad" (holy war) against Israel, that (even more than Libya or Nigeria) holds the oil cartel together,[10] and that is the most viciously racist state in the Arab world (although *Time* has called it the "desert democracy"). Then there is "moderate" Jordan, whose reasonableness consists of its willingness to accept American aid while flirting with the Russians, refusing all negotiation with Israel, boycotting the Camp David accords, and flouting every American effort to achieve a negotiated settlement. References to the "moderate" wings of the PLO and to the "moderate" Arafat, increasingly common in anti-Israeli editorializing in *Time* (starting in January 1975), the *Washington Post,* and elsewhere, have begun to find their way into news reports as well.

Whereas reporters and editorialists classify Arab nations according to their greater or less moderation (Iraq and Syria are often "less moderate"), Israelis are classified ornithologically, as "hawks" or (less frequently) "doves." In the British press the epithet "terrorists" is generally reserved for Irishmen and Jews, and it is a point of honor in the "quality" news media always to refer to Arafat and his followers as "moderate." The BBC's Philip Short solemnly warned in November 1981 that if the Saudi "peace" plan were rejected, "Yasser Arafat may conclude that moderation does not pay." During the war in Lebanon, Robert Fisk of the *Times,* in addition to making the ritualized gestures of respect toward "Mr. Arafat and the more moderate PLO leaders," expressed his intense regret that Mahmoud Labadi, the PLO's "eloquent" spokesman in Beirut, had been coerced by a bigoted public opinion into "wearing a small pistol at his waist as a symbol of his presumed militancy" (17 July 1982). So resistant is Fisk to applying the label "terrorist" to the world's leading terrorist organization that he adds *sic* after the word when quoting it from Israeli sources (*Times,* 13 July 1982), a standard device of grade-school journalists less secure in their Latin than in their partisan fervor. The American magazine *Newsweek* was distressed because Israel's war against the PLO, instead of destroying the movement, had "sorely weakened its more moderate elements." *Newsweek* feared that if the extremely moderate Arafat lost charge, the PLO "seems likely to turn . . . toward terrorism" (19 July 1982). Six days later, David Shipler, no great friend of Israel, published in the *New York Times* a detailed account—one that helped to explain why the Israeli invasion was welcomed by several factions in Lebanon—of "the terror of six years of living under the PLO." If gruesome accounts of the bloody reign of terror in Lebanon by the PLO and its hired mercenaries have unsettled the faith of *Newsweek* in Arafat's moderation, the magazine has yet to reveal that fact to its readers.

Tactful silences and ingenious euphemisms permeate reporting and commentary on contemporary events in the Middle East. Rare was the American journalist who thought it necessary to report (much less deplore) the fact that Jamil Baroody, the representative of Saudi Arabia in the UN, had (in March 1976) read into its protocols the neo-Nazi claim that the Holocaust never happened. In December 1980, when Hazem Nuseibeh, Jordan's UN delegate, made an openly anti-Semitic speech in which Jews were said to "control and manipulate and exploit the rest of humanity by controlling the money and wealth of the world," the *New York Times* primly reported that "a notable feature" of his ravings was "several hostile references to Jews." Although he could muster none of that moral severity characteristic of *Times* reporters chronicling Israeli behavior, Bernard Nossiter did helpfully annotate Nuseibeh's speech by saying that a certain Rothschild was a London bullion dealer and a certain Oppenheimer was a South African mogul. Whether the *Times*'s treatment of this display of Jew-hatred by moderate Jordan and also by Senegal (identified by Nossiter as "a political moderate") was better or worse than that of the *Washington Post, Christian Science Monitor,* ABC, CBS, and NBC, all of which chose not to mention it at all, we leave it to the moral philosophers of the future to decide.

To them we also leave a crucial question that has thus far been deliberately evaded in this survey. What is the underlying cause of the journalists' war against Israel? One answer, proposed by many liberals and especially Jewish liberals during the period 1977–84, was that what some of us mistakenly supposed to be hostility by the news media to the state of Israel was in fact only disapproval of the Likud government; once that aberration was removed, the hostility would vanish like morning mist at sunrise. As I write, it is more than two and a half years since the fall of the Likud government, and it would seem that there is little evidence to support this liberal explanation. After all, it was not Menachem Begin or Yitzhak Shamir but Shimon Peres who in March 1985 incurred the terrible wrath of the president of CBS for being the commander in chief of an army that specialized in "attacks . . . on innocent journalists in Lebanon," an army whose tank crews "deliberately fire . . . on unarmed and neutral journalists." It was Shimon Peres and Yitzhak Rabin of the Labor party who enraged the head of CBS by refusing to do for him what a Likud government had done in the spring of 1984 for David Shipler of the *New York Times* after the Ashkelon bus hijacking, namely, satisfy the journalistic conception of Israel's system of government as one vast commission of inquiry into its own misdeeds. The attempt to explain journalistic hostility toward Israel by blaming the misbehavior of the Likud government is as convincing (and derives from the same sources) as the attempts made over the centuries by self-hating Jews to divert the hatred directed against all Jews onto a particular subgroup—backward Jews, Yiddish-speaking Jews, poor Jews, or rich Jews. A more likely explanation is the fact that the ideology of anti-Semitism, embarrassed into hiding for twenty-two years after the Second World War, has since June 1967 regained its old vigor and openness as well as a new acceptance by the intelligentsia, which is (not surprisingly) impressed by the fact that the Arabs always base their arguments on "rights" and never (like Israel, even under Begin and Shamir) on "security."

I suggested, at the outset of this essay, that the task of describing and analyzing and thereby "revealing" the hostility of large numbers of journalists to Israel has now changed from what it used to be. It has been rendered, in a way, too easy by the shameless admission of journalists themselves, especially the Middle East "experts" among them, that, yes, they really do hate Israel, and they certainly do take the side of the Arabs. Until fairly recently, there still existed some margin between speculation and proof in this matter; but now the margin no longer exists. The facade has come down. Journalists whose disinterestedness was for years angrily challenged by their critics and as laboriously defended by their employers now openly, even defiantly, acknowledge their hostility.

Generally, the confession, or rather boast, is made in books rather than in newspaper articles or on television programs. Jonathan Randal of the *Washington Post* has published a book entitled *Going All the Way: Christian Warlords, Israeli Adventurers and the War in Lebanon,*[12] a title whose subtlety accurately mirrors the subtlety of its author's mind. Randal first gained notoriety outside of narrow journalistic circles when his employers revealed that he, the *Post's* Beirut correspondent, had been among the journalists held for nearly twenty-four hours by Palestinian Arab terrorists without the *Post* ever bothering to report the occurrence. The paper, as noted above, only reluctantly and belatedly admitted that Randal had been arrested, and argued that a seasoned veteran of wars and revolutions could hardly be expected to take account of so minor an affliction as captivity by the PLO. Previously, Randal's distinction among Middle East reporters was that he was widely recognized as the master of the unattributed source. He had only to talk to the nearest lout leaning on his Kalatchnikov in a Palestinian refugee camp, and this anonymous victim of Israeli oppression would deliver an eloquent discourse about Palestinian Arabs living in "Diaspora" or in camps that were replicas of Auschwitz, a discourse that bore a remarkable similarity to Randal's own conception of

Palestinian Arabs as the true Jews in the Middle East. He had only to consult an anonymous former aide of Menachem Begin to be regaled with a psychosexual analysis of the arch-villain of Israel-haters, an analysis that, by a happy accident, turned out to be exactly his own: "all Begin has to do is see a general and he has an orgasm."

In his book, however, as Rael and Erich Isaac have shown,[13] Randal dispenses with the tedious business of invoking anonymous sources. Israel is here nothing less than the embodiment of evil, engaged in "large scale murder," reneging on signed agreements in "the most insulting and murderous fashion," and outdoing all other countries in "ruthlessness," except perhaps the United States, which has been so irredeemably tainted by its support of Israel that Randal is "ashamed of being an American." If in his reporting Randal's sexual obsessions found their realization in his portrait of Begin, here his lurid excremental imaginings are literalized in the entire army of Israel, whose soldiers, according to Randal, "left distinctive calling cards [all over Lebanon]: human excrement in drawers, in beds, in closets, in churches and mosques and on the floor of hospitals." The picture of Jonathan Randal diligently sifting, analyzing, and labeling excrement in every corner of Lebanon is not a pretty one. But it is as fitting an emblem as one is likely to find of analytic journalism as practiced by the staff of the *Washington Post* stationed in Beirut.

Among Randal's Beirut colleagues was Tony Clifton, who covered the Lebanon war for *Newsweek* (and was subsequently rewarded for his distinguished work there by being appointed *Newsweek*'s bureau chief in London). His book *God Cried*[14] expresses the same curious sexual obsession that characterizes Randal's lucubrations on Israel, although—difficult as this may be to credit—on a still lower level. Begin, Clifton alleges, ended the war "because he had got what he wanted, just as a rapist stops humping after he has had his orgasm." Clifton has no hesitation about referring to the PLO as "our side," boasts that "of course we all [in the Beirut press corps] became anti-Israeli," and declares that only a fool would ask why Clifton and his friends told only the PLO side of the conflict with Israel: "There is no other side to tell."

Another journalistic pursuer of truth in an Arab capital who has published her personal views on the Arab-Israeli conflict is Doreen Kays, head of the Cairo office of ABC-TV from 1977–81. In *Frogs and Scorpions: Egypt, Sadat and the Media,*[15] she depicts Sadat as a gullible fool entrapped by the satanically clever Israelis who, once having lured Sadat into the Camp David agreements, "no longer bother camouflaging their nefarious intentions." Freed from the constraints, mild as they were, imposed upon her when she was dispensing news and opinions on ABC, Kays expresses at every opportunity her "loathing" for the "insufferable Begin" and "all he stood for . . . a pygmy, ill-equipped to stand besides a giant." Not that she had much use for the "giant" either. Since Sadat had betrayed the Arab cause, she "felt nothing but relief" as she watched him bleed to death after being gunned down. She acknowledges that her strong pro-Arab bias might possibly have affected, however slightly, her reporting, but any bias on her part was, she says, "nicely offset by the pro-Israeli position emanating from my Jewish colleagues in Tel Aviv and Jerusalem." At least Doreen Kays has a sense of humor.

Such is a mere sampling of the ideological and temperamental disposition toward Israel of some of the journalists who supply countless millions of readers and television viewers with their version of the Arab-Israeli conflict. Anyone who is tempted to believe that the depredations committed by the journalists of the *Washington Post* or *Newsweek* or ABC television in dealing with Israel result from ignorance and incompetence would do well to read these books, vile and semiliterate as they are. He will then have to face the possibility that what is now called for in the realm of "media criticism" is not sober analysis of error and rational recommendation for correction and improvement, but a reconsideration of the basic premises we have long taken for granted, namely, that a "free" press is a guarantee of democratic freedoms and a means of bringing us into some reasonable relation to truth. In Orwell's Oceania the basic premise with respect to journalism is far different; it is that, given modern technology and a contempt for moral tradition, anything is possible—anything can be done with the human mind, with history, and, above all, with language.

Notes

1. See Robert B. Heilman, "Writers on Journalists: A Version of Atheism," *Georgia Review,* 39 (Spring 1985): 37–54.
2. Chafetz's views on the misreporting of Middle East news were later articulated more fully in his book *Double Vision: How the Press Distorts America's View of the Middle East* (New York: Morrow, 1984).
3. That CBS has a special problem with Jerusalem is suggested by the propensity of (for example) Bob Simon for standing in front of the Knesset or the Western Wall in Jerusalem and concluding his report with "Bob Simon, reporting from Tel Aviv."
4. Renata Adler, "Annals of Law," *New Yorker,* 23 June 1986, pp. 61, 44.
5. When, years later, he did get around to replying to criticism of this column—in his letter to the *Jerusalem Post* of 4 June 1982—he claimed that he couldn't recall having written it (though a paragraph later he proceeded to quote from it).
6. Another leftist journalist much disturbed by the Jewish conspiracy is Alexander Cockburn, who wrote in the *New Statesman* (27 August 1982) that "the cowardice of almost all American reporting on Israel has long been a source of wonderment. . . . It was plain that the US Press was—by and large—obediently catering to Zionist fantasies. . . ."

7. Christopher Sykes, *Cross Roads to Israel* (London: New English Library, 1967), p. 388.
8. See Melvin J. Lasky, "Lies have long legs," *Jerusalem Post,* 2 May 1982.
9. Geyer invariably takes it for granted that all Moslem religious sensitivities are sacrosanct, that all Arab assertions of "historic right" are unquestionable, and that Saudi monarchs cannot rest in their beds at night so long as a single Jewish dwelling stains the soil of Judea. But no sooner does she hear an Israeli Jew refer to the Bible than shock waves of secularist indignation burst forth in her column (see, e.g., her columns of 5 August 1977, 29 April 1981, and 17 June 1981 [Universal Press Syndicate]).
10. For a shrewd analysis of how Saudi Arabia manipulates both the oil market and the news media, see J. B. Kelly, "Yamani's Book of Revelations," *National Review,* 10 July, 1980.
11. The extent of Nossiter's confusion over the meaning of this word may be gauged by his *Times* article (20 September 1982) entitled "U.N. Carries Moderation to Extremes."
12. Jonathan Randal, *Going All the Way: Christian Warlords, Israeli Adventurers and the War in Lebanon,* (New York: The Viking Press, 1983).
13. Rael and Erich Isaac, "Enemies in the Extreme," *Midstream,* 30 (September 1984): 45–48.
14. Tony Clifton and Catherine Leroy, *God Cried* (London, Melbourne, and New York: Quartet Books, 1983).
15. Doreen Kays, *Frogs and Scorpions: Egypt, Sadat and the Media* (London: Frederick Muller, 1984).

9

Strangers in the Land of Israel

In Jewish tradition, the treatment accorded "strangers" has always been assigned the highest importance. In Leviticus (19:34) we are told: "The stranger that sojourneth with you shall be unto you as the home-born among you, and you shall love him as yourself; because you were strangers in the land of Egypt." The injunction to love the stranger, to treat the stranger as an equal, both legally and ethically, is repeated no fewer than thirty-six times in the Pentateuch.

There are at least three reasons for this emphasis on the equitable treatment of the stranger. One is that it is intrinsically just. A second is that the persistent admonition to Israel to love the stranger "as thyself" is a necessary complement to the doctrine of Israel's chosenness, because it is a reminder that the chosenness of Israel does not depend on ethnic "exclusivity" but is directed toward the ultimate unity of all mankind. A third reason for the insistence on the precept of loving the stranger is, as Cynthia Ozick has written, to establish "a moral connection . . . with the memory of bondage." Israel's own bondage in Egypt becomes "a metaphor of pity for the outsider."[1]

Over the centuries, the biblical term "stranger" became synonymous in Jewish tradition with proselytes, converts to Judaism. Attitudes toward proselytism have varied greatly over the span of Jewish history. Some Jewish leaders, such as rabbis Johanan and Eleazar of the third century, actually claimed to deduce from scriptural texts that "the Holy One, Blessed be He, exiled Israel among the nations only in order to increase their numbers with the addition of proselytes." Others discouraged proselytism, citing historical evidence of the unreliable character of proselytes during times of travail for the Jewish people. Yet at all times the biblical declaration that "you shall have one manner of law, the same for the stranger as for the homeborn" (Lev. 24:22) has determined the treatment of those who, with or without benefit of Jewish encouragement, joined

143

themselves to the Jewish people. This element of joining one's fate to that of the Jews rather than replacing one set of theological opinions with another has usually, for obvious historical reasons, been paramount. Maimonides clearly understood this when he wrote that "Toward father and mother we are commanded honor and reverence, towards the prophets to obey them, but toward proselytes we are commanded to have great love in our inmost hearts. . . . A man who left his father and birthplace and the realm of his people . . . and who attached himself to this nation which today is a despised people . . . the Lord does not call you fool but intelligent and understanding, wise and walking correctly, a pupil of Abraham our father. . . ."

In view of this tradition of respect for the convert and of insistence on "one law for the citizen and for the stranger that dwelleth amongst you" (Exod. 12:49), how does one begin to explain the order issued by Israel's interior minister, Rabbi Yitzhak Peretz, in June 1986, that the word "converted" be stamped onto the identity cards of anyone who immigrates to Israel after being converted to Judaism? The immediate cause of Peretz's astonishing order, so clearly at variance with Torah and with Jewish tradition and condemned as such by former Chief Rabbi Goren, is a legal anomaly in the state of Israel. In Israel, only those persons who are converted in accordance with Halachah (Jewish religious law) are registered as Jews. In the case of immigrants to Israel, however, conversion by Conservative and Reform rabbis has been accepted by the civil authorities as sufficient for those immigrants to be registered as Jews even though their conversion was not accepted by Israel's Orthodox rabbinate. Peretz was trying, by administrative fiat, to change Israel's Law of Return, which states that a Jew is "a person who is born of a Jewish mother or who is converted and is not a member of another faith." Since neither the courts nor the Knesset had been willing to amend the law to say "converted according to Halachah," Rabbi Peretz thought he would take this short and ready way to enable the Orthodox rabbinate in Israel to identify and then investigate persons whose conversions it did not deem authentic.

That an Orthodox rabbi, seeking to encompass a narrow political goal, should so casually and thoughtlessly violate one of the most deep-seated of Jewish traditions (Goren likened Peretz's action to "spilling blood") suggests that the immediate cause of his order is not its ultimate explanation. For this, I think, one needs to examine the emotional uneasiness of certain elements of Israeli society occasioned by the stranger, since the granting of legal equality to the stranger is in the Bible predicated on the granting of emotional equality—"you shall love him as yourself"—and also on the moral understanding of the stranger's history—"you know the heart of a stranger, seeing you were strangers in the land of Egypt" (Exod.

23:8). I propose therefore to discuss a few incidents of recent years involving the plight of strangers (in the old sense of the term) and of actual converts in Israel in order to suggest the extent to which Rabbi Peretz's inflammatory and impious action (repudiated by Israel's Supreme Court in December 1986)[2] is an outgrowth of unresolved conflicts between Halachah and modern Jewish history and of ethnicity masquerading as religion.

Halachah and Jewish History

On 21 November 1984 Meir Agassi and David Ehrenfeld, two employees of the *chevrah kadishah* ("burial society") of the town of Rishon Lezion, were sentenced to three months in prison by the Rehovot Magistrates' Court for removing the remains of Tereza Anghelovici (dead since December 1982) from her grave in the Rishon Lezion Jewish Cemetery in the darkness of the night of 1 March 1984 and dumping them in a Moslem cemetery in Ramle. The two had been adjudged guilty on 31 October on all nine charges brought against them, including violating health regulations, trespassing, breach of trust (of the burial society), and—surely the one most immediate to their professional task—"dishonoring the dead." They had carried out their grisly deeds in the wake of objections by ultra-Orthodox circles to the burial in a Jewish cemetery of an Israeli woman born Christian and never converted to Judaism in accordance with Halachah. The court president, Shlomo Yifrah, stated that the defendants, whom he called two of the most prodigious liars ever to appear in his courtroom, were better at talking about respect for the dead than at practicing it. They, for their part, kept invoking their "religious mission" as the excuse for what to the unappreciative eye of an *apikoyres* might look like a crime. They had very much wanted, for example, to bury Anghelovici "in the place deserving of her religion," but, insufficiently versed as they were in the niceties of comparative religion, mistook the Moslem cemetery for a Christian one.

The other two judges, although they concurred in the verdict of guilt against the black-coated graverobbers, placed considerable responsibility for stirring up this "senseless hatred" on Anghelovici's daughter, Adina Harpaz. She had accomplished her mother's burial in the Jewish cemetery fraudulently in the first place, by falsely claiming that her mother was Jewish when she provided details to the burial society.

The announcement of the court's verdict in November brought back to the mind of the Israeli public the untidy controversy that surrounded this affair in the spring, when it was debated in the newspapers, on television, and on the floor of the Knesset. Since many of the apopleptic utterances made about the case were made in relative ignorance of the details, it may be useful to review these briefly. During the turmoil of the Holocaust in Rumania, Tereza voluntarily followed her Jewish husband Josef to a forced labor camp. In 1964 she chose to settle with him in the Jewish homeland, knowing all the hardship this might entail. The Anghelovicis had two daughters, Miriam and Adina. Adina applied to the Israeli Chief Rabbinate for conversion over a decade before the controversy, at which time she stated, in reply to a direct question, that her mother did not wish to join her in conversion. The other daughter, Miriam, deceased by 1984, never converted to Judaism, although she had had a religious Jewish marriage in Rumania and had her son circumcised in accordance with Jewish law. This son, named Robert Pollack, was brought up by his grandparents after his mother's death. He was now doing regular service as a soldier in the Israeli army. In one of the many graveyard scenes featured in connection with this story on Israeli television, he told (on 9 March) of being raised as a Jew, of becoming a bar mitzvah, and of having not the slightest "identity" crisis about being a Jew. He did ask pointedly, since he was about to return to his unit in Lebanon, whether, should he die there, he would be denied burial in a Jewish cemetery and, like his grandmother, be dumped into a Moslem graveyard.

The members of the Anghelovici family claimed that Tereza had been the most Jewish of them all, that she had brought Shabbat candlesticks from Rumania with her and put them to their proper use in Israel, and that she alone of the family had taken the daughters to shul on Shabbat. But none of these testimonials, given by a family that in Israeli eyes is distinctly secular, could make much impression on the religious in Israel or gainsay the fact that when this very "Jewish" woman came to Israel in 1964 she listed her religion as Christian and later (1979) applied for naturalization as a non-Jew.

If we can credit Adina Harpaz's claim that she declined help from Amnesty International in her struggle with the rabbis because she anticipated that the resultant controversy would bring disgrace on the state of Israel, then her foresight is to be applauded. For most of the combatants in the national debate incited by the graverobbing looked very much like foot soldiers enlisting to join Matthew Arnold's "ignorant armies clash[ing] by night." Shlomo Lorincz, then an Agudat Yisrael member of the Knesset, was mainly worried that the two body snatchers, who in his view (*Ma'ariv*, 23 March) had done their work with commendable neatness and respectfulness, would be unable to get a fair trial because of the unprecedented "lynch" atmosphere that had been created by the news media, the Knesset, and even a judge of the Supreme Court. Most rabbinic authorities did not condone the actions of the graverobbers but thought the opportunity afforded by the robbery to repurify the Rishon Cemetery should not be missed. For the most part, they insisted that Halachah was an iron law that could not be bent to meet historical crises (like the Holocaust) or to suit Zionist definitions of Jewish identity, or to satisfy the exigencies, however compelling, of family unity.

Israel's anticlerical left, always able to match the arrogance and ignorance of its black-coated adversaries, saw in the Anghelovici affair an ideal occasion for venting its hatred of Jewish religion through epithets such as "Khomeiniism," "ghetto Judaism," and "orientalism." Philip Gillon of the *Jerusalem Post* found in this defilement of graves evidence that the Jews have become the new Nazis. Shulamit Aloni, suddenly very concerned with fidelity to Halachah, opened the Knesset debate by announcing that Halachah not only permits but requires the burial of Christians and Jews in the same cemetery, a novel interpretation of a statement in the *Shulhan Aruch* that (it later turned out) entered her head in the form of a half-understood remark she had heard on a radio program.

Yet not all of the debate took place on this level. Even among the staunch defenders of Halachah, like Chief Rabbi David Volpa of Rishon Lezion, there was a half-conscious recognition that Tereza's actual experience during the Holocaust was relevant to the decision about burial. What other reason could there have been for his going to the trouble of checking with Chief Rabbi Moshe Rozen of Rumania to try to find out just what had happened during the war to Jews who came from the Anghelovicis' area of Rumania (and ascertaining that they had been sent not to concentration camps but to forced labor camps)? What possible difference could this have made from the point of view of Halachah? Yehuda Ben-Meir expressed the National Religious party's denunciation of the body snatching and tried (unsuccessfully) to discourage Knesset members from exploiting the incident for political ends.

The "secular" position in the Anghelovici debate, where it was not vitiated by the Aloni-like inanities that would excite laughter in a well-ordered kindergarten, stressed the apparently insane anomalies of the Halachic definition of Jewishness and the inability of traditional Jewish religion to incorporate the central experiences of the Jewish people in modern times: mass migrations of unprecedented magnitude, the destruction of European Jewry, and national rebirth in Zion. Why should Karl Marx, baptized at age six into Lutheranism and founder of a political movement that condemns all religions as false but Judaism as the falsest of all, be considered Halachically Jewish? Why should a woman who voluntarily took upon herself the fate of the Jews during World War II and again joined her fate to theirs in Israel and—in the aftermath of the Holocaust—raised her children as Jews, be denied, in the very state that claims to have created a new kind of Jew, the right to die, as in all essential ways she had lived, as a Jew? Did Ruth, the archetypal Jewish convert, having declared "whither thou goest I will go; and where thou lodgest, I will lodge; thy people shall be my people, and thy God my God" also have to undergo rabbinic catechism and ritual immersion to prove that she had joined the Jewish people?

The most sober and balanced reply made to these arguments by a defender of Halachic authority came from Rabbi Menahem Hacohen, a Labor party MK, in the Knesset debate. Human sympathies, he argued, cannot by themselves invalidate Halachah; neither can a political body decide religious truth. Although Tereza Anghelovici was a virtuous woman and a dutiful citizen of the state of Israel who may indeed have considered herself Jewish, "120 Knesset members cannot decide that she is Jewish any more than they can decide that Meir Vilner [a Communist pro-PLO MK] is not Jewish . . . Let us not blur the distinction between Israel and the nations."

It is precisely this idea of *distinction* that is most difficult for secularized Israelis (like assimilated Diaspora Jews) to fathom. That is why the television editorialists on Mabat News (Friday, 9 March) contrasted the scenes of contentious bitterness in the Rishon Lezion Cemetery with the scene of peace and harmony at the British military cemetery on Mt. Scopus, where Jews and Christians lie side by side. Unfortunately, distinction is the central principle of Judaism—between good and evil, meat and dairy, weekday and Sabbath, man and woman, and, yes, Jew and gentile.

Yet Rabbi Hacohen's impressive statement finally showed no more ability to encompass his opponents' demand for the religious assimilation of modern Jewish experience than they showed ability to understand that a body of teaching claiming divine origin cannot yield to every human whim. For Hacohen, like other defenders of the Halachic fortress, has forgotten that the strength of a fortress is also its weakness; it cannot move to take the offensive against its enemies and conquer new ground.

Judaism vs. Ethnicity

On 19 June 1984, the Israeli courts lifted their ban against publication of the names of the twenty-eight men accused of participation in acts of terror organized by the "Jewish underground." Photographs and short biographies of all of them immediately appeared in the press and on television. The biographies usually mentioned the army experience, if any, of the accused, the particular deeds or plots in which he was implicated, and the yeshivot in which he had studied or taught. Since all of the accused were religious, individual religious histories went unmentioned—except for that of one man. This was Dan Be'eri, identified by the television reporters and by *Ha'aretz* as a *ger tzedek* (sincere proselyte, or proselyte by conviction), and by the English-language *Jerusalem Post* as "originally a French Catholic [who] immigrated to Israel some 15 years ago and became a deeply religious convert to Judaism."

In a country where it is considered normal and indeed necessary to identify and label converts at every opportunity (though Yitzhak Peretz seems to have been the first to suggest stamping the label in their identity cards), very few people are likely to have been surprised by descriptions that elsewhere, certainly in the United States, would have caused a scandal. Even a weak imagination can conceive the storm that would ensue if an American television reporter felt called on to reveal that of twenty-eight members of a recently captured gang of Christian fundamentalist terrorists, one was a convert from Judaism and now, odd though it might seem, a "deeply religious" Christian. But in Israel it is routinely accepted that a convert never sheds the skin of his old, gentile self.

Questions regarding the Halachic definition of Jewish identity receive much attention in Israel because the religious political parties periodically attempt to coerce their coalition partners into bringing to the floor of the Knesset a "Who is a Jew" bill (one version of which was defeated in January 1985). The intent of such bills is to amend Israel's Law of Return so that it would apply only to those Jews born of a Jewish mother or converted in strict accordance with Halachah. The question receives even more attention among Diaspora Jewry because of the contention between Orthodox Jews and those Jews who resent the Orthodox desire to "monopolize" conversion. The irony in all this fire and fury is that it is much ado about nothing. The attention that the "Who is a Jew" question receives is grotesquely out of proportion to its human relevance. The number of Diaspora converts to Judaism whose non-Halachic conversion might, under a new Law of Return, cause them difficulties when they come to settle in Israel is very small.

The real question about converts in Israel has much less to do with Halachah than with the degradation of Jewish religion into ethnicity. It is this that causes Israeli society such trouble in accepting Jews who have been converted in complete accordance with Halachah. In Israel as in America, these Jews are to be found in all walks of life, among the secular and the religious, the uninstructed and the educated; but in Israel, far more than in America, their status as strangers is likely to be a permanent one.

One cannot live in Israel for long without being assaulted on all sides by illustrations of this problem. When I began to teach at Tel Aviv University, no fewer than three of my colleagues took it upon themselves to inform me that a student in my graduate seminar was a convert to Judaism from Roman Catholicism. It was not clear to me why I needed this information.

Was it to explain in advance any peculiarities in his manners, or perhaps the fact that, unlike some other students, he might *have* manners? Was it to excuse him for some deficiency in Jewish learning, or to justify some unseemly endowment of Christian knowledge? Since no explanation was forthcoming I could only guess.

In the *Jerusalem Post* of 24 May 1985 an article on converts quoted an American convert, the wife of a rabbi, who said that she was shunned by her neighbors in an Orthodox Ashkenazic neighborhood in Jerusalem from the moment they discovered her to be a convert. After twelve years of living in Israel, she alleged, "We're on the periphery knocking on the wall, with bloodied knuckles, trying to get in."

A convert's history almost invariably becomes a subject for research and an occasion for uneasiness when marriage is contemplated. Some converts claim that matchmakers consider them damaged goods and therefore do not examine very carefully the prospective grooms or brides for the convert. An observant (not to say ultraobservant) friend of mine came to me in distress over the doubts that had been raised about his daughter's "Jewishness" by her fiancé's family. Upon emerging from the Bais Ya'akov religious school system she had become engaged, after the fashion of Orthodox matchmaking, to a yeshiva *bocher*. But her pedigree was called into question because her mother is a convert to Judaism. There was not the slightest doubt about the Halachic validity of that long-ago conversion or about the rigid Orthodoxy of the mother's life as a Jew. Nevertheless, her daughter clearly lacked *yichus* ("pedigree") and was looked down on as an unworthy match for the scion of a rabbinic family.

Despite the fact that Israel's population is one of the most ethnically diverse in the world, and physical appearance varies from the "blackness" of Ethiopian Jews to the preternatural "whiteness" of many of the inhabitants of Meah Shearim, converts who do not "look Jewish" to the ignorant are in for a hard time, especially (a further irony) among the most secular and "assimilated" Israelis. Members of families that include converts to Judaism tell me that they can count on an average of five incidents a month in which they are "shamed in public" because of what strikes Israeli connoisseurs of physical appearance as "non-Jewish" looks. One of them told me how one of his colleagues—a university professor, no less—made a point of phoning him to report her amazed impression that "Your son looks like a real goy!" The son himself told me that his classmates in school often say to him (without any hostility) things like, "You look like a Christian! What are you doing here?" From sheer fatigue, this blond, fair-skinned, Hebrew-speaking boy now routinely responds to all inane questions about why he doesn't "look Jewish" with the ready retort: "That's because I'm a Falasha."

Since Jews are a "people" and a "nation" as well as adherents of a religion, it was perhaps to be expected that Halachic standards of admission to Jewish identity would prove inadequate in the actual world. But if Jewish religion is something less than Jewish peoplehood and nationality, surely Jewish peoplehood and nationality are more than mannerisms and appearances and transient political prejudices. If some Israelis think that kinky hair and bad manners constitute Jewishness, others are sure it consists of universalist ethics and leftist politics; and still others have a vague notion that someone demonstrates his Jewish identity when, in arguing a point, he strikes two fingers of one hand in the palm of the other. The difficulty that many Israelis have in accepting converts is in exact proportion to their attachment to these grotesque travesties of Jewish identity. Indeed, the converts themselves afford a kind of litmus paper for distinguishing between what is genuinely Jewish and what is meretricious, transient, and merely "ethnic" in Israeli Jews.

The degradation of Judaism into ethnicity did not, of course, begin in the state of Israel. Every illustration of it just given will be only too familiar to Jews of the Diaspora. Indeed, if we can trust the historical imagination of Isaac Bashevis Singer, it had already begun as far back as the seventeenth century in Poland. In his novel *The Slave* the hero Jacob converts Wanda, the Polish widow of a drunken peasant, to Judaism. When she comes to live with him in a Jewish community, she is re-created as "Dumb Sarah." She feigns muteness because her imperfect Yiddish would very likely reveal her gentile origins, and Polish law punished by death the "crime" of converting a Christian to Judaism. But she also feels keenly the need to conceal her gentile origins from her Jewish neighbors. "True, Dumb Sarah behaved as a Jewess should, went to the ritual bath, soaked the meat and salted it, on Friday prepared the Sabbath pudding . . . blessed the candles; on the Sabbath, she stood in the woman's section of the synagogue and moved her lips as though praying." This is all very well, but it cannot eradicate the taint of her "non-Jewish" manners and looks. She sometimes walks barefooted, has "unblemished peasant-like teeth," works like a country woman ("and for nothing"), and swims naked in the river. For these unspeakable offenses Sarah is slandered and rejected by the Jewish community, none of whose members appears to recall that Moses himself took an Ethiopian as his wife. An emissary from Palestine whom Jacob meets after Sarah's death tells him that " 'before the Messiah will come, all the pious gentiles will have been converted.' " He does not add, since the entire book makes this irresistibly clear, that these righteous converts will find it easier to be Jews in the next world than in this one.

But it is not in the land of fiction that the tendency of Jews to slide from religion into ethnic clannishness has been expressed in its most extreme form. In the *Antisemitism* volume of her *Origins of Totalitarianism* (1951), Hannah Arendt called attention to the fact that in nineteenth-century Western Europe, "assimilation as a program led much more frequently to conversion than to mixed marriages." She refers to the widespread tendency among baptized Jews to marry only other Jews, whether baptized or not. Jewish religion had come to mean far less to such people than "Jewish" family, familiarity, and manners. It goes without saying that these apostates felt more at home with other Jews who had become Christians than with Christians who had become Jews.

It would be a poor conclusion to one crucial aspect of the Zionist enterprise if, in its desire to create a new, "normal" Jew, it only led us back to these desperate perversions of Judaism. For it was precisely these perversions, as much as external persecution, that justified the longing for an independent Jewish state in the first place. Ethnic homogeneity is neither possible nor desirable in a country whose inhabitants have been ingathered from every corner of the Exile, bringing with them a rich variety of physiognomy, of culture, and of manners. That Israeli identity is not based on religion according to Halacha is self-evident. But it is based on religion, for—as even very "secular" Israelis understand only too well—merely to live in this country, a country hedged around by enemies bent on its destruction, a country whose war for independence has already lasted nearly forty years and may never be won, is to belong to what Hillel Halkin calls "a community of faith." "Many a man," wrote John Henry Newman, "will live and die upon a dogma; nobody will be a martyr for a conclusion." The Israeli version of this dogma is that there is a transcendent meaning in Jewish collective existence that justifies the hardship and suffering that life in this country entails. Few people are better situated to recognize this truth with perfect clarity than those converts who, by choosing to live in Israel, have taken on themselves not only the God but the fate of the Jews; for they know that to the idea of transcendent meaning ethnicity contributes exactly nothing.

Notes

1. Cynthia Ozick, "The Moral Necessity of Metaphor," *Harper's Magazine*, May 1986, p. 67.
2. On 2 December 1986, the Supreme Court ruled in favor of a new immigrant from the United States who had challenged the Interior Ministry's labeling her a convert to Judaism in her Israeli identity papers. On 31 December Interior Minister Peretz submitted his resignation.

10

Liberalism and Zionism

"Liberalism is always being surprised." That was how Lionel Trilling used to describe the characteristic liberal failure to imagine what reason and common sense appeared to gainsay. During the past century few things have surprised and offended the liberal imagination more than the weird persistence of the Jewish nation. Liberal friends of the Jews expected that their emancipation would put an end to Jewish collective existence. Count Stanislas de Clermont-Tonnerre, the French revolutionary, told the French National Assembly in 1789 that "the Jews should be denied everything as a nation, but granted everything as individuals." Wilhelm von Humboldt, the great liberal reformer of Prussia whose ethical idealism is celebrated in Mill's *On Liberty,* considered the disappearance of the Jews as a distinct group a condition for taking up the cause of their emancipation.

When the Jews failed to live up to their sponsors' expectations, the reaction against them could be fierce. George Eliot wrote in 1878 that modern English resentment of Jews for maintaining themselves in moral isolation from their fellow citizens was strongest among "liberal gentlemen" who "usually belong to a party which has felt itself glorified in winning for Jews . . . the full privileges of citizenship." Eliot had herself once belonged to that party, and in 1848, when her revolutionary ardor was at its height, predicted that the Jews as a "race" were "plainly destined to extermination." But between 1848 and 1874, when she began to write *Daniel Deronda,* her liberalism was tempered by a wider experience of mankind and a deeper reflection on the meaning of nationality in general and of the organized memory of Jewish national consciousness in particular. She came to cherish the idea of "restoration of a Jewish State planted on the old ground," not only because it would afford the Jews a center of national feeling and a source of dignifying protection, but because it would contribute to the councils of the world "an added form of national genius," and one of transcendent (though not Christian) meaning. At the conclusion of her essay on the Jewish problem ("The Modern HEP! HEP! HEP!"), she pleads with Millite liberals to enlarge their master's ideal of individuality to include nations: "A modern book on Liberty has maintained that from the freedom of individual men to persist in idiosyncrasies the world may be enriched. Why should we not apply this argument to the idiosyncrasy of a nation, and pause in our haste to hoot it down?"

The relation among liberalism, democracy, and the Jewish nation is directly addressed in two ambitious books on Zionism and Israel by liberals. Bernard Avishai, author of *The Tragedy of Zionism* and self-styled elegist of Zionism, has cast himself in the role of Epimenides coming to Athens or Plato, to Syracuse, sternly ignoring the contemptible traditional and local idiosyncrasies of the natives in order to bestow on them the blessings of "British liberal tradition," "secular democracy," "liberal decency," and "a written constitution." Unlike Epimenides and Plato, who landed before dispensing advice, Avishai is doing so from afar, long after having departed Israel. In his prologue he describes how, in 1972, he and his wife left Canada to become Israelis. But by 1973 they began to feel that they were victims of "cultural enslavement" whose "English spirit" was being blotted out by Hebrew. The instrument of their unconversion from Zionism was television; American and English programs revealed to them that they were "living among foreigners" and that their true home, to which they soon returned, was Canada and the English language. Although he momentarily blamed himself for failing to become an Israeli, Avishai quickly decided that the blame lay with Israel, which, if you are American, turns your children into strangers, and with Zionism, which, "like old *halachic* norms," represses "individual life . . . equivocation, sexuality," desiderata of the "culture of liberalism" that he now pursues in Massachusetts. Five pages after describing how he saved himself from the clearest and most dangerous siren call he had ever heard, Avishai announces that it is time "to retire" Zionism in favor of democracy. Ten pages later he contemptuously describes political Zionists such as Leo Pinsker, Theodor Herzl, and Vladimir Jabotinsky as people who invented an ideology to assuage "personal disappointment," for they "were themselves people who had tried to assimilate and . . . failed."[1] The ironic vision of this tragedian-elegist does not extend to himself.

Conor Cruise O'Brien also begins his massive study of Israel and Zionism, called *The Siege,* by describing those elements in his national, religious, and family background that drew him to the subject. In the late 1950s that most unphilosophical principle called the alphabet conspired with destiny to situate O'Brien, as Ireland's UN representative, between Iraq and Israel, a revealing perspective for a shrewd observer. In 1961 he left Ireland's foreign service but subsequently went into politics at home, where he served four years in the opposition and four years as a member of the Irish government. He is a liberal, but it was not his liberalism that made him see the Return to Zion, which took place under "harsher necessities" than any ever imagined by liberals, as "the greatest story of modern times." As an Irish Catholic he had no trouble recognizing, at the heart of Zionism, a powerful bond between religion and nationality. As the child of a lapsed or "enlightened" Catholic father, whom he labels a *maskil* (Hebrew for "enlightened one"), O'Brien grew up sufficiently "alienated" from Catholic society to feel yet another link with Jews living as strangers in Exile. Finally, he was moved by the conviction that "Irish Catholics . . . have had a greater experience of persecution, oppression and stigmatization than any other people in Western Europe *except* the Jews."[2]

Throughout his book, O'Brien freely and candidly uses his experience as an Irishman and a diplomat to shed coruscating light on the story of the Zionist movement as well as on the play of forces around that movement. This means that in his view of the Mandatory government, the British Anglo-Saxon constitutional system, which to Avishai is a second (and superior) revelation from Sinai, sometimes appears to be just what Matthew Arnold called it: "a colossal machine for the manufacture of Philistines." O'Brien remarks that among such Philistines "antisemitism is a light sleeper" and offers as an instance the use in British official circles, starting in 1941, of the epithet "Jewish Nazi state."[3] For Avishai, anti-Semitic remarks by Bevin are "tactlessness," something akin to eating soup with a fork.[4]

O'Brien's saga of Israel and Zionism is in two volumes. The first recounts the story of Zionism from the assassination of Czar Alexander II through the expiration of the British Mandate in 1948 and includes detailed analysis of the whole spectrum of Zionist ideologies; portraits of such central actors as Herzl, Weizmann, Ben-Gurion, and Jabotinsky; and accounts of the Dreyfus Affair, Eastern European pogroms, and British motives and actions in Palestine. The second, longer, volume tells the story of Israel from its bloody beginning through the completion of the withdrawal from Lebanon in summer 1985. It comprises lengthy chapters on the inner life of Israel as expressed in its literature, on Israel's Oriental-Jewish population, on the Arabs of Israel and the administered territories, and on the complex relations between international diplomacy and Israel's wars. *The Siege* is the work of a writer of open, flexible intelligence and boundless curiosity. The book therefore has a kind of noble imperfection, like that of large Victorian novels lovingly called loose and baggy monsters.

Avishai's tragedy, by contrast, has the completeness of a limited mind.

The first part of the book analyzes the development of Zionist ideas, especially in relation to certain crossroads in the development of the *yishuv* (Palestinian Jewish community), with favorable emphasis on cultural as opposed to political Zionism. The second part of this book traces, in just three chapters, the rapid disintegration of Labor Zionism from its victory at the 1931 World Zionist Congress to "the end of Zionism" on the eve of the Six-Day War. The last, most aggressively polemical, section of the book presents the various tragedies and failures, from 1967 to the present, that resulted from Ben-Gurion's "post-Zionist matrix" of "power, Bible, defiance, settlement, economic growth." Avishai's is a much narrower book than O'Brien's in scope because it tells comparatively little of what the gentiles, apart from Palestinian Arabs, are thinking and doing. His description of the 1938 Évian conference on Jewish refugees, for example, includes a polite, passing allusion to the failure of the Western democracies to accept Jews, followed by a detailed, acerbic description of Labor Zionist hopes that the conference would fail. This is also a narrower book in its quality of mind. O'Brien's discussion of Israeli literature ranges widely from Abba Kovner, Aharon Appelfeld, David Shahar, and Yehuda Amichai to Amos Oz and A. B. Yehoshua. Avishai's is limited to books and plays that illustrate "the liberal, post-Zionist curve of Israel's leading writers," especially if these writers deal with an Arab-Jewish love affair or depict Israelis as Nazis.[5]

Both books are unusually personal and enlivened by anecdote. O'Brien's invocations of experience often reveal the hypocrisy or hatred that is part of the burden Israel must bear. Recalling how in 1974 the UN delegates of every Western European nation, including Ireland, joined in the standing ovation for Arafat, O'Brien says, "I asked our Foreign Minister, Garret FitzGerald, whether it was altogether wise for Ireland to be so fulsome about the P.L.O.: might there not be a precedent in relation to the I.R.A.? Garret thought not . . . Arafat and his Fatah were the moderates." On another occasion, as Ireland's representative at the 1946 conference on refugees in Geneva, O'Brien had to meet with a monsignor representing the Vatican who frankly told his interlocutor of his feelings about Jews: "I'm not antisemitic. I just hate them."[6]

Avishai's anecdotes serve mainly to cast a warm glow over his debating skills marshaled in combat against illiberal, paranoiac Jews. In Israel, he vanquished a taxi driver whose experiences in Lebanon had embittered him toward Palestinian Arabs. In North America, he joined an Israeli in heaping scorn on Diaspora Jews who still brood over the Holocaust and "now need to invent anti-Semites to feel like Jews, to perform the commandment of Auschwitz." (It is characteristic of Avishai to suppose that the power exercised over ordinary Jews by Emil Fackenheim's commandment not to give Hitler posthumous victories is merely that of a smart syllogism, on the order of "since Hitler didn't want Jews in Germany, we must live there.")[7]

The stark contrast in method, tenor, and tone between the two books is everywhere apparent. For O'Brien the Jews, for all their political inaptitude, are a great people, and the state of Israel, despite its "Panglossian" professors, proud, overweening politicians, and a national character "so democratic as to be almost unworkable," is the culmination of a movement whose power over gentiles as well as Jews is a "mystery" that cannot be explained except by the divine power of the Bible. For Avishai, full of acrid contempt for those who sense "something mysterious and wonderful about Jewish history," the Jews are a small people, but a nasty one. Their country has become the devil's own experiment station, where the state is "superior to all other moral values," where young people increasingly succumb to their primordial instincts for "domination, lockstep, revenge," and where the Bible impedes peace by deluding "new" Zionists into calling the West Bank Judea and Samaria (always enclosed by the author in whining quotation marks) and impedes "liberal democracy" by imposing on Hebrew speakers an archaic vocabulary in which the word for "freedom" *(cherut)* is national rather than individual in meaning. O'Brien expresses admiration for the heroism of the outnumbered Jewish defenders of the settlements of Yad Mordechai, Degania (helpfully identified by Avishai as Umm Juni, its Arab name), and Geulim. Citing several sources, he writes that in the War of Independence "the numbers actually engaged on the two sides seem to have been about equal. But the Arabs had a huge initial superiority in . . . equipment and firepower, heavy weapons, armor and aircraft." Avishai, judging the efforts of the Jews by the severe conceptions of gallantry that obtain at MIT, where he teaches, is unimpressed. He writes, citing no sources at all, that "Jewish forces outnumbered the combined strength of the Arab forces and Palestinian irregulars by 2 to 1—a fact which should dispel misty notions about how courage alone vanquished the Arab Goliath."[8]

In both books the immigration to Israel in the 1950s of large numbers of Oriental Jews, strangers to democracy, receives detailed attention. O'Brien describes the lives these people led as second-class citizens in their lands of origin, where they were held in contempt by the aggressive "trimphalist creed" of Islam. He argues persuasively that they were something more than a mixed multitude, incapable of appreciating the socialism and atheism of Israel's founders. Rather, they were Zionists, from "national traditions kept alive through religious observance." For Avishai, the Oriental Jews were not merely, like many of the children of Labor Zionist veterans, not Zionists; they were also destitute of liberalism, hence poor material for secular democracy. It was in order to mobilize such a rabble, he argues, that Ben-Gurion had to sacrifice the revolutionary ideas of Labor Zionism in favor of statism and militarism, and diplomacy in favor of retaliation. The best of the Oriental Jews, that is, their "liberal intelligentsia," had gone to Montreal or New York rather than Israel, and the rest were deaf to the blandishments of socialism and democracy. Incapable of appreciating "secular categories," they came to Israel because it afforded them a "chance to be strong against the Arabs." Explicitly, Avishai bewails the fact that so few Yemenite cobblers and North African policemen have learned the true, "European" meanings of democracy and freedom at Hebrew University; implicitly, what bothers him is that so many have learned about Arabs from experience and not from, say, the country's institutes of Middle East studies, where they would have received instruction in how to hallucinate moderation in their enemies.[9]

Ascribing moderation to the enemies of Israel and blind, willful extremism to her leaders is characteristic of Avishai's approach. There are assorted "tragedies" scattered through his account of Zionism, starting with the Histadrut (General Federation of Jewish Workers) establishment of a "dictatorship of the proletariat." But for Avishai the underlying meaning of "tragedy" is that the protagonist, Zionism, has brought about its own destruction by *hamartia* ("arrogant pride"). He describes King Feisal of Iraq in 1919 "offer[ing] protection for Zionism under a united Arab state." O'Brien points out that the real intent of the agreement with Chaim Weizmann was, as even the Royal Commission Report of 1937 confirmed, that "If King Hussein and Emir Feisal secured their big Arab state, they would concede little Palestine to the Jews." The agreement, wrote a British intelligence officer, Colonel French, at the time of its signing, "is not worth the paper it is written on." Avishai depicts the present King Hussein of Jordan intrepidly arguing for recognition of Israel at the Khartoum conference of Arab nations following the Six-Day War. But how, asks Avishai, could he dream of making peace without getting back Jerusalem? We are not told why Hussein showed no interest in peace or recognition between 1953, when he came to the throne, and 1967, when he led his country into war against Israel. In any event, the ascendant political figure in Israel by this time was Moshe Dayan, who, allegedly, made any settlement impossible. For Avishai, Dayan is "a modern pharaoh" who virtually created Palestinian Arab "radicalism." So fond is Avishai of this conceit whereby (in the familiar style of Arab propaganda) Arabs become Jews and Israelis their gentile oppressors, that he tells how Dayan's heart, like Pharaoh's, "had been hardened by terrorist attacks such as the one at Ma'alot." This is to say that Arafat does not murder but only executes divine sentence. Avishai claims that "in 1968, Arafat was still an unlikely guerrilla, crisscrossing the West Bank on a motorcycle. . . ." O'Brien, however, reminds us that in March 1968, at Karameh, this pathetically enterprising cyclist, in league with a Hussein who now called himself a *fedayee,* murdered twenty-three Israeli soldiers. Avishai indignantly reports that in 1976 only the dove Yossi Sarid recognized that the newly elected pro-PLO mayors of the West Bank, graciously willing to set up a state "in whatever part of the homeland would be liberated," represented "a new opportunity for Israeli diplomacy." O'Brien quotes "moderate" Palestinian Arabs who unblushingly declare that "the step that follows liberation is the dismantling of the racist . . . structure of Israel as a state." He offers, too, the sobering reminder that the organizers of the massacre of Israeli schoolchildren at Ma'alot "were well-known Palestinian 'moderates' who had been in dialogue with Israeli 'doves.'"[10]

Avishai's generosity toward Israel's adversaries is epistemological as well as political. He sneers at claims of Revisionist Zionists that most Palestinian Arabs were as much immigrants to the country as most Jews were. He does not deny the fact, but argues that Arabs who moved to Palestine from Damascus or Amman were, "in their own eyes, . . . doing no more than moving from one part of the Arab homeland to another." How such people could consistently also claim, after 1948, to be homeless refugees if they lived anywhere outside the borders of Israel is not a question to interest Avishai, though he castigates Labor Zionists for causing the displacement of Arab residents "from their country." Later he refers gingerly to Joan Peters's "highly controversial book" about Arab immigration to Palestine, promising that a friend of his—the infamous Norman Finkelstein—will soon explode Peters's thesis. But in the meantime we must rest content with the view that "the number of Arabs who came, and their actual place of origin, beg the question of the subjective feelings of the people who came to call themselves Palestinians." That is to say, it does not much matter what things are in themselves, but only what they appear to be to Arabs.[11]

O'Brien points out that among the "subjective feelings" of Israel's Arab adversaries, belief in Enlightenment principles of secular democracy barely exists. Nevertheless, it is in this language that they have chosen to make their case to the West, knowing that it will be music to the inward ear of liberals. "In terms of the governing code of debate, based on the Western Enlightenment value system, this puts the Arab states—and the cause of Government by Consent—permanently in the right, and Israel—with its archaic Right of Return and Jewish State—permanently in the wrong." Of course, O'Brien adds, Muslim spokesmen who appeal to Enlightenment principles "are engaging in double-talk, masking the realities of what is fundamentally, on both sides, a religious-nationalist culture conflict." He notes that the terrorist group *Fatah,* whose spokesmen repeat "secular democratic state" with the regularity of a steam engine, is an organization whose name means the opening of a country for conquest by Islam.[12] The archetype of the relation of Palestinian Arabs to democracy is for O'Brien their outright rejection of the Palestine Constitution proposed by Palestine High Commissioner Herbert Samuel and Colonial Secretary Winston Churchill in 1922. Although Weizmann accepted this commitment to representative democracy, the Arab majority scorned an arrangement that did not abolish the Balfour Declaration and bestow on them the power to exclude Jews from Palestine. Then, as now, only "the prestige of the absolute" could enrapture Palestinian Arabs.[13]

For both writers the nature of democracy in Israel is bound up with religion; beyond that point they diverge in every particular. In the first part of his book Avishai insists, often to the point of absurdity, on denying Jewish religion any role in the development of Zionism; but his account of events after 1948 alleges that religious influence poisoned Zionism, prevented territorial concession, and maimed by compression, like a Chinese lady's foot, every libertarian impulse of Israeli citizens. On the very first page of his tragedy, Avishai states that Czar Nicholas I "had been dismayed by Jewish sympathies for Napoleon's occupation."[14] The statement is typical Avishai for two reasons. First, it is wrong. Nicholas, not famous for his love of Jews, wrote of them in his diary: "Surprisingly . . . in 1812 they were very loyal to us and assisted us in every possible way even at the risk of their own lives."[15] Second, it is wrong because Avishai cannot admit that, given the choice, many Jews preferred their traditional religious observance under a tyrant to emancipation under the aegis of French Enlightenment.

Avishai's account of the origins of Zionism is diametrically opposed to that of O'Brien, who insists that Jewish nationalism drew its ultimate strength from Jewish religion and that even Ben-Gurion and Weizmann were, and could not but be, essentially religious Jews. Avishai never even mentions such early religious Zionists as Yehudah Alkalai and the widely read Zevi Hirsch Kalischer, declares that the Eretz Yisrael of religious Jews "corresponded to no actual territory," even though Weizmann had somehow got the impression that Jews in the East End of London who prayed for dew in the summer and rain in the winter were attached to Palestine (and not Atlantis), and reports (falsely) that all religious Zionists at the congresses supported Herzl's scheme for emergency settlement of Jews in Uganda. He lashes Ben-Gurion and Golda Meir for not entering into a *Kulturkampf* against religious forces. He depicts Rabbi Abraham Isaac Kook, who held out a welcoming hand to Labor Zionism, as a parasite, but reserves his harshest epithets for the new, religious Zionists who do work the land. Although Avishai's single reference to Jewish daily prayers—"the daily prayers stated that Jews had been exiled 'for their sins' "—indicates he has not said them for a long time, he is filled with a visceral loathing for those who do, which reminds one that the French Enlightenment whose child he is was not only liberal and secular—it was also anti-Semitic. "Scripture hawks," "ultra-nationalist settlers," and "fringe romantics"—these people have, in Avishai's view, lost the human status.[16]

The relatively small number of religious Jews in the fledgling state and the much larger number of citizens for whom religious symbols had become, through the agency of the state, a kind of civil religion, kept Israel from becoming a secular, democratic state in two ways, according to Avishai. First, they made it impossible to promulgate a comprehensive bill of rights and constitution, and thus enabled the discriminatory Law of Return, which grants citizenship to all Jews who request it, to be passed and maintained. In the long list of liberal nostrums prescribed by Avishai for the de-Judaization of Israel, abolition of the Law of Return has a high place. He is not, however, a dogmatic egalitarian; he does not want Arabs to be bothered with that little matter of serving in the army from the age of eighteen to fifty-five, and he does not object to the principle of "affirmative action" as such. In fact, he recommends it—for the Arabs. Second, the religious and their allies stand accused of fostering an atmosphere of intolerance, especially in Israeli schools, that permeates all aspects of society. For his information on the "anti-democratic views" of Israeli high school students Avishai relies on the tendentious polls conducted by Jerusalem's leftist Van Leer Institute, Israel's version of the Institute for Policy Studies. His complaint that "Israeli schools have taught children much more about the tribes of Israel than about the Enlightenment" will elicit a bitter laugh from people whose children have actually attended these schools, the kind of laugh invited by one who cries fire in the midst of a flood.[17]

In his epilogue to *The Siege*, O'Brien argues cogently against exchanging the territories of Judea and Samaria for an illusory peace. This notion can be espoused only by well-intentioned fools or ill-intentioned rogues. By a strange irony, O'Brien adds, "Those in the West who urge that the effort to rule over large numbers of Arabs may eventually destroy Israel itself might do well to note that Meir Kahane is making the same point, while drawing from it an inference radically different from what the Western critics have in mind."[18] Avishai, who favors yet another partitioning of Palestine, "the only democratic solution," is not exactly making "the same point" as Kahane, yet there is an uncanny resemblance between the mental worlds they inhabit. In both, the opposition between Zionism and democracy is inevitable and Manichaean. In both, the "problem" of marriage between Jew and Arab is obsessive. Kahane wants to outlaw it, and Avishai, speaking for those few Israelis who combine the liberal craving for forbidden fruit with the liberal craving for legality, wants Israel to institute civil marriage.[19]

In flagellating Israel with half-understood, misapplied, and uniquely inappropriate slogans about the "tyranny of the majority" that he has gleaned from Tocqueville and Mill, while demanding that Israel surrender her Jewish character, Avishai shows a poor grasp not just of his liberal sources (for whom "liberal" democracy was nearly an oxymoron)[20] but of something far more important. Mill once wrote that in the makeup of every state there must be *"something* which is settled, something permanent, and not to be called in question: something which, by general agreement, has a right to be where it is, and to be secure against disturbance."[21] In the state of the Jews, a state (as O'Brien keeps stressing) under siege and likely to remain so, that "something" can never be liberalism but only Jewish religion, a Judaism freely and variously interpreted, but always including the conviction that Jewish life leads somewhere because it began somewhere. Men live and, if need be, die for values, not for procedures; for beliefs, not for conclusions. This religion may not suit the most refined tastes, and some of its devotees may be raw and blind in their gropings. Early Labor Zionists seemed to do very well without it because, as O'Brien recognizes, they were sustained by the very religion they denied. The same was not true for their children and grandchildren, for whom no traditional faith existed that could endow gestures of rebellion with meaning.

It is a gloomy thought that the enemies of Israel neither slumber nor sleep. But there is comfort, too, in remembering that the first elegist to crow over the demise of Zion was a fellow named Merneptah, a ruler of Egypt who announced that "Israel is desolated; its seed is no more." That was in the year 1215 B.C.E.

Notes

1. Bernard Avishai, *The Tragedy of Zionism* (New York: Farrar, Straus, Giroux, 1985), pp. 6, 12, 25, 230, 309, 319.
2. Conor Cruise O'Brien, *The Siege: The Saga of Israel and Zionism,* 2 vols. (London: Weidenfeld and Nicolson, 1986), pp. 21, 18–19, 329–30, 656. In her essay "The Modern HEP! HEP! HEP!" George Eliot likened the situation of the Jews among the English to that of the Irish. The Jews are blamed for rejecting Christianity, the Irish for rejecting Protestantism. " 'No Irish need apply,' parallels the sentence which for many polite persons sums up the question of Judaism, 'I never *did* like the Jews.' "

3. O'Brien, *The Siege,* p. 258.
4. Avishai, *The Tragedy of Zionism,* p. 170. Avishai is equally charitable toward the constitutional democracies of the U.S. and Canada, which, he says, closed their doors to mass immigration "in the depths of economic depression." In fact, those doors were closed in the boom years of the twenties. Irving Abella and Harold Troper *(None Is Too Many)* have demonstrated that Canada's distinction of admitting fewer Jewish refugees from Hitler than any other Western country had nothing to do with economics, and everything to do with that "tactlessness" called anti-Semitism.
5. Avishai, *The Tragedy of Zionism,* pp. 152, 301, 313, 321–22.
6. O'Brien, *The Siege,* pp. 485, 266.
7. Avishai, *The Tragedy of Zionism,* pp. 309, 352–53.
8. Ibid., pp. 221, 249–50, 180, 309; O'Brien, *The Siege,* pp. 18, 153, 291, 443, 540. According to American military historian Trevor Dupuy, the Arabs committed 40,000 men to the conflict; the Jews had 30,000 under arms, and 10,000 more ready for mobilization.
9. O'Brien, *The Siege,* p. 348; Avishai, *The Tragedy of Zionism,* pp. 210–11.
10. O'Brien, *The Siege,* pp. 144, 479, 462; Avishai, *The Tragedy of Zionism,* pp. 106, 275, 277, 280.
11. Avishai, *The Tragedy of Zionism,* pp. 140, 148, 368 n. 8. The best account of the controversy over Joan Peters's *From Time Immemorial: The Origins of the Arab-Jewish Conflict Over Palestine* (New York: Harper & Row, 1984) is the essay "Whose Palestine?" by Erich Isaac and Rael Jean Isaac in *Commentary,* 81 (July 1986): 29–37. See also " 'Whose Palestine?'—An Exchange," in *Commentary,* 82 (October 1986): 2–22.
12. O'Brien, *The Siege,* pp. 654–55. Avishai's Palestinian Arabs not only appear indifferent to religion; the ones living in Israel are reported to be powerfully attracted to "Israel's libertarian style of life" (Avishai, p. 317). Apparently, if we believe anything Avishai says about Israel's illiberalism, Israeli Arabs are easily satisfied.
13. O'Brien, *The Siege,* pp. 162–64.
14. Avishai, *The Tragedy of Zionism,* p. 15.
15. Simon Dubnow, *History of the Jews in Russia and Poland,* 3 vols. (New York: KTAV, 1975), 2:14. (Originally published 1916.)
16. Avishai, *The Tragedy of Zionism,* pp. 20, 65, 94, 252, 285–86, 323.
17. Ibid., pp. 189, 319–20, 305. The biased and unreliable character of Van Leer surveys has been analyzed by Professor Shlomo Sharan of Tel Aviv University (see *Ma'ariv,* International Edition, 27 September 1985).
18. O'Brien, *The Siege,* pp. 649–50.
19. Avishai, *The Tragedy of Zionism,* p. 9.
20. In a letter of 1855, Mill wrote: "Almost all the projects of social reformers of these days are really liberticide."
21. J. S. Mill, "Coleridge," in *Autobiography and Other Writings,* ed. Jack Stillinger, Riverside ed., (Boston: Houghton Mifflin, 1969), p. 276.

11

Jewish Anti-Semitism, Enlightenment Evenhandedness, and the Arab-Israeli Conflict

Comprehensive studies of how the state of Israel came into being and of its current social, cultural, and political condition generally include accounts, however brief, of the often troubled history of Jews in their various lands of exile, of the kinds of hostility, ranging from vilification and discrimination to expulsion and murder, visited by gentiles on Jews. Knowledge of this dark background is assumed to be needful to the understanding of what propelled the Zionist movement, of the events that led, by circuitous paths, to the establishment of the state of Israel, and of the state of mind of its present inhabitants.

In these accounts of the anti-Semitism that forms part of the history of the Zionist enterprise, relatively little attention is paid to the anti-Semitism of the Jews themselves, although it plays a large role in Jewish history. Indeed, self-hating Jews have made such large contributions to the ideology and politics of anti-Semitism that it may fairly be called a product, perhaps the only genuine one, of the "Judeo-Christian" tradition. Before Pope Gregory IX ordered the Talmud to be seized, examined, and publicly burned in Paris and Rome, he was presented in 1239 with a detailed analysis of the manifold evils of the Jews' religious books from the Dominican brother Nicholas Donin, a Jewish convert possessed of the "special" knowledge of these poisonous books that only a Jew could have. In the sixteenth century Martin Luther's seemingly innovative program of burning synagogues, destroying Jewish homes, and confiscating the Talmud and all other Hebrew books, was in fact derived from the proposals of Johannes (formerly Josef) Pfefferkorn, the Jewish convert who had years earlier exhorted his German countrymen to "drive the old Jews out like dirty dogs and baptize the young children" and "take their goods and give them to those to whom they belong." Christians appear to have invented, all on their own, the belief in Jewish male menstruation, but doubters among them received reassurance from Jewish converts such as Franco da Piacenza, who in 1630 revealed to the world the shameful secret that Jewish males of the lost tribe of Simeon menstruated four days a year. The belief of Luther and his acolytes that Yiddish was the language of thieves and constituted a sin against the German tongue was actively supported by many Jews from his own time through that of Moses Mendelssohn, who alleged that Yiddish degraded culture.

This fruitful interaction between Christian anti-Semites and Jewish self-haters, a process in which it is difficult to disentangle cause from effect, continued after the Enlightenment. The German anti-Semites who said that Heine smelled—devilish Jews have not only the horns, tail, beard, and sexuality, but also the smell, of the goat—found confirmation of their views in Heine's own depiction of the Polish Jew with "his lousy beard, with his garlic breath, and his bad German." Socialist anti-Semites heard from the converted Jew Karl Marx the assertion that capitalism is nothing other than the Talmud written in the "real" language of the Jews, which is neither Hebrew nor Yiddish, but "haggling." Feminist anti-Semites (we are very familiar with them today) could find in the same "Jewish" source the revelation that "in the Jewish religion . . . woman is bartered." Perhaps the ultimate instance of the "German-Jewish symbiosis" is the relation between attacks by such Jewish self-haters as Karl Kraus on Jewish perversions of the pure German tongue and Hitler's demand that works written by Jews in German be labeled translations.

This pattern whereby "in inexorable dialectic, each self-hating text generates new anti-Jewish texts" is studied in great detail in Sander Gilman's brilliant book, *Jewish Self-Hatred: Anti-Semitism and the Hidden Language of the Jews*.[1] Gilman claims that the form of self-abnegation called self-hatred has existed throughout Jewish history, and that it is a term interchangeable with "Jewish anti-Semitism."

The form that Jewish self-hatred took in the eighteenth and nineteenth centuries has a special relevance to the condition of modern Israel because Zionism derived in significant measure from the Enlightenment and absorbed some of the Enlightenment's revulsion from the culture of the ghetto and the shtetl. Jewish enlighteners such as Moses Mendelssohn shared the belief of their gentile fellow enlighteners that sectarian religious strife was the world's besetting evil, and that the antidote to fanaticism was the exercise of and devotion to reason. Mendelssohn therefore worked under the most compelling sense of obligation to show that Judaism was none other than "the religion of reason" and that its moral law, far from being absolute and eternal, was only the epitome of secular philosophy. If the Jewish religion was to be made acceptable by Enlightenment standards, it must divest itself of the trappings of distinctiveness, of the (unequal) claim of chosenness, and of peculiarities of dress and language. Like the converts of earlier centuries, the German-Jewish intellectuals of the Enlightenment tried to deal with their own self-doubt and insecurity by deflecting the charges that were being made against Jews in general—as following barbaric, "Oriental" practices and speaking a corrupt jargon—onto other Jews, especially Yiddish speakers. Thus Mendelssohn referred to Yiddish translations of the Bible as written in "a language of stammerers, corrupt and deformed, repulsive to those who are able to speak in correct and orderly manner."[2]

Other Jews did not see why, given Mendelssohn's Enlightenment premises, they should be satisfied with such a halfway house as "rational" Judaism when improving Judaism out of existence altogether could make so much greater a contribution to the realization of Enlightenment ideals. Ludwig Börne (Judah Low Baruch before he became a Lutheran) fled from his religion, from his native Yiddish language, and then found, to his discomfiture, that he was still seen as a Jew because "he bears the stigma of the new language of the Jews, not Yiddish but irony."[3] Desperate for acceptance, he then espoused the anti-Semitic views of the 1819 "Hep-Hep" rioters and re-created himself as the liberal journalist excoriating the bad, moneyed Jews—only to find that "liberal journalist" had now become synonymous with "Jew."

Baruch-Börne served as a model for Johann Christian Heinrich Heine, who before *his* baptism was Harry Heine. No sooner had he converted than he condemned his friend Eduard Gans for committing the "unforgivable felony," namely, converting. Subsequently, he too found that no matter where he fled, he was confronted by himself. His Lutheran "ticket of admission" to European culture proved worthless; he was now hated by Christian and Jew alike, sorry that he had permitted himself to be baptized, and condemned to endless suffering by "that never removable Jew" that he would be no matter what discourse he used.

Whereas Börne and Heine projected all their own faults onto their Jewish identity, Karl Marx—converted at age six—found himself perceived as a Jew even though his Jewish identity was virtually nonexistent and he tried to make his life into the antithesis of the image of the Jew, outdoing most of his contemporaries in pouring scorn and hatred on the Jews. The worst thing Marx could think to say of the German-Christian state was that it was "Jewish" in its corrupt art and language. The only good Jew was the ex-Jew, but since the Jews lacked free will they could never alter their essence and so inevitably poisoned their environment. Gilman reveals how Marx, in the tradition of Jewish anti-Semites since the

Middle Ages, imputed to Jews other than himself false language, bad manners, and sexual aggressiveness. Of the "Jewish nigger" Lassalle (himself a Jewish anti-Semite of formidable derangement), Marx wrote: "Always this constant babble with the falsely excited voice, the unaesthetic, demonstrative gestures, . . . and also the uncultivated eating and the horny lust of this 'idealist.' . . . As his skull shape and hair prove, he is a descendant of those Blacks who accompanied Moses on the exodus from Egypt. . . . Now this combination of Jewishness and Germanness upon the Black basic substance must bring forth a strange product. The pushiness of this fellow is also nigger-like."[4] Of course it came as a shattering disappointment to Marx when his new, "non-Jewish" language of revolution was labeled—Jewish. Indeed, one could almost be moved to commiserate with the shade of this fierce Jew-hater as he now contemplates the sorry spectacle of his adoration in many a library, many a museum, many a kibbutz dining hall, and countless professorial minds in the Jewish state itself.

It was one of the hopes of Zionism that a Jewish state would put an end to the almost lunatic persistence of Jewish self-hatred throughout the centuries. That it has failed to do so in the Diaspora, where much of the propaganda campaign against Israel is conducted by Jews—the assorted Kreiskys and Chomskys and Navaskys—is self-evident. But what about the land of Israel? Is it possible that self-hatred, like other afflictions of the Jews in exile, has taken up residence in the country of the Jews itself?

David Shipler's recent book, *Arab and Jew*,[5] although it never touches on this topic, is a virtual treasure house of evidence about it. *Arab and Jew* purports to be a study of the attitudes, images, and stereotypes that are at once the effect and the cause of the relations that obtain between the two groups in Israel and the administered territories. Shipler, too, is a child of the Enlightenment, committed to notions of pluralism, relativism, tolerance, and the equality of cultures and religions. He therefore falls into what Leszek Kolakowski calls the typical Enlightenment error—stretching tolerance to include fanaticism itself. "To deny 'absolute values' for the sake of . . . rationalist principles," says Kolakowski, "threatens our ability to make the distinction between good and evil altogether."[6]

The structure of Shipler's ambitious study is one of "symmetry" or "balance" or what has come to be called evenhandedness. But to be evenhanded or morally impartial between two sides in a conflict when one side advocates the destruction of the other, is to become a moral nonentity. To avoid the appearance of being such a nonentity, one must either redefine the conflict in the Middle East from one between Jewish nationalism and Arab nationalism to one between Jewish nationalism and the nationalism of Palestinian Arabs exclusively; or one must dodge this unpleasant business of destructive intention altogether by stressing the cultural identity of Palestinian nationalism. Shipler does both.

At the outset he announces his intention to "allow the larger Arab world to recede into the background."[7] This makes much more manageable the problem of depicting Palestinian Arabs as the victims of Israeli Jews, and of presenting their displacement from their home villages (the Arab definition of refugee status) as a burden infinitely heavier to bear than the constant burden of peril of Israelis surrounded by enemies who have destroyed sixteen thousand of them in six wars. It is as if some journalistic ancestor of Shipler's had in 1936 written a book about relations between Czechs and ethnic Germans in Sudetenland, showing preternatural sensitivity to the Sudeten Germans' complaints of discrimination and mistreatment while "allowing the larger German world to recede into the background," and blithely ignoring the fact that neither perfect equality for the Sudeten Germans nor expulsion of every German from Czech territory would mitigate by one iota the Nazi campaign to destroy Czechoslovakia.

Shipler's chapter on "Nationalisms" devotes three pages to Jewish nationalism and the rest to Palestinian Arab nationalism and Israeli blindness to or suppression of it. The chapter uses many of the locutions mandated by the rhetoric of balance: "Palestinian diaspora," "Palestine, like Zion," "Like Jews in the Diaspora," and so on. But the crucial moment of the discussion, the one that is to prove that Israelis will not admit to "a symmetry of claims," is Shipler's story of the "dramatic Israeli move against Palestinian nationalism," which consisted in the (temporary) confiscation of the archives of the "research center" of the PLO in West Beirut in September 1982. This, according to Shipler, "was as if Israel had tried to steal the Palestinians' past and identity, as if the Israelis could not stand to see the Palestinians have a historical archive."[8] Lest he be suspected of bias in this matter, Shipler invokes the authority of another "archivist," the Israeli Meron Benvenisti of the "West Bank Data Project," who confirms that his countrymen wanted "to take from them their history."

The archivists at this center had indeed been diligently at work, assembling files on Israeli military officers, monitoring Israeli police, military, and civilian broadcasts, and exchanging the fruits of their abstruse researches with terrorist organizations all over the world. The center's "director," Sabri Jiryis, was an advisor to Arafat; and its "faculty" included Elias Shufani, Arafat's military deputy. It was, in short, a main PLO intelligence center. As Cynthia Ozick wrote in the *New York Times* (March 1983), "To represent the military capture of a camouflaged military arm as an 'erasure' of culture and history is a stunning falsehood. But what would be worse yet is if it were not a falsehood." That it may not be a falsehood, that what Shipler and Benvenisti call the distinctive Palestinian Arab culture and history may be nothing other than the desire to destroy a living nation, is a possibility that runs like a red thread through *Arab and Jew,* whose author at one point admits that "much of the Arabs' nostalgia for their pre-1948 Palestine . . . was the product less of sweet memories than of current anti-Zionism."[9] If the possibility occurs even to Shipler, how must it haunt the citizens of Israel? Few of them are likely to be reassured by his sanguine claim that Arabs "who think logically" are now willing to settle for a little "West Bank" state alongside Israel, especially if they happen to have seen the results of a poll conducted under joint Arab-American-Australian auspices and supervised by none other than the ubiquitous Benvenisti showing that (according to the *New York Times* of 9 September 1986) "78 percent of West Bank Palestinians said their preferred ultimate solution to the Palestine problem was the establishment of a 'democratic Palestinian state in all of Palestine' while only 17 percent favored a Palestinian state limited to the West Bank and Gaza strip." Perhaps the pollsters failed to stop at the homes of those Palestinian Arabs "who think logically."

In the second part of his book, Shipler compares the images that Arabs and Jews have developed of each other during their years of interaction in Palestine. He makes no attempt to conceal the blood lust that permeates Arab literature depicting Israelis; his problem comes in persuading the reader that "Arab and Jewish stereotypes of each other attain remarkable symmetry." In this effort he is helped not only by his unchanging conviction that all cultures are created and forever remain equal but by assorted Israeli researchers, ranging from the young woman who copies down anti-Arab graffiti scrawled in the lavatory she frequents at Hebrew University, to the Tel Aviv University expert on Israeli children's literature whose ponderous analyses reveal that many books that are standard fare in Israeli schools depict Arabs in general as hostile and prone to violence against Jews. These books also, to be sure, often show that Israeli "fears [of Arabs] turn out to be unfounded" and that generalities about Arabs do not necessarily tell us the truth about individuals. Nevertheless, Shipler expresses his horror that such books still remain "available in libraries" and are used in schools.[10]

But why stop with half measures? If a literary text is objectionable because in depicting the Hebron riots of 1929 it shows Arabs threatening to kill Jewish children, though ultimately leaving them unharmed, how much more objectionable are the historical accounts and memoirs of that event (for example, by Pierre van Paassen[11] or the lone British policeman on the scene), replete with actual killings, including beheadings, "severed sexual organs," and other inflammatory indelicacies? Why balk at literary texts that depict Arabs attacking with the cry of "Palestine—our land; the

Jews—our dogs!" and allow Jewish children to read historical texts that depict Arabs attacking with the cry of—for this was what they really shouted—"Death to the Jews!"'?

In order to fashion his artifice of balance and symmetry Shipler, as we have seen, abstracts Palestinian Arabs from the larger Arab world. This is objectionable, yet less productive of distortions than his removal of the Israeli Jews from their Jewish world and his assumption that they can be understood "essentially on their own terms, without much need for reference to the Jewish Diaspora from which many of them originated."[12] For the rhetorical strategy of the book depends on the skillful use of certain Jews, usually Israeli leftists, to condemn their countrymen and their country's religious heritage in a manner so extreme that Shipler's own criticisms appear moderate and restrained by comparison. He also cites Jews in whom, in Shipler's colorful idiom, "a grinding guilt works at the bowels" so fiercely that they abase themselves before hostile Arabs in a manner so sycophantic that Shipler is embarrassed by it.

There is Shimon Avidan, who, when he looks at the famous picture of the Jewish children in the Warsaw Ghetto, sees Arab children. There is the journalist Benny Morris, who has made it his special object in life to prove that the Jews forcibly expelled Arabs from Western Palestine in 1948. There is Rabbi David Hartman, who tells Shipler that in the Hebrew Bible "you don't have welcoming of the stranger," that Judaism "is fundamentally reactionary," and, on the positive side, that after 1967 "the whole world fell in love" with Israel. There is Elhanan Naeh, talmudic scholar of the Hebrew University, who reveals to Shipler that the reason why Jews admire Jehudah Halevi's *Kuzari* is that "the best-known things in it are racist." There is Aviezer Ravitsky, he, too, of Hebrew University, who argues that Arabs who commit terrorism have more justification than Jews because they "might feel in real distress." There is Danny Rubinstein of *Davar,* who tells Shipler that "There is nothing wrong in terrorism" and helpfully explains that Arabs must use terror because they do not have Phantoms. (Just why an organization whose assets are estimated by the *Economist* to be ten billion dollars cannot afford Phantoms, or why the Syrians and Libyans, lacking Phantoms but amply supplied with Migs, persist in terrorism, the usually glib Rubinstein does not explain.) There are the Interns for Peace, who, on the evidence of this book, appear to spend most of their time off from peacemaking in scorching the ears of journalists with accounts of Israeli "racism." There are the liberal Jewish students whom Shipler meets at Hebrew University, who in their "moderation" and "tolerance" never—for they also are too enlightened to be intolerant of fanaticism—under any circumstances demand that an Arab reject terrorism, since this would entail denouncing "the only institution that represents his nationalist aspirations as a Palestinian." There is

Mordechai Bar-On, Peace Now leader and Knesset member, who listens to an Arab woman declaring that there can never be peace with a nation like Israel, which wants only to dominate other nations and grab as much land as possible, and replies: "You are a very beautiful human being." There are the several Israelis who try to persuade Shipler that he is wrong to "boil and rage" over the exploitation of the Holocaust by Palestinian Arabs who present Ansar as Auschwitz, themselves as Jews, and Israelis as Nazis; for, they explain—and they are all prolific explainers—the use of this inversion (manufactured for Arab use, as surely as their weapons have been, by the USSR) is really "a search for a Palestinian history." And Shipler, by no means immune to that form of liberal condescension that denies to Palestinian Arabs moral responsibility for their words and actions, is not unwilling to be persuaded.

If Shipler had taken the trouble to view his Israeli subjects in relation to their Diaspora history instead of in isolation from it, he might have been less inclined to bow and nod in obeisance before every absurdity uttered to him by his guilt-ridden informants. He might, intelligent observer that he is, have recognized that the centuries-old tradition of Jews who internalize the hatreds and fantasies of anti-Semitic gentiles and then project them onto other Jews did not simply cease when the Jews returned from Diaspora to Zion. Amos Oz, the Israeli novelist, once wrote that "I am a Zionist because I cannot live and have no desire to live like the reflected image of a symbol imprinted in other peoples' imaginations, neither as symbol of a crafty and diabolic vampire nor as the symbol of a piteous victim to who one must offer compassion and compensation. That is why there is no place in the world for me other than the country of the Jews."[13] Now we know that Oz was too sanguine. Donin and Pfefferkorn and Börne and Marx and Kraus and Walter Lippmann and Bruno Kreisky, anxiety-ridden Jews eager to substantiate the most outlandish allegations brought against Jews by anti-Semites, have their continuators in Zion itself. Does Shipler suppose it a mere coincidence, for example, that ever since the UN (then led by Kurt Waldheim) passed its Zionism-racism equation in 1975 many Israeli intellectuals have busied themselves in combing the land of Israel for instances of the "racism" of their less Western, less enlightened fellow citizens, and in proclaiming their discoveries to receptive gentiles in precisely the style practiced by self-hating Jews since the Middle Ages?

Notes

1. Sander Gilman, *Jewish Self-Hatred: Anti-Semitism and the Hidden Language of the Jews* (Baltimore: Johns Hopkins University Press, 1986).
2. Ibid., p. 102, from Mendelssohn's pamphlet *Or lantetive* (Berlin, 1783).
3. Ibid., p. 162.

4. Ibid., p. 206.
5. David Shipler, *Arab and Jew: Wounded Spirits in a Promised Land* (New York: Times Books, 1986).
6. Leszek Kolakowski, "The Idolatry of Politics," *New Republic,* 16 June 1986, p. 32.
7. Shipler, *Arab and Jew,* p. xv.
8. Ibid., p. 75.
9. Ibid., p. 70.
10. Ibid., pp. 184–87.
11. Pierre van Paassen, *Days of Our Years* (New York: Hillman-Curl, 1940), p. 371.
12. Shipler, *Arab and Jew,* p. xv.
13. Amos Oz, "Homeland," in *Under This Blazing Light,* in Hebrew, (Tel Aviv: Sifriat Poalim, 1979), p. 75.

Part III
EVENTS

12

The Quandaries of Terrorism: Three Instances

The Jewish Terrorist Underground

In April 1984 the war in Lebanon still weighed like an incubus on the existence of every Israeli. Barely a day went by without a report of injury, barely a week without a report of death, for soldiers on patrol in Lebanon between nowhere and nowhere. Yet the most riveting subject, almost two years after the beginning of "Operation Peace for Galilee," was neither the war nor the fate of the political coalition that began it in the forthcoming July elections, but terror—terror at home.

Given the fiendish inventiveness of Arab terrorists over the past sixty years, the Israelis might have been thought incapable of surprise at any sort of terrorist tactic, except perhaps at lurid variations on the old themes. But revelations in this month about the Jewish terrorist underground that had been operating since 1978 proved otherwise, as did the storm of controversy that arose over the killing of two Arab terrorists after their capture in the Ashkelon bus hijacking of the same month.

At the end of April, twenty-five Jewish men, mostly settlers in Judea, Samaria, and the Golan Heights, but also including three army officers involved in military government or local security, were arraigned in Jerusalem on charges ranging from theft of army property to membership in a terrorist organization to premeditated murder. Among the deeds they planned or perpetrated were bomb attacks on three Arab mayors in 1980 (one lost both legs, one a foot, and one escaped injury), a grenade attack in Hebron's market, an attack on students at Hebron's Islamic University, and the sabotage of five Arab buses in East Jerusalem. This last, abortive exploit on 27 April gave the General Security Services and the police the occasion for mass arrests. Eventually the men were found guilty of crimes,

including activity in a terrorist organization, manslaughter, causing grievous bodily harm, attempted murder, and murder. The heaviest sentence
was meted out to the three defendants who murdered Arab students at the
Islamic University—they received life in prison.

Among the terrorists were some of the leaders of the settlement movement. Menachem Livni, allegedly the leader of the terrorist organization,
had moved to Hebron in 1970 and become a central figure among the
settlers, who elected him chairman of the Kiryat Arba Council in 1977. He
was also, at the time of his arrest, chairman of the Committee for the
Renewal of Jewish Settlement in the City of the Patriarchs, that is,
Hebron. Yehuda Etzion, charged with involvement in the plot to blow up
the mosques on the Temple Mount and the three Arab mayors, was one of
the founders of Ofra, one of the main Gush Emunim settlements. Ze'ev
Friedman, charged with a series of crimes including attempted murder, had
been chairman of the Kiryat Arba Council and the town's security coordi-
nator.

A public-opinion poll conducted by *Ha'aretz* in June indicated that 60
percent of the Israeli public condemned the activities of the underground
and thought the culprits deserved heavy punishment; just over 14 percent
thought the underground justified in its actions; and 17.5 percent found
justification in specific instances. The last group no doubt had in mind the
distinction pointed out by Yuval Ne'eman between the indiscriminate
assaults on students or bus passengers and the attacks on Arabs who had
themselves been frequent inciters to violence against Jews. Ne'eman,
however, was careful to indicate his disapproval of all these violations of
the law, and to describe in stark terms the moral damage that the Jewish
terrorists had done to their own people. "The students at the Islamic
College were attacked for being Arabs just as the yeshiva students in
Hebron were assaulted for being Jews. No distinction was made . . .
between guilty and not guilty. . . . This was an attack in the style of the
Corsican vendetta or the common Arab blood feud. . . . This is the
accepted moral code in Lebanon and is shared by Bedouins in the Negev
and clans in the villages of Galilee . . . a tradition to which we have grown
accustomed in our Middle East neighbors and in the entire Mediterranean
area, but which we thought we, as Jews, had left behind in biblical times."

Also arrested and held for eleven days for questioning was Rabbi Moshe
Levinger, the pioneer of political settlement in Hebron, the father-in-law
of one of the terrorists, and allegedly a powerful "spiritual" influence in
the lives of underground members. Although the Labor party in its
election platform, and many of its supporters in the press, described the
underground as a result of Likud policies, many people recalled that
Levinger's Hebron activity had begun during Passover of 1968, and that

Kiryat Arba had been established in 1970 with the full support of Yigal Allon. Intimates of Levinger report that he speaks nostalgically of Labor party leaders, who were not only easily manipulated but had a warmer feeling than Likud people toward the idea of settling the land. Only when it was too late did Allon plead, "How could we have known then what Levinger and Katzover would become?"

The enormity of what "they" have become was only gradually revealed to Labor and Likud and, indeed, Gush Emunim, the majority of whose leaders, including Hanan Porat and Israel Harel, strongly condemned the terrorist underground and its apologists. They had good reason to be alarmed by the state of mind as well as the actions of their colleagues. Newspaper reports described how, in a two-hour hearing of the Jerusalem District Court on 31 May, "defendant No. 1 paid little attention to the proceedings, preferring instead to study a page of Talmud." For "defendant No. 1" and his collaborators, neither the courts nor the laws nor the political institutions nor the defense forces of the state of Israel have authority, any more than if they were the courts, laws, institutions, or army of Albania. No more gruesome illustration of this fact emerged than the story of how one of the army officers among the plotters knew a bomb had been placed outside the garage of the former mayor of El-Bireh (Ibrahim Tawil) and said not a single word about it to the army sapper as he watched the latter begin his search. The sapper touched a trip wire and was blinded. Prime Minister Shamir, interviewed in *Ma'ariv*, stated tersely that the activities of the Jewish terrorist organization constituted "a denial of governmental authority." Since the blowing up of the Temple Mount would, as an Israeli Middle East expert of distinctly rightist views said to me, "have brought us an all-out war on every front," this was something of an understatement.

Apologists for the underground, Levinger foremost among them, have offered numerous justifications for the acts of violence begun in 1980. According to him, the very existence of the underground must be ascribed to "shortcomings of government." The accused (and subsequently convicted) men were "frustrated" by the inability of the state to provide complete security for the settlers. The "accused" in the trials ought therefore rightly to have been the state of Israel itself.

Ironically, the apologia for the underground resembled nothing so much as the liberal-left justification of terrorist violence with which we have all become so familiar; everyone is guilty of the crime except the poor fellow who happens to commit it. In Israel the desire to exculpate the terrorist and inculpate society, or even the victim, had previously been expressed by leftists like Yossi Sarid and Shulamit Aloni. The latter at times justified Arab violence against Jews as the inevitable result of "frustration." If someone feels frustrated, he absolutely must go out and bomb his Jewish neighbor. This smelly little orthodoxy of leftist criminology has now been adopted by the Jewish underground and its defenders. According to old wisdom, extremes meet. His brother, Professor Yaacov Levinger, reported that one of Rabbi Levinger's ideological heroes is none other than Yeshayahu Leibowitz, the aging leftist enfant terrible. Leibowitz, like members of the underground, is fond of declaring that Israel, if it fails to heed his warnings, is irrevocably doomed regardless of which perfidious political party wins elections.

Terrorists, Journalists, and National Security

To left-wing journalists the world over, including those in Israel, the discovery of a Jewish terrorist underground was a godsend, the opportunity at last to use the terrorist label without inverted commas and to assume a moral equivalence between Jewish and Arab terror, despite the fact that while Arab terrorists were universally acclaimed by their people, Jewish terrorists were generally abhorred and condemned by theirs.

Although the *Jerusalem Post*'s "West Bank" specialist began to refer to the Jewish underground as "the most serious subversive organization in Israel's history," citizens with a less jaundiced eye continued to be far more troubled by the activities of other, more familiar subversive organizations called the PLO and PDFLP. In December 1983, PLO bombs had turned a bus crowded with passengers into an abattoir on Mt. Herzl. On 2 April 1984, Arab terrorists threw hand grenades and sprayed bullets at every Jew in sight in the very center of Jerusalem, killing one person and wounding fifty-eight. The culminating incident in the series of attacks came on 12 April, when four Arab terrorists hijacked the Tel Aviv–Ashkelon bus. By the time security forces captured the bus, a nineteen-year-old Israeli woman soldier who had been a passenger was dead, and eight other passengers were wounded. But what made this incident, and this alone of the three, into a cause celebre for journalists and politicians was not the fate of the victims but the fate of the terrorists. For it gradually emerged that although all four terrorists were killed during the episode (in which they had threatened to blow up all passengers), only two were killed as a result of the attacking force's gunfire.

The inalienable right of captured terrorists not only to all the rights due prisoners of war but even to all niceties of peacetime legal procedure has long been a strident demand of most journalists. But in this instance journalists reacted with more than customary indignation because the army and security forces also violated the inalienable rights of the journalists—among them, the right to go wherever they like, to photograph and say whatever they like, and to publish whenever they like. Photographers at the scene took pictures of one of the terrorists being led away from the bus, apparently uninjured. The military censor prevented publication of the pictures, and the tabloid *Hadashot* was briefly shut down for disregarding the prohibition. Israeli journalists swiftly retaliated for the injury inflicted on them by then Minister of Defense Moshe Arens by invoking the help of outside forces they correctly assumed capable not just of flouting the censor but of intimidating the Israeli government itself, namely, David Shipler and the *New York Times*. *Hadashot* took its pictures to the home village of the terrorists in the Gaza Strip for identification, then turned the pictures and information over to Shipler, who covered the whole matter in ample detail in several stories in the *New York Times*.

The reverence of numerous Israeli journalists for Shipler was not mutual. In his book *Arab and Jew* he sneers at the Israeli journalists, in particular the *Ma'ariv* photographer who allowed his journalistic zeal to be compromised by his inability to choose correctly "between journalism and patriotism." "The Israeli press," Shipler complained, "with little exception, devoted more anger to *Hadashot* for evading the censor than to the authorities for trying to cover up."[1]

In fact, the campaign begun by Shipler in the *Times* to force the Israeli government to appoint yet another investigatory commission had a good deal of support from Israeli journalists. A whole cadre of professional communicators concerned for the rights of terrorists took up the cry. Phillip Gillon, the *Jerusalem Post*'s television critic, not only wanted Moshe Arens to establish a commission of inquiry, but to grovel in the dust and "apologize" to David Shipler. *Mabat,* Israel's evening television news program, made a point of dividing interview time equally between the father of Irit Portuguez, the dead passenger, and the mother of one of the terrorists killed by security forces.

The Israeli public was less capable of such impartiality. The results of a public-opinion poll released on 1 June revealed that 64.9 percent of the public opposed the appointment of a commission to investigate the deaths of the terrorists, and 57.2 percent opposed publication of the conclusions of such a commission, should it be established.

Moshe Arens did what the news media, not the general public, demanded. He established a commission of inquiry headed by Major General (Reserve) Meir Zorea, which came to the conclusion, released by the Defense Ministry on 28 May 1984, that although the blows dealt to the terrorists during the operation to retake the bus were necessary to prevent their detonating the bomb that was on the bus, they had also been dealt severe blows after their removal from the bus that resulted in their deaths.

The penultimate section of the report stated that "the minister of defence regards with the utmost gravity, and strongly condemns the behaviour that led to the deaths of the two terrorists captured on the bus, behaviour that is in clear contradiction to the basic rules and norms incumbent on all, and especially the security forces."

The further inquiry ordered by the Zorea Commission and propelled by the zeal of Attorney General Yitzhak Zamir resulted, over a year later, in the court martial of the senior army officer at the scene, Brigadier Yitzhak Mordecai. He admitted striking the terrorists in order to gain vital information about the bombs allegedly planted on the bus, but he was acquitted of the charges brought by the panel. The story did not, however, end here, for the Arab terrorists proved to be far more potent and destructive as ghosts than they had been in their bodily presence, and their evil spirits continued to haunt some of Israel's major institutions for well over two years after the hijacking.

In May 1986 it was revealed that Zamir had ordered an investigation of the head of Shabak (the acronym for Sherut Bitachon Klali, the General Security Services), Avraham Shalom. This was the first time in Israel's history that the identity of a serving head of the security services was made public. He had come under suspicion because his own deputy alleged that Shalom and three of his agents had lied to the various panels of inquiry into the killing of the terrorists in order to divert suspicion from themselves and Shabak onto the army and Brigadier Mordecai. In this dispute, Prime Minister Peres chose to support Shalom and also Shalom's decision to suspend the accusing deputy and two other Shabak agents. At this point, apparently in March 1986, the deputy tried to persuade Zamir to initiate yet another investigation. Zamir said that he would do so unless Shalom and those agents who had cooperated with him in the alleged acts of perjury and subornation of witnesses resigned.

The stain of the Ashkelon hijacking, having already marked the army and the security services, now spread into still other respected Israeli institutions, formerly assumed above politics. Zamir's request to the police to examine evidence against Shabak was opposed by Peres and Shamir and their respective blocs on the grounds that it would harm Israeli security and efforts to fight terrorism. Zamir, for his part, would not back down, insisting that the issue "is law, not security." The leftist Citizens Rights Movement, supporting Zamir, introduced a no-confidence motion in parliament, alleging that "the behavior of the Prime Minister and his ministers in this affair has brought their commitment to the rule of law in Israel down to a new low."

In June, Peres, influenced by his justice minister (and also least favorite cabinet colleague) Yitzhak Modai, dismissed Zamir and replaced him with a district court judge named Yosef Harish. Harish said that some kind of investigation into the killings and alleged cover-up was necessary, but in the meantime yet another branch of the Israeli government became embroiled in what had begun as a garden-variety terrorist depredation. President Chaim Herzog was persuaded by the government to grant, on 25 June, immunity from possible future prosecution to Shalom in exchange for his resignation; three of his top deputies also were granted immunity but allowed to keep their jobs. This move prompted no fewer than four no-confidence motions in parliament by left-wing opposition parties. Harish denied that he had been a party to any deals, and insisted that "There was no harm done to the rule of law if the President saw fit to advance the pardon before there were charges." But since the president had pardoned Shalom before a police investigation could be begun, Harish said, an investigation now seemed "pointless." All members of the inner cabinet of key Likud and Labor ministers endorsed the resignation-for-amnesty arrangement with the exception of Ezer Weizman.

The "Shabak Affair," as it had now come to be called, was something that no one seemed able to touch without being defiled. Criticism of the government and of President Herzog came from all sides. Many charged that Peres and Shamir were fearful that an investigation of Shalom for covering up the murder of the two hijackers would provoke him to cite as precedents in his defense previous extralegal or at least unconventional actions against terrorists that were approved by the political leadership; and they also pointed out that the political leader at the time that Shalom's actions against the hijackers were taken was Yitzhak Shamir, the prime minister in 1984 and soon, in November 1986, to become prime minister once again. Jurists also reminded the government that when Zamir was asked, in 1985, about the possibility of granting amnesty to suspects in the Jewish terrorist underground cases, he had said such a move would be illegal while their trials were still in progress. A pardon could not be granted before someone was convicted as a criminal. Former Justice Minister Haim Zadok argued that Modai had no legal right to request Herzog to grant amnesty, and the president had no authority to pardon the Shabak chief Shalom before he had been tried or convicted: "In this case, the amnesty was not out of mercy, but with one object: to prevent an investigation and an exposure of the truth. This is a black day for the rule of law."

From the president's office the taint of the Shabak affair then spread to the High Court of Justice, or nearly did so, when several applications were made requesting that the Court nullify the pardons and begin yet another investigation of the affair from its beginnings. But the High Court upheld the president's right to issue pardons to persons not yet formally charged with crimes, and the critics of the government had to settle for the new attorney general's recommendation of a police investigation. "The devil's dance is over," said Ronnie Milo, deputy foreign secretary. Shamir and Herzog justified the amnesties granted to the Shabak officials, and urged that this apparently endless case be terminated before the domestic intelligence agency became totally demoralized. This, not surprisingly, was what the majority of the public also wanted. A poll published in *Yediot Aharonot* on 13 July found that 57 percent of the public were against any further investigation and accepted the view that the pardon took into account, in a balanced way, both the apparent offenses of the security men and the implications for national security of endless probing of the wound. A still more interesting poll by the tabloid *Hadashot* conducted in July found that, when asked who was "guilty" in the Shabak affair, 34 percent named the Israeli press itself.

No group attacked the resolution of the Shabak affair more savagely than what Shamir and Herzog called the "barking dogs" of the Israeli press, who seemed to be trying belatedly to fend off charges of overseas colleagues like David Shipler that they had put patriotic ahead of professional loyalties. They had, after all, been intimately involved in this miserable affair from the night back in April 1984 when the powerful lights of their television cameras had nearly blinded the Israeli troops just as they prepared to charge the bus and rescue the hostages, and Yitzhak Rabin complained angrily that "Care should have been taken to prevent journalists from running around beneath the feet of the rescuers during the operation." Now, *Ma'ariv* attacked Peres for political interference in the legal process "under the pretext of 'security considerations,' " and an editorialist in *Ha'aretz* proudly accepted the label of "barking watch dogs" for the press and defiantly asserted that true security "means being able to look into the mirror and tell ourselves the truth."

The ramifications of this story are complex and manifold, a web of interconnectedness among political, military, and spiritual considerations. At some level of awareness, most Israelis sense that, in the very nature of things, violence does even justice unjustly; and surely the way in which the mud flung up by the killing of the terrorists eventually spattered so many of Israel's hitherto sacrosanct institutions demonstrated how good may corrupt itself to evil in the very act of combating it. On a more mundane level, it has long been evident to the citizens of this country under siege that if terrorists know they will be executed when captured, they are likely to hold the lives of their Jewish hostages even more cheaply than they do now; that information can be extracted from live terrorists, not dead ones; and that violent treatment of captured terrorists can jeopardize Israeli prisoners of war held by Syria or the PLO, who recognize no distinction between terrorists and regular soldiers. On the other hand, the awareness that their every action will be submitted to the refined scrutiny of moral idealists sitting miles away from the battlefield cannot but have an inhibiting effect on soldiers and security men struggling against ruthless terrorists. Neither, perhaps, can these Israeli soldiers and security men be expected to do their demanding jobs without being allowed the consolation of the belief expressed by Solomon that "In the destruction of the wicked there is joy."

The most memorable response that I heard to the Shabak affair was expressed to me by one of Israel's (and the world's) greatest living novelists, a survivor of the Holocaust, and a man of almost preternatural gentleness who has nevertheless fought in all of Israel's wars: "When I listen to the hysterical reactions of our intelligentsia to the killing of the terrorists, I think, no, it's hopeless, we can never become a normal people. We will never recover a certain kind of life-wisdom that we must have had before we went into exile because in most countries it's the common property of every peasant. Still, when I listen to ordinary people in Israel it seems to me that, yes, we *have* recovered here in this land some of the old understanding about life and death—the difference between legality and justice. I, at least, am glad to count myself one of these ordinary people."

Exchanging Terrorists for Soldiers

On 20 May 1985, Israel released 1,150 terrorists, more than half of the security prisoners held in the country, in exchange for three Israeli soldiers who had fallen into the hands of terrorists in Lebanon in 1982. Although there were self-interested references by various cabinet ministers to "long months" of negotiation with Ahmed Jibril's Popular Front for the Liberation of Palestine general command, a minor-league terrorist organization (numbering about 400 members), the actual negotiations with Jibril, a Syrian-backed functionary, lasted only from September 1984 to March 1985. Newspaper reports kept referring to the presence of Jibril's nephew in an Israeli jail as one of Israel's "main cards" in negotiation, despite the fact that it had to be supplemented by 1,149 other "cards," including 930 from the forces of Jibril's rival, Yasser Arafat. On 1 April (not yet known in Israel as April Fool's Day), the Israeli inner cabinet of Shimon Peres's government of national unity voted unanimously to approve the agreement for exchange of prisoners.

Astonishment and outrage at the news arose not only from the quantity but also the "quality" of terrorists involved. One hundred and sixty-seven of the terrorists (most but by no means all Palestinian Arabs) had been convicted of involvement in attacks in which people were killed, and 116 others had been involved in attacks that wounded and maimed people. Their number included many whose pitiless cruelty and animal barbarity had often shocked a world that had thought itself inured to bestial violence. Among the released was Kozo Okamoto, who had been sentenced to multiple life terms for his part in the 1972 massacre of twenty-seven arriving passengers at Lod Airport. Also freed were terrorists responsible for the 1978 coastal road massacre of thirty-four people out for a holiday; one of the killers of Danny Haran and his two little girls in Nahariya in 1979; the murderer of the two Aroyo children in Gaza; the killer of the yeshiva student–soldier Aharon Gross in Hebron; the bombers of the Hebrew University cafeteria in 1969; the man whose bomb killed fifteen people in the Mahane Yehuda market in Jerusalem in 1968; and so on and on and on, ad nauseam. Jibril's organization, with which a sovereign Israeli government negotiated this exchange, was itself known to have been responsible for the massacres at Kibbutz Shamir and Kiryat Shmona, and at Moshav Avivim, where they destroyed the children on a school bus.

The information about the three captive Israeli soldiers to be released did little to strengthen the government's case for what it had done. Two of them had been captured (along with six other members of their unit) in circumstances that, in the view of several high army officers, justified their being court-martialed. Some of the relatives of the freed soldiers made tempers worse by insensitive statements to the press to the effect that it did not matter how many terrorists were freed in order to release their flesh and blood.

The intermediary in the negotiations had originally been Bruno Kreisky. In addition to being one of the most flamboyant Jewish anti-Semites on the world stage, Kreisky had given his unstinting support to the PLO, and was the first Western leader publicly to embrace Muammar Khadafy, just as he had been the first to embrace Arafat. His labors in negotiation were ultimately brought to fruition by Herbert Amry, Austria's ambassador to Greece. The press reported that, at one point in the bargaining, Israel had submitted a list of thirty-six names of terrorists whose crimes were so revolting that they could under no circumstances be released; but Kreisky persuaded the Israelis to reduce their sense of revulsion by half, and the number dropped to eighteen.

Israel's humiliating surrender to terrorist extortion was not limited to the quantity and quality of killers released. Israel was also persuaded, apparently by the Red Cross (which does not recognize Israel's Magen David Adom), to allow nearly six hundred of the released terrorists to return to their former homes in Israel and the administered territories. The negotiators also demanded, and received, Israel's consent to distribute to the terrorists, along with jaunty red shirts, light slacks, and sneakers, a letter from their benefactor Jibril congratulating his "militant brothers and comrades" on their past heroic deeds, which were "highly appreciated," and their "long-standing patience" during the years (or months) in Israeli jails from which he had just obtained their release. The letter was a means of telling the terrorists, most of whom had probably never heard of Jibril, to whom they were indebted (and obligated) for their liberation.

Perhaps in anticipation of the storm of outrage that was bound to follow announcement of the exchange agreement, rumors began to spread that one or another member of the government had strongly dissented from the agreement, only to be coerced into acquiescence by pressure from his colleagues. Minister of Tourism Avraham Sharir was reported to have spoken against the agreement at cabinet meetings. Former President and now Education Minister Yitzhak Navon, too, some claimed, had vigorously opposed the surrender to terrorist demands. Perhaps most remarkably Shmuel Tamir, former justice minister and now chief of Israel's negotiating team, had, according to *Ma'ariv* (30 May 1985) at one point submitted his resignation to Rabin in protest against the heavy price that the agreement would exact from Israel; but the Minister of Defense and Chief of Staff Moshe Levy pressured him into withdrawing his resignation.

Still, in a country where the tradition of collective cabinet responsibility is generally weak, and in a government of national unity that came, soon after its formation in 1984, to be known as the "government of national paralysis," the unity of government ministers in defending this, of all their decisions, was astonishing. For once, Peres and Shamir spoke in harmony, and even Menachem Begin broke the self-imposed silence of his exile to give his approval. Many people drew from this rare unanimity the optimistic conclusion that there lay, behind the official explanation of the deal, a secret, hidden explanation that, for reasons of security, could not be disclosed.

The public justifications of the exchange were intellectually feeble and even morally offensive, no matter which minister offered them. To judge from the stridency of his apologias for the agreement, Yitzhak Rabin appears to have been the key government figure urging the agreement with Jibril. Like Prime Minister Peres he kept repeating that, since an Entebbe-style rescue was not possible in this case, Israel "had no choice," and had obtained "the best terms we could." But Rabin also insisted that Israel's obligation to its soldiers was infinite, and exhorted all citizens tempted to criticize the government to put themselves into the place of the families of the three captives. "What would you expect of me as defense minister if it was your son sitting there?" He did not try to explain why, in 1978, when Ezer Weizmann had released seventy-six terrorists in exchange for a single soldier, he and Yigal Allon had been Weizmann's harshest critics, and the Labor Alignment had proposed a motion of no confidence in the Begin government. Neither did Rabin address himself to the more pressing question about families of hostages, put to him and Peres repeatedly and with considerable heat by Israelis who had lost sons and daughters, husbands and wives, in the dozens of terrorist attacks in which Arabs had taken Jewish hostages: "Why were *our* sons, *our* babies, sacrificed to uphold the principle that Israel does not surrender to the demands of terrorists?" Rabin may have to face still harder questions in the future from parents whose children will fall prey to the hordes of killers released in 1985.

Angry reactions by Israelis who had felt on their own flesh and in the inmost recesses of their souls the cruelty of the freed killers began to reveal the nearly boundless ramifications of the exchange. Dora Rosenfeld's husband David had been stabbed to death, with flagrant brutality, while performing his duties as a caretaker at the Herodion archaeological site in July 1982. Since his two Arab killers were among the released terrorists allowed to return to their homes in Israel or the administered territories, they were greeted in their villages as heroes, not only for having committed murder, but for having done it with impunity. "There's no justice in Israel," she declared. Haim Mark, a survivor of the 1979 Tiberias bombing that killed two children, including a two-year-old who died in his arms, and maimed his wife, threatened to kill the terrorist who had carried out the attack and was now free. Since, in his view, the Israeli government had brazenly flouted justice, he would carry it out himself. The friends and family of Aharon Gross, the yeshiva student murdered in the Hebron market in 1983, now had to watch his murderers walking through that very market, or, rather, being carried through it on the shoulders of their admirers. (Not only Israelis felt aggrieved by the government's release of the killers. Reuters reported that the Japanese police would now place Okamoto, the mass murderer of Lod Airport, on its list of most wanted criminals.)

If the human sense of justice and the moral imagination were violated by the immunity that had been granted for murders committed in the past, reason could not accept what Israel's surrender might mean for the future. Those who condemned the exchange most strongly spanned the political spectrum from the Likud MK, Meir Shitrit, who answered Rabin's slightly demagogic question by saying he would *not* want his son freed at such a price, to the United Kibbutz movement, which said it was not even convinced that the three POWs' lives were in danger; and they posed unanswerable questions about the future implications of the exchange. Are Israel's secret agents and soldiers and border guards to continue risking (and often losing) their lives to capture terrorists who will eventually be released to ply their trade again? Does it make sense to blow up the houses of Arabs suspected of terrorism, or to deport them, while those guilty of terrorist acts freely walk the streets of the same village? How can Israel ever again urge foreign governments to uphold the principle of not surrendering to terror and of punishing terrorists, now that she has herself violated this principle on a massive scale that not even the most greedy and pusillanimous nations of Western Europe have matched? What steadfastness can be expected of Israeli ministers in future political negotiations with Palestinian Arabs if they demonstrate such weakness, such lack of policy and resolve, in negotiations over prisoners?

There were, of course, some differences in emphasis between leftist and rightist critics of the prisoner exchange. Many of those on the right hoped to link the exchange to the fate of the imprisoned members of the Jewish underground, a link that the left vigorously opposed as undermining the "rule of law" in Israel. Neither side was convincing in trying to make partisan political profit out of the mess. Rightist insistence on linking the fate of the Jewish underground to that of the freed Arab terrorists tended to confirm allegations that this was the main reason why Likud ministers had agreed to freeing the 1,150 terrorists in the first place. On the other hand, leftist insistence on the need to uphold the rule of law sounded hollow in view of the fact that some Arab terrorists had been allowed hastily to change their pleas from innocent to guilty so that they could be done with mere legal formalities in time to be released along with those already found guilty; and in one case of ecumenical terrorism, the Arab members of the team had been freed while the Jewish member stayed in jail. The fact that the rule of law had already been scandalously violated did not necessarily mean that further violations of it were justified. But many Israelis who opposed pardons for members of the Jewish underground, and even thought they belonged in cells to which the keys had been thrown away, could nevertheless understand the fury of settlers in Hebron who watched as gloating Arab killers were cheered by their admirers while the Jewish culprits languished in prison.

The great majority of Israel's political commentators, indeed, all but the most doctrinaire leftists (and even they were discomfited by the fact that Jibril was a fierce rival of their favored "moderate," Arafat), did not merely object to the flouting of all judicial norms for political purposes or to the likely reestablishment of the terrorist political and military network in Judea and Samaria, or to the increased incentive that had now been given to the enemy to try to capture Israeli soldiers. They were stunned by a recognition that the Israel of 1985 was no longer the Israel that had undertaken the Entebbe rescue—that the leaders of Israel were people who no longer felt themselves masters of their own fate and therefore had lost all sense of perspective and proportion and even their own strength. And, in a situation that seemed ideally suited for the emergence of a strong, articulate leader to challenge the government, no serious opposition leader emerged to channel the widespread public discontent into political action.

About a week after the news of the exchange became public, I asked two wily veterans of Israeli politics, one a Herut member of Israel's first Knesset, the other a longtime Labor Zionist executive in the Jewish Agency, both on intimate terms with many of the ministers in the inner cabinet, whether there was in fact some secret explanation of the government's accession to the extravagant demands of the terrorists. "The 'secret' explanation," said the former, "is more disturbing than the public one; it's that there's *nothing* behind what they've done, except the acknowledgment that Israel nowadays will always back down when the other side stands its ground." The Laborite's answer was not much different: "There's no secret at all, I'm afraid; it's just the result of emptiness and exhaustion. You also mustn't underestimate the power of sheer stupidity in human affairs."

Perhaps these verdicts are too harsh. The obligation to ransom or redeem captives, powerfully felt at all times by Jews, must have seemed uniquely compelling in the wake of so catastrophic a misadventure as the war in Lebanon. The talmudic saying that whoever saves a single life saves a whole world has exercised, especially since the Holocaust, a powerful sway even over the secular Jews who dominate Israeli governments. But in the world that the state of Israel inhabits, the noblest motives, if not tempered by unrelaxing awareness of the nation's constant burden of peril, can have the most disastrous consequences, and saving single lives may involve endangering a whole nation. The authors of that talmudic saying were themselves fully aware that failure to punish the wicked is failure to uphold the honor of their dead victims.

Notes

1. David Shipler, *Arab and Jew: Wounded Spirits in a Promised Land* (New York: Times Books, 1986), p. 89.

13

"We Will Drive this Country Crazy": Reflections on Meir Kahane and the Elections of 1984

In his book on representative government, published in 1861, John Stuart Mill, who for more than two decades had sought a means of diluting the power of the numerical majority in British democracy, endorsed Thomas Hare's scheme for proportional representation in parliament. Its great virtue, according to Mill, was that "it secures a representation, in proportion to numbers, of every division of the electoral body: not two great parties alone . . . but every minority in the whole nation, consisting of a sufficiently large number to be, on principles of equal justice, entitled to a representative." Something very like this system has been tried in Israel, and the elections of 1984 proved more conclusively than ever before that it does not work. The application of the principle of proportional representation in Israel has not, as Mill hoped it always would, preserved the voice and spiritual influence of that "truth and reason" supposed by him to be embodied in the liberal minority. Instead it has exaggerated the power of unreason and fanaticism, and burdened Israel with a parliament that often seems a Jewish version of what Burke once called "the dissidence of dissent and the protestantism of the protestant religion," and with governments that cannot govern.

The elections of 1984 failed to produce a government because neither of the "two great parties" came close to securing a majority of the 120 Knesset seats. The Labor Alignment, led by Shimon Peres, won forty-four and the Likud (Coalition), led by Yitzhak Shamir, won forty-one. Since what Mill called "a sufficiently large number to be . . . entitled to a representative" was adjudged by Israel's founding fathers to be 1 percent of the total votes cast, many small parties, including what in Israel are called "one-man factions," won Knesset seats. They ranged from Meir

191

Kahane's Kach party (one seat), whose main principle is expulsion of the Arab population, to the two pro-PLO parties, the (Communist) Democratic Front for Peace and Equality (four seats) and the Progressive List for Peace (two seats).

A pervasive paradox of the Israeli electoral system is that winners often turn out to be losers and losers, winners. Although the Alignment received three more seats than the Likud, even a visitor from Mars watching the reactions to election returns on television could tell from their faces that the Alignment leaders felt themselves to be losers, and the Likud leaders were surprised and elated by their "victory." This was not only because most of the opinion polls had predicted a solid Labor (Alignment) victory, but because, as one unnamed Likud minister quoted in the newspaper *Ma'ariv* the morning after the elections said, "If after 400 percent inflation and 600 killed in the Lebanese war, these are the results, then the public is even stupider than we thought." If the Labor party could not win an election under these circumstances, just when and how could it win one? The question acquired greater force from postelection studies showing that younger voters and Oriental voters (who comprise the fastest-growing sector of the population) continued to vote more heavily for the Likud in each election. A headline in the local paper *Jerusalem Voice* read: "Every day new Herutniks are born and Laborites disappear."

If the Labor party, apparent winners, were in fact widely perceived to be losers, then some of those small parties that at first appeared to have done (and indeed did do) very badly in the voting turned out—such are the vagaries of proportional representation—to hold the key to forming a new government. This was especially the case with Ezer Weizman's Yahad ("together") party, and Aharon Abu-Hatzeira's Moroccan Tami party. Weizman and his colleagues, despite a very well-financed and highly professional campaign, could manage only three seats, and the party of Abu-Hatzeira, whose abandonment of the Likud government had brought on the early elections in the first place, did even worse, winning only one seat. Nevertheless, in the weeks after Peres received from President Chaim Herzog the mandate to try to form a new government, it turned out that without Weizman and Abu-Hatzeira he was unlikely to succeed. Weizman, once a minister in a Likud government, gave both sides ample opportunity to outbid each other for his three votes by offering him cabinet portfolios and safe places in the next election. Eventually he decided that the Alignment was willing to pay a higher price than his former comrades could, and he signed an agreement with Peres.

During the endless speculation about possible coalitions that would add up to a sixty-one-vote majority, it was generally assumed that three parties would remain beyond the pale of hypothetical coalition partners: Kahane's

Kach movement on the far right and the Communists and the Progressive List for Peace on the far left. That is why the Alignment, even as it courted the small parties, heeded Herzog's recommendation to try to form a national unity government with the Likud. If Labor could woo one or more of the religious parties to its side, then it could form its own narrow government, albeit one dependent on elements that both its own left wing and its allies in the liberal Shinui ("Change") and leftist Citizens' Rights parties found repellent. Once it failed to gain the adhesion of, say, the National Religious party (four seats) or the non-Zionist religious Agudat Yisrael party (two seats), then it could form a government only by relying on the votes of the two pro-PLO parties to give it a "blocking majority" that would make formation of a government by its Likud opponents impossible. Certain figures in Labor, among them Abba Eban, appeared to see nothing wrong with this. Others strongly objected to it in principle, and still others pointed out that such a move might bring Labor into power but would involve the major inconvenience of suicide in the long run, since the main reason for its disappointing showing at the polls was that it had been perceived by many moderate voters as overly inclined to see Arab moderation where none existed.

Despite sharp disagreement over who would become prime minister and over the distribution of ministerial portfolios, many supporters of both the "great parties" hoped and believed that a national unity government would be formed. Likud and Alignment positions were, after all, nearly identical with respect to withdrawal from Lebanon; and their views on healing the economy and on revising the electoral laws in order to break the paralyzing stranglehold of the small splinter parties were also very similar. In addition, the Alignment was riven with disunity because seven of its seats were now held by the once-Stalinist and still rigidly leftist Mapam party, strongly opposed in principle to any agreement with "the class enemy." If Labor risked suicide by moving leftward toward dependence on Communists and PLO supporters in order to form a narrow government, it risked the dismantling of its alignment with Mapam if it moved rightward to form a national unity government. That is why Shimon Peres, sensing that this was his final chance to become prime minister, was reduced to ingratiating himself with the small parties in a manner that began to remind Israelis of Swift's saying that climbing and crawling are done from the same posture. Eventually, Peres sensed the futility of this effort and preserved his dignity by entering into the national unity government with Shamir and the Likud, with the understanding that he would serve as prime minister until the autumn of 1986, when he would be succeeded by Shamir.

The only political fact created by the elections that elicited more editorial comment than the fevered negotiations between large and small parties was the election of Rabbi Meir Kahane to the Knesset. No sooner had the election returns indicated that, because his Kach party had amassed 1.2 percent of the total vote, he would occupy a seat in the next Knesset than Kahane announced: "We will drive this country crazy. We will make this country Jewish again." Although the first part of this unintentionally comic prediction struck nearly everybody who heard it as a commitment to carry coals to Newcastle, subsequent events were to demonstrate that Kahane really is capable of driving many ordinary Israelis to do still more abundantly what they already do very adequately, namely, give free rein to their penchant for political hysteria.

During the election campaign the Central Elections Committee, supported by its chairman, Supreme Court Justice Gavriel Bach, voted to disqualify Kahane's list altogether on the grounds that it incited racial hostility toward one segment of the population. (The committee also, without the support of Bach, voted to disqualify the Progressive List for Peace because its leader had been a member of an illegal organization dedicated to the overthrow of the state.) Although the Supreme Court overturned these rulings, it did not publish its reasons for doing so. Very likely it recognized the danger inherent in panic-ridden measures to resist undemocratic parties by suspending democratic procedures, and therefore allowed both Kach and the PLP to run.

After Kahane's election hardly a day passed without some prominent individual or group proposing a new law to "fight Kahane" with measures that would likely do more harm to Israeli democracy than Kahane himself ever could. Jerusalem Mayor Teddy Kollek called for a "law banning racist talk." Ephraim Urbach, president of the Israel Academy of Sciences, warned that "those who insist on the strict application of democratic principles" to Kahane would destroy Israeli democracy. Journalist Yosef Goell urged the Knesset to "bend its own regulations" to keep Kahane from speaking. Assorted leftist politicians called for denying Kahane his seat or stripping him of his parliamentary immunity or organizing the other 119 Knesset members (among them such lovers of Zion and democracy as the PLP and Communist members) to boycott or heckle any speech made by Kahane. President Herzog refused to meet with Kahane on the same day that he dutifully consulted with leaders of fringe parties, among them the editor of a pornographic newspaper, who had urged abolition of Israel's Law of Return (the very foundation of the state). It was the first refusal of a president to meet with an elected party head in the history of the state.

Commentators were puzzled by the fact that there were Kahane voters in nearly every Arab town and village. The likeliest (and least condescending) explanation is that these voters anticipated the orgies of "craziness" that Kahane's election would excite among liberals in Israel and abroad. It must have been with wry satisfaction that these Arab voters observed the delegations of solemn Jewish "peace" groups and Conservative and Reform rabbis daily parading through their neighborhoods to "prove" to them that, in the words of Rabbi Jeremy Milgrom, "a rabbi doesn't mean a racist."

If Kahane seemed to be making good on his promise "to drive this country crazy," he was definitely successful in driving some overseas "friends of Israel" into spectacular displays of outrage. Leaders of the American Jewish Congress, finding themselves in Jerusalem just after the elections, called Kahane "Israel's Farrakhan." They studiously avoided calling him "Israel's Jackson," for to do so might have stirred the unsettling thought that Jackson and his mass following represent a far greater danger to American Jews than Kahane does to Israel. It might also have prompted some to wonder why Jewish leaders had not, during the preceding ten years (and not merely ten months) when Jesse Jackson was attacking Jews as the source of nearly every evil on the globe, denounced him, as they now denounced Kahane, as a racist agitator. With all Israel astir over Kahane, a British journalist interviewed on Israeli television took it upon himself to scold the Israeli electorate and to boast that although Britain also had its racist demagogues, they did not get elected to parliament. It never occurred to his Israeli interviewer to ask whether the British people, too, ought not to cover themselves with sackcloth and ashes and ask pardon from the liberals of the world because Enoch Powell had been sitting in the House of Commons for thirty-four years, despite the fact that since 1968 he has advocated the repatriation of "colored" immigrants. In the 1983 British election Powell received 32, 254 votes from his little constituency of South Down, 7,000 more votes than Kahane received from the entire state of Israel.

Among the few who saw any good coming from Kahane's election were those at the opposite end of the political spectrum who share his view that the Arab population of the land of Israel is a demographic time bomb, and that Israel cannot coexist with a substantial Arab minority. Ruth Gavison of the Association for Civil Rights in Israel publicly thanked Kahane for "doing us all a signal service by forcing us all" to recognize that Kahane's position was no different from that of all Israeli parties that call for integration of the "territories." The *Post*'s David Bernstein went a step further by angrily blaming Likud, Tehiya, and Gush Emunim politicians for not supporting Kahane; this was "intellectually dishonest" of them because by repudiating him they were "imparting to themselves an aura of moderation that belies their true political identity." By Bernstein's standard of guilt by nonassociation, every Jew, from Chaim Weizmann and David Ben-Gurion onward, who believed in the Jewish right to sovereignty in a land of Israel containing a sizable Arab minority was a secret Kahaneite, hypocritically concealing his monstrous designs.

Israel's leftist literary intellectuals found themselves in disarray after the election. In the days before the vote, the novelist A. B. Yehoshua was loudly warning his Labor party colleagues that he and his fellow doves would give them no respite after their victory but would lay down the law regarding withdrawal from Lebanon, repair of the economy, and resumption of the "peace process." When it became clear that not even the Lebanese morass and the 400 percent inflation rate could induce the Israeli electorate to restore Labor to power, Yehoshua and three other writers of the Peace Now persuasion—Amos Oz, Haim Gouri, and S. Yizhar—swallowed their disappointment and called for the establishment of a national unity government. This, they claimed, was the only just response to "an outcry from a people torn and split." Though they made it clear that this national unity government was to be headed by Peres and to be inspired by the continued adhesion of Mapam, their call for unity was instantly denounced by five literary figures even farther to the left. Their denunciatory statement, whatever its political merits, should give pause to those of us who have been taught to believe that the study of literature is conducive to a sense of the dangers of pride, vanity, and self-righteousness. The literary quintet of Natan Zach, Meir Weiseltier, Yair Hurwitz, Dan Miron, and Menahem Peri expressed feelings of "repulsion and disgust" for their colleagues. "The call for a covenant between the man of blood and the man of culture, the responsible man of conscience and the scoundrel," they modestly declared, "is nothing but erroneous and misleading, if not completely stupid."

One wonders whether it was with the help of literature that these literary intellectuals acquired so powerful a conviction of their own infallibility and their opponents' wickedness. Sophocles, who understood something of the tragic nature of all political action, wrote in the *Antigone* that "lofty words are not becoming to mortals."

Yet it was not the arrogance of the writers that provided the election's most lasting image of the intellectual's inability to cope with the stubborn actualities of politics. Rather, it was the pathos in the photograph of Arie (Lova) Eliav proudly holding up the picture of himself shaking hands with the late PLO official Issam Sartawi when the two were awarded the "Bruno Kreisky Peace Prize" in 1979. Eliav, a man of unquestionable character and achievement, was denied a place on the Labor list because he really does believe that his country's salvation lies in the hands of people like Kreisky and the leaders of the PLO. Running on his own, he failed to achieve the paltry 1 percent required for a Knesset seat. Whatever the shortcomings of the Israeli electorate, it still recognized, even if its intellectuals could not, that, as Cynthia Ozick has often pointed out, the result of hallucinating moderation in one's most deadly enemies is, especially in the Middle East, like the result of hallucinating an oasis in the midst of the desert: one ends up choking to death on sand.

14

Operation Moses

"I Rejoice: There Are White Jews Too!" This exclamation came from the mouth of one of the newly arrived Jews from Ethiopia in his first day at Israel's national absorption center for his people in the seaside town of Ashkelon. However ironic the remark may have seemed to those who read it in Israel's newspapers on 4 January 1985, it had not a trace of intended irony in it, for this man, like nearly all of his ancestors and a large majority of his contemporaries, believed that the Beta-Yisrael, called by their Ethiopian countrymen Falashas (the pejorative Amharic word for "strangers"), were the only Jews left alive in the world. His exclamation of joy was followed by one of apprehension about how he and the thousands of his brothers and sisters just rescued from the Gehenna of Ethiopia's chaos and famine would be treated by their exotic white coreligionists: "I am fearful about how they will receive us."

If this new immigrant had been speaking exclusively on the basis of what he might have heard about his people's past relations with white Jews, his fears would have been justified. By the nineteenth century, when the Beta-Yisrael had already been reduced, by mass executions and enslavement, from a powerful tribe of one million to a vulnerable remnant of two hundred thousand, they became a special target of Christian warfare in the form of Protestant missionary invasions supported by the emperor of Ethiopia. Typically, the missionaries were apostate Jews who represented themselves to the Beta-Yisrael as "white Falashas." Probably the most intrepid of these was Henry Stern, a German-Jewish convert who had been ordained by the Prussian-Jewish apostate Anglican bishop of Jerusalem, Michael Solomon Alexander.[1] His evangelizing bore unintended fruit in 1862 when the Ethiopian Jews fled en masse from the missionaries in what they supposed to be the direction of Jerusalem. This attempt to reenact the story of the Exodus led to disaster, with many dying of hunger and malaria. "Had they succeeded, they would have been among the first modern olim to Jerusalem—20 years before what Zionist history calls the First Aliya ['immigration'].''[2] It is not by accident that the Beta-Yisrael celebrate Passover with unique immediacy and with special understanding of the biblical injunction to every Jew that he view the story of enslavement in Egypt and rescue to Israel as his own.

European Jewry became aware of the Beta-Yisrael only as a result of the publicity attaching to the efforts of the Church Militant in Ethiopia. In 1868 Professor Joseph Halévy, a Turkish-born, French-Jewish linguist, was sent by the Alliance Israélite Universelle to assess the situation of the Beta-Yisrael. He made the mistake of introducing himself, as the missionaries had done, as a "white Falasha" and got the deserved rebuke: "You are laughing at us. Are there any white Falashas?" The skepticism and suspicion were allayed only when Halévy could persuade the Beta-Yisrael that the people Israel still lived and flourished outside of Ethiopia, that Jerusalem was a living reality for modern Jews, and that its Jewish inhabitants were indeed white.

Halévy was less successful in persuading his European sponsors that the Ethiopian Falashas were a living Jewish reality, and that they needed and deserved help. Although he brought back with him an Ethiopian *siddur* written in Ge'ez (ancient Ethiopic) and two young Ethiopian Jews as living witnesses, the Alliance, despite publishing his report in its *Bulletin semestrial* in 1868, would not permit publication in book form.

Halévy later succeeded in inspiring one of his students at the Sorbonne, the Orthodox Jew Jacques Faitlovitch (originally from Lodz), to devote his life to understanding, preserving, and rescuing the Beta-Yisrael and their distinctive Jewish culture. Faitlovitch had to struggle not only against the Christian missionaries but against the Jews, including some rabbis, who were only too pleased to turn the "Falashas" (for strangers is all they were to these Jews) over to the evangelists. Faitlovitch undertook expeditions to Ethiopia in 1904 and 1908. The second began just a few months after Rabbi Haim Nahum, the representative of the Alliance, arrived in Addis Ababa. The reason for the apparently pointless duplication was that Faitlovitch believed that the Alliance had largely ignored Halévy's recommendations and was cool to the whole idea of involvement in the plight of the Ethiopian Jews. Faitlovitch disapproved of Nahum because he did not speak Amharic, offended the Beta-Yisrael by traveling on the Sabbath, and allowed himself to be duped by local Ethiopian officials into underestimating the Jewish population by something like 87 percent, an error that buttressed his opposition to establishing Jewish schools (even though he praised the Christian missionaries for their educational efforts).[3]

From the vantage point of the Ethiopian Jews, it must have seemed that Rabbi Nahum found his continuators among leading politicans of Israel's

Labor party during the twenty-nine years of their rule. But then the Ethiopian Jews were not, and are not, well situated to recognize that for a state like Israel there are such things as impossibilities in this world. Whether they viewed the Ethiopian Jews as unpromising raw material for development into socialists or feared that involvement on their behalf would hurt Israel's relations with Haile Selassie and thus impede realization of Labor's aspirations in Africa, it is difficult to say. What does seem certain is that arrogance, ignorance, and thoughtlessness pervaded the attitude of Labor politicans toward the black Jews. For whatever reasons, many years passed without a single shaliach being sent to this substantial community of Jews eager to come on aliyah, and in danger of physical extinction. In his important book on *The Lost Jews*,[4] Louis Rapoport singles out Abba Eban, foreign minister during the years of Israel's campaign to woo black Africa, for special blame. Eban condescended to the Ethiopian Jews and to those interested in their fate: "That is a subject on which my ignorance is vast. . . . I do recall that Norman Bentwich bothered us about the Falashas. And David Kessler of London's *Jewish Chronicle* talked to me about it—I suppose it's a 'gentleman's interest' for him. I believe the embassy used to send prayer books to the Falashas. But it was never considered to be an important issue." All Eban did know for certain about the Falashas was that they were "a very marginal problem."

Another architect of Israel's African assistance program, Golda Meir, was fond of likening the African experience—of oppression, discrimination, enslavement, and murder—to the Jewish historical experience. But her attachment to the metaphorical Jews of Africa often seemed to be matched by her caution about involvement in the fate of the real ones, whom she never mentioned publicly. Rapoport quotes sources who claim that she consistently opposed their immigration to Israel because "they would be miserable here, objects of prejudice" and because trouble was a sufficiently plentiful resource in Israel so that it did not have to be imported from Africa. One of her party colleagues, the late Yisrael Yeshayahu, former Speaker of the Knesset, returned from his visit to Ethiopia convinced that the best solution for the Ethiopian Jews was—to become Christians. This would make the Ethiopian government "happy" and would entitle the Beta-Yisrael to an autonomous region. Yeshayahu did not live to be confronted by those Ethiopian Jews who arrived in Israel with the sign of the cross branded on their foreheads, courtesy of the missionary efforts sponsored by that former linchpin of Israel's African policy, Haile Selassie (whose name, not coincidentally, means "Holy Trinity").

Until the election of Menachem Begin as prime minister in 1977, there were only about two hundred Ethiopian Jews in Israel, and no government minister had ever consented to meet with a representative of the group. Begin, fortified by the 1975 ruling of Sephardi Chief Rabbi Ovadia Yosef that the Beta-Yisrael were indeed Jews, members of the lost tribe of Dan, and by his own conviction that all Israel are indeed brothers, reversed the policy of his socialist predecessors and initiated an active program to help them and to bring them to Zion. But in February 1978, Moshe Dayan (whether inadvertently or by design) destroyed the immigration program by telling the press that Israel was supplying arms to Ethiopia. (Dayan was never fortunate in his public pronouncements concerning blacks. Some years later, it will be recalled, he created a scandal in the United States by declaring that the poor condition of the American army was due to the fact that most of its soldiers were illiterate blacks.) In 1980 Begin intensified what came to be called Operation Moses as the civil war in Ethiopia began to take a heavy toll of lives in the northern provinces of Gondar and Tygre where most of the Ethiopian Jews lived.

Official secrecy about Israel's program to rescue thousands of Ethiopian Jews and bring them from famine-ravaged Ethiopia to the homeland obtained until 2 January 1985, when Yehuda Dominitz, director general of the Immigration Department of the Jewish Agency, told the settlers' newspaper *Nekuda* that "a majority" of the Ethiopian Jews were now in Israel. On 3 January the government reluctantly acknowledged that "more than 10,000" of the Beta-Yisrael had been brought to Israel during the last few years. (Other estimates are that twelve to fifteen thousand have come since 1980, and that six thousand of these came in the last two months of 1984.) Although Israel's program of rescue had been an open secret in certain circles before January, and Arye Dulzin, Jewish Agency executive chairman, had all but revealed it in a statement to the press in early December of 1984, the American and Israeli press had, in general, showed rare and admirable self-restraint in withholding the story, and—as it turned out—for good reason. As soon as Dominitz and then Shimon Peres acknowledged the truth of the rumors, Operation Moses was stopped—by an embarrassed Sudanese government.

Up until 5 January the Ethiopian Jews had been going by foot to Sudanese refugee camps at Gedaref, just across the Ethiopian border, from whence they were trucked to Khartoum, where they boarded planes to Brussels and then were flown to Israel. Although Sudan denied any role in the operation, a spokesman for the Belgian charter airline that had ferried the Jews to Brussels announced that it was halting its participation in the airlift because of pressures coming from the Sudan. According to the Jewish Agency, the last planeload of immigrants arrived on 5 January. At this date, at least four thousand Jews were thought to remain in Sudanese camps, and several thousands more in Ethiopia itself. Dominitz was suspended from his duties by his supervisor in the Immigration Department, Haim Aharon. His claim that he had granted the interview to *Nekuda* on condition that it not be printed was greeted with skepticism, especially among those who recalled that back in 1975 Dominitz had said: "Take a Falasha out of his village, it's like taking a fish out of water. . . . I'm not in favor of bringing them."

The Ethiopian Jews knew that one-eighth to one-tenth of their community had already lost their lives on the trek from Ethiopia to Israel. To this knowledge was now added the bitter news that thousands more of their relatives and friends would be stranded in Sudan and Ethiopia as a result of the loose tongues of Israeli officials. Anger was felt by some of the new immigrants toward officials and journalists. Eyewitnesses described how one group in Ashkelon, when 120 reporters and photographers descended on their absorption center, fled to their rooms "as if from an approaching earthquake," leaving behind them a spokesman who said, "Israel is making publicity for itself, but at whose expense? At ours."

Yet, even among families torn asunder during Operation Moses, this was not the dominant reaction. For the Ethiopian Jews understood quickly that the "white Falashas" who had saved them from hunger and death had brought them not out of self-interest but out of brotherly love. Because the Ethiopians' knowledge of the land of Israel derived from the Bible more than from the world press, they came to Zion expecting a land flowing with milk and honey—and their expectations were, in large part, fulfilled. Food, so lacking in Ethiopia, was lavished on them, and doctors in Petach Tikva's Hasharon Hospital were shocked to see Ethiopian patients hiding slices of bread under their bed sheets for fear that someone would steal their food. They also received in abundance the milk of kindness and the sweetness of fellowship. Rarely has there been such an outpouring of love and sympathy in Israel as that which greeted these immigrants. They are immigrants, one must remember, the great majority of whom arrived not only with black skins, but with bare feet, with emaciated, undernourished bodies covered only in rags, and, in many instances, with tropical diseases like typhus and malaria, the mere mention of which is generally sufficient to strike terror into the hearts of the citizenry of industrialized countries.

To outward view these immigrants looked more resistant to integration or (the official term) "absorption" than any of their predecessors since the founding of the state. They would have to be taught to wear shoes, to use knives and forks and toilets, to take medicines, and to understand that electrical wires are not worms, that gas can be dangerous, and that one cannot take food from groceries without giving money in exchange. Having been rescued from Ethiopia's Marxists and Christians and Moslems and famine, they would also have to be rescued from a state of shock.

Virtually every report on the new immigrants remarked on their preternatural silence, a silence that bespeaks the shock of people transplanted from one planet to another.

None of these obstacles prevented the people of Israel from taking the Beta-Yisrael to their collective heart. Nearly everywhere in the country, the reaction to these black immigrants was: "Thou art bone of my bone, flesh of my flesh, one God made us." Doctors and social workers and even Jewish Agency bureaucrats were efficient, generous, and tactful in dealing with this largest wave of immigrants since the massive influx of Soviet Jews in the 1970s. In a typical episode, a group of two hundred parentless children (out of about fifteen hundred placed in Youth Aliya centers), children who a few days earlier had been without a home, without hope, and without help, arrived in Ashkelon and were housed in a sick fund medical center that had been transformed into an absorption center. The menu for their first meal, which had to take into account both their malnutrition and their unfamiliarity with Western food, was prescribed by doctors. Each child was looked after by workers from the departments of aliyah and *klitah* ("absorption"). An Amharic-speaking volunteer presided as social workers showed the children by hand motions how to cut a potato and eat an egg. The children remained in Ashkelon for just two days, during which time they were washed, clothed, examined by doctors and, depending on their condition, sent either to hospitals or to absorption centers all over the country. (It was deliberate government policy to disperse the immigrants to a variety of towns.) Nevertheless, the seventy absorption centers and thirty youth aliyah institutes were filled to capacity with the Beta-Yisrael, and hotels and convalescent homes had to be rented to accommodate them.

Nearly everywhere there was good will and generosity towards the new immigrants. In Nahariya, for example, the local residents carried their used finery to the 600 Beta-Yisrael who had been lodged in local hotels, and soon the immigrants who arrived in rags were strolling the streets of this "yekke" resort town in a queer sort of *shaatnez* compounded of Adidas and Pierre Cardin. At the Israel Broadcasting Authority efforts were quickly under way to start radio programs in Amharic. Calls for black dolls went out to the United States and were promptly answered. Schools began teaching Israeli children about the history and customs of Ethiopian Jews. Snow was brought in from Mt. Hermon for the amusement of children who had never seen any. Every wedding among the immigrants, every baby born to them, and every diploma granted to one of their college graduates was greeted as a communal triumph. The front page of the tabloid *Hadashot* featured a large photograph of the wedding of a young immigrant couple with the caption: "How Do You Say 'Mazel Tov' in Amharic?" A still larger photograph in *Ma'ariv* showed a small blonde girl with her arm around a smaller Ethiopian girl, with the caption: "Zionism as it used to be: the young will once again teach their parents the language of the new land."

Occasionally, perhaps inevitably, the good will that expressed itself in the desire to integrate the Ethiopian Jews ran afoul of the officially declared policy of encouraging them to retain their own Jewish culture— their prayers, music, and dances. On the one hand, the Voice of Israel ushered in the Passover holiday with a lengthy program about the Passover customs of the Beta-Yisrael; on the other, Jewish Agency officials distributed Haggadot translated into Amharic for people whose traditional celebration of the holiday is derived directly from the Bible and not at all from the Haggadah. A "veteran" immigrant, interviewed on the aforementioned program, recalled with good-humored resignation that when he saw all the shiny metal utensils laid out at his first Israeli seder he thought he had been brought to an operating room.

It is worth remembering that the welcome accorded by the people of Israel to the Ethiopian Jews is not the universal practice of mankind with respect to distressed immigrants, and particularly penniless, starving, black immigrants. It is, of course, true that from its inception one raison d'être for the state was to be a safe haven for Jews fleeing persecution. It is also true that Israel's very existence is predicated on continuing and increasing aliyah. Nevertheless, a merely rational observer of Israeli life might well have predicted a very different and much icier reception for the Ethiopians at that particular point in the country's history. Israel in 1984 was a country seared by war, a country that every night turned with sick dread to the television screen to see the burials of soldiers, mostly very young, killed not in purposeful battle but in retreat from a conflict widely viewed as one of Israel's greatest misfortunes since the founding of the state. It was a country beset by grave economic difficulties, including rampant inflation, a severe shortage of housing for young couples, a ruined currency, and rapidly increasing unemployment. These are not as a rule the circumstances that conduce to the warm reception of thousands of destitute new immigrants, who will need not only Hebrew, but housing and jobs. At a time when all budgets, including the crucial one for defense, were being cut, the Israeli government was spending hundreds of millions of unbudgeted dollars on absorption of Ethiopian immigrants.[5]

Why have the people of Israel, so often sermonized by their Diaspora coreligionists for their lack of ethical idealism, their inadequate relation to Torah, and their gross materialism, opened their hearts and their purses to the Jews of Ethiopia? Why, for example, did the Moroccan community of Jews in Israel, which has a history of bitterness over its unsuccessful absorption in the early 1950s, which continues to claim that its members are discriminated against by Ashkenazi-dominated institutions, and which is disproportionately harmed by spreading unemployment in development towns, go out of its way, at its annual Mimouna[6] festivities, to extend a special hand of welcome to the Ethiopian Jews and give them a central role (the priestly blessing of President Herzog) in the official celebration in Jerusalem?

Part of the answer, to be sure, has to do with the intrinsic value of the immigrants themselves. Those who have worked with the Beta-Yisrael invariably speak with admiration of their gracious manners, filial devotion, and elementary decency. Teachers at the absorption centers have expressed amazement at a dedication and devotion "not of this world"; they have described students of Hebrew at their desks half an hour before class starts in hopes the teacher will arrive early, and have found children poring over their books until midnight in dormitories where the lights are turned out at ten. Uri Gordon, head of Youth Aliyah, even predicted that the Ethiopian Jews would prove to be the rescuers of those who have rescued them—that they would help raise Israelis from the depression in which they are sunk and inject new life into the Zionist enterprise.

But beyond this, many Israelis sensed that they shared with these outcast people something more than the human status, namely, a common history and common hopes and aspirations. The photographs of joyous family reunions, of grievous family separations, and, above all, of orphaned children, brought to the mind's eye of countless Israelis the pictures of European Jewish survivors of the Holocaust. The overriding wish of the Ethiopian Jews has been the same as that of the remnants of European Jewry after the Second World War: to reach Israel. Israelis with a longer historical memory also recognized the similarity between the religious persecution of the ancient Jewish community of Ethiopia and that of ancient (if not equally ancient[7]) Jewish communities of Eastern Europe by Christian establishments eternally fearful of a primal Jewish taint.[8] Finally, Israelis for whom the Hebrew Bible has a unique resonance—and they are still the vast majority of the population—could not but feel that the great themes of the story of Joseph and his brothers and of Jacob and his sons were being reenacted before their eyes. The brotherhood between Israeli and Ethiopian Jews was reaffirming itself, in despite of decades of betrayal and neglect; and among the Beta-Yisrael the ties that bind the souls of sons and fathers showed their magical capacity to survive unspeakable suffering and shattering upheaval. One young man who had years earlier left his father behind in Ethiopia, apparently forever, told a reporter: "I began a new life here, learned Hebrew, married, had a son. And now suddenly my father arrives and discovers that he has a grandson. I did not believe that I would see my father alive again."

It must be stressed that the Israeli sense of a bond of unity between herself and the Jews of Ethiopia is national and religious, not ethnic. The Ethiopian Jews do not look or eat or dress or dance or talk or sing like any of the major ethnic groups of Israel. But, like every other Jewish "tribe," they have been called into existence by God, chosen by Him to accept Torah and chosen by the world to be punished for having done so. The phenomenon of their ready acceptance by the people of Israel suggests that in this allegedly secular country Jewish religion is, after all, a principle of unity that is ultimately far stronger than the centrifugal forces nourished by the advocates of ethnicity.[9]

Ironically, the only major group in Israel that finds ethnicity more important than religion in estimating the Jewishness of the Ethiopian Jews is the Chief Rabbinate and its followers. The current occupants of this office, whose very authority is shamelessly defined by ethnic boundaries, the Ashkenazi Chief Rabbi Avraham Shapiro and the Sephardi Chief Rabbi Mordechai Eliahu, have ruled that the Ethiopian Jews are not "full" Jews because their marriage ceremonies were not valid, or because their divorce proceedings were improper, or because they received converts who were not converted according to Halachah, or because they had customs "strange to the spirit of Judaism," or whatever the chief rabbinic whim of the moment may be. Equally whimsical have been the Chief Rabbinate's conditions for the Ethiopians' conversion (to the Beta-Yisrael it must seem that the "white Falashas" always want them to convert to something other than what they are); one week it is ritual immersion, then it is symbolic circumcision, then a vow of loyalty to Torah, and then various combinations of the three. Some of the more zealous acolytes of the chief rabbis have prevented the Beta-Yisrael from praying at the Western Wall. The Chabad movement, well known for the stringent standards it applies to *baalei teshuvah* in the United States and Europe, in 1985 refused to accept any more Ethiopian children in its schools and was "checking the Jewish status" of those already enrolled (in Beersheva, it was doing so in the dark because the municipality, in retaliation, cut off electricity to Chabad's Uziel school).

The short and ready condemnation of the Chief Rabbinate's stand as predictable resentment of a Jewish tradition that developed without benefit of the oral law and therefore without benefit of rabbis, is inadequate, as is the labeling of it (for example, by Israel's most aggressive anticlerical parliamentarian, Shulamit Aloni) as "racism." Rabbinic resistance to acceptance of the Beta-Yisrael as Jews is essentially, if not exclusively, modern. Another chief rabbi, David ben Solomon Ibn Avi (known as "Radbaz"), who served in this capacity for forty years in Egypt, ruled that the Beta-Yisrael were indeed Jews. But that was in the sixteenth century. The nineteenth-century German orthodox scholar, Azriel Hildesheimer, supported this view, as did Israel's first chief rabbi, Avraham Yitzhak Ha'Kohen Kook. The recent history of rabbinic refusal to accept the Beta-Yisrael as Jews, both in Israel's National Religious party and in its Chief Rabbinate, is mainly an instance of modern Judaism's tendency to slide from religion into ethnicity. As Howard Sachar remarked of a 1968 court ruling about the rabbinate's refusal to register a Falasha for marriage: "The Falashas . . . were suspected by the rabbinate of having intermarried in Ethiopia generations before, and therefore since they weren't Jewish by *nationality* (ethnic identification), they were not entitled to Jewish *religious* rights."[10]

If it is ironic that Israel's appointed guardians of talmudic tradition comprise the only group in the country that places ethnicity ahead of religion in this matter, it is scandalous that they have made a subject of daily public discussion out of the Jewish identity of people who are religiously observant, who have suffered for countless generations because of their Jewish identity, and who have been brought to Israel under a law that applies only to Jews. In a sharp attack on the rabbinic authorities, Shmuel Katz pointed out that their daily pronouncements on the Jewishness of the Ethiopian Jews showed them to be either ignorant or contemptuous of the talmudic dictum that "putting your friend to shame in public is equivalent to shedding blood." Indeed, a small group of the immigrants responded to the Chief Rabbinate by threatening, on 4 January, to shed their own blood if they were not recognized by Israel as complete Jews equal to all others. But such reactions are not representative of the community at large, which, despite its profound resentment of the rabbinic demand for conversion, is not given to the language of threat and violence.

The humane and generous reception of the Ethiopian Jews by the Israeli people and the decision by the Israeli government to treat them not as remnants of the Stone Age who might be taught enough Hebrew words to enable them to become hewers of wood and drawers of water, but as full citizens of a free and independent state, seemed to offer conclusive proof that Zionism is not racism. But it was naive of politicians to voice the hope that Israel's permanent enemies would view the matter in this light. Assorted Marxists around the world echoed, with local variations, the official statement issued by the Marxist Ethiopian government's Foreign

Ministry that "It is a serious affront to the sensibilities of world public opinion that the current drought and famine in Ethiopia should be invoked as an excuse for the Israeli-engineered . . . massive kidnapping of the Falashas. . . . The entire operation conjures up the revival of the slave trade. . . . [an] act of brigandage . . . based on the claim that the Falashas are Jews."

But it was not only Marxists who spewed fire and vitriol at Israel for its rescue mission. In Germany, for example, the prize for moral obscenity was won not by any of that country's large number of certified crazies and anti-Semites among Greens, Reds, and Browns, but by the Israeli experts of Germany's main television news program on the first network (ARD), watched nightly by tens of millions of Germans. The main message of the report, which came within days of Israel's official acknowledgment of the rescue operation, was that here was the culminating, irresistible demonstration that Zionism was another version of South African racism. The network's reporter in Israel, Peter Dudzig, conveyed the first lesson of the evening, which was that the Israelis do not want the Ethiopian Jews at all. Why else would they have intentionally leaked news of the airlift to the press? The second lesson, which was taught by the network's commentator on Israeli affairs, Hans Leschleitner, was that Israelis are racists because they did indeed airlift the Ethiopian Jews to Israel. Leschleitner inveighed mightily against the "selectivity" and "egoism" of a state and religion that uprooted hungry people from native soil and transplanted them to an alien land, all as part of a cynical arms deal posing as "humanitarianism." He then trotted out the, by now, formulaic equation of Israelis with Nazis. Once the yellow patch had the word "Jew" inside it, but now it enclosed the label "hungry"; and now the selections and transports were being conducted by the Jews themselves. Did not all this prove, Leschleitner concluded with a rhetorical flourish, that all the resolutions of the UN and of the African Solidarity congresses equating Zionism with racism were in fact true? It must have come as a disappointment to some of Leschleitner's viewers, given the rich inventiveness of modern German imagination where Jews are concerned, that he neglected to identify as the ultimate instance of Israel's racism her failure to ship her own citizens southward to starve along with the Ethiopians.

Rarely have the enemies of Jacob offered more convincing evidence of the truth of the old saying that what matters is not what the gentiles say but what the Jews do. In fact, if no one is watching too closely, this might be one of those rare moments when Israel can take the risk of congratulating herself on the greatness of her people and the littleness of her enemies. Operation Moses has demonstrated that it is the Jews and not their adversaries who have rightly understood the Lord's question (Amos 9:7): "Are you not like the children of the Ethiopians unto Me, O Children of Israel?"

Notes

1. Alexander was at the center of the Jerusalem bishopric affair of 1841, the event that shattered the faith of John Henry Newman in the Church of England.
2. Shoshana Ben-Dor and Jeff Halper, "Fasika and the Beta-Yisrael," *Jerusalem Post,* 5 April 1985.
3. Faitlovitch deals with these matters in *Quer durch Abessinien* (1910).
4. Louis Rapoport, *The Lost Jews,* (New York: Stein and Day, 1979).
5. On 17 April 1985 Shimon Peres told students at Tel Aviv University that the absorption process had thus far cost $300 million. "This was not budgeted. But I think you all agree it was worth spending less on other things to save lives."
6. From Maimon, the North African sage who was father of the Rambam.
7. Yitzhak Ben-Zvi, in *The Exiled and the Redeemed* (1963) enumerates three theories as to the origins of the Beta-Yisrael. One traces their ancestry to King Solomon's men who brought the Queen of Sheba back from Jerusalem and then settled in Ethiopia; a second claims they were direct descendants of the Jewish mercenaries of Yeb (Elephantine) and Sweneh (Assouan), who migrated south and settled in Ethiopia; a third holds that they were the direct descendants of Arabian Jews who came to Ethiopia in the sixth century C.E. Ben-Zvi favors the second theory.
8. In 1267 the Church Council of Breslau declared: "In view of the fact that Poland is a *nova plantatio* in the body of Christianity, there is reason to fear that her Christian population will fall an easy prey to the influence of the superstition and evil habits of the Jews living among them, the more so as the Christian religion took root in the hearts of the faithful of these countries at a later date and in a more feeble manner." When the Jesuits descended on Ethiopia in 1541 they came quickly to the conclusion that there was a "dangerous Hebraic mould" to the Abyssinian Christian Church, from which it required urgent rescue.
9. Israel's only ethnic political party, the Moroccan Tami group, virtually collapsed in the last election.
10. One of Israel's voluble professorial experts on Africa, Mordechai Abir, also rejects the Beta-Yisrael as ethnically insufficient to be as Jewish as he is: "I say they are converts of converts."

15

Denis Goldberg, Jerry Falwell, and the Wise Men of Chelm

"A blind horse," according to the Yiddish proverb, "makes straight for the pit." This is as close as we are likely to get to a plausible explanation of one of Israel's exercises in international rescue in 1985.

Leading Israeli politicians, having apparently learned exactly nothing from the earlier Jacobo Timerman episode about the extreme risks involved in prying Jewish radicals loose from the jails in which they sit for assorted crimes against reactionary regimes in the Diaspora, succeeded in February 1985 in bringing to Israel the South African insurrectionary, Denis Goldberg.

Goldberg arrived after twenty-two years of imprisonment in South Africa on 189 counts of sabotage and terror alleged to have been committed by him (in collusion with other leaders of the military wing of the banned African National Congress) between December 1960 and July 1964. Among those involved in the long, complicated, and difficult campaign to secure Goldberg's release were MK Avraham Katz-Oz, one (thus far unidentified) "senior minister in the government of former Prime Minister Yitzhak Shamir," President Chaim Herzog, Herut Lapid of the United Kibbutz movement's Prisoner Rehabilitation Committee, and Eliahu Lankin, Israel's ambassador to South Africa.

Indeed, so many Establishment figures worked so long and so hard to win Goldberg's release that Russian immigrants in Israel might have been forgiven for wondering aloud why the Jewish tradition of redeeming captives from gentile prisons seemed so much more compelling with respect to a Jewish Communist in a South African prison than to a Jewish Zionist in a Communist labor camp. No diplomatic campaign comparable to that undertaken for Goldberg was ever attempted for Anatoly Shcharansky, who was, of course, held in conditions that did not lend themselves to "studying for several degrees and potting plants," as Goldberg did in his Pretoria accommodations.

The first reports of Goldberg's arrival from Pretoria barely mentioned, and even then fleetingly and in the vaguest terms, his application of his engineering expertise to the production of explosives for terrorists. The stress was rather on the "humanitarian" aspect of the rescue, and on the reunion of Goldberg with his daughter, who had lived at an Upper Galilee kibbutz for two years, and his wife, who flew in from London for the occasion.

Less emphasis was given to the fact that Goldberg had been separated from his wife and two children not by imprisonment but by his own decision, made in May 1963, that the revolution was more important than domestic responsibilities. No emphasis whatever was given in these early reports, glowing with euphoria and self-satisfaction, to Goldberg's doctrinaire Marxism, his anti-Zionism, his wide-ranging bloodthirstiness, or his support of the PLO. But the terrible secrets gradually began to emerge. Goldberg had no sooner arrived at Ben-Gurion Airport than he launched into an attack on the Israeli government for maintaining ties with the South African regime. Even this did not disturb Israel's more sanguine journalists, who assumed that a man so splendidly attached to principle would naturally want to show, at the first possible opportunity, that he was not disinclined to bite the hand that fed him.

Goldberg's next public appearance came on 4 March, on the television program called "This is the Time," conducted by Ram Evron. Preceding him on that evening's show was Jerry Falwell, the prominent American evangelical minister and active supporter of Israel in the United States. Nothing could be more instructive about a large segment of Israel's educated classes than the difference between the treatment meted out to Falwell and to Goldberg, both on this program and in the published reviews of it.

Scowling darkly at his first guest, moderator Evron made it clear that poor Falwell had much to answer for, much to justify—his support for Israel and for Zionism, his opposition to abortion and homosexuality, and his continued adherence, despite his apparent friendliness to Jews, to the doctrines of his own religion. Surely Falwell had ulterior motives for supporting Israel? Surely his real aim was to convert Jews? And, beyond these parochial Jewish issues, how could Falwell, as a professing Christian, expend so much energy fighting abortion and so little on genuine "moral issues" like those the Bible stresses? Evron dismissed with contempt Falwell's mention of the millions of dollars his organization had contributed to the poor in America and to the starving in Sudan: "that's charity, not social justice," Evron sneered.

Viewers eager to discover precisely what Evron meant by dedication to moral issues and social justice were presently to be enlightened. The camera moved to Goldberg; instantly, Evron became a different person. The sudden transformation of his countenance from glowering hostility to smiling benignity suggested the lurid metamorphosis of the hideous Mr. Hyde back into the kindly Dr. Jekyll. The icy hostility displayed to Falwell melted into oily sycophancy in the presence of Goldberg. Whereas the Christian Falwell had, repeatedly, to justify his Zionism, the Marxist Goldberg, who had been announcing his anti-Zionism at approximately hourly intervals since his arrival, was not asked a single hard question about his past involvement in terror or his continuing dedication to violence.

Evron took it for granted that, in these matters, so delicate a conscience as Goldberg's not only had the right to go its own way, but to go its own way without any questions asked. Indeed, Goldberg was offered to viewers as a living embodiment of that devotion to "social justice" lacking in Falwell, who is not known ever to have designed or thrown any explosive devices. Few viewers could have missed the implied suggestion that if only Jerry Falwell would take moral instruction from a prophetic voice like that of Denis Goldberg, he, too, on his next visit to Israel, would be received with the beggarlike gratitude that journalists like Evron now reserve for the enemies of Israel who deign to set foot in the country.

It goes without saying that for Israel's leftist media critics, Evron had been "too Israel-orientated" [sic], insufficiently fierce with Falwell, and deplorably lacking in respectful awe for Goldberg's utopian convictions, stern dedication, and heroic deeds. Philip Gillon of the *Jerusalem Post* was outraged to the point of incoherence by the extent to which "Falwell was allowed to get away with murder" by Evron. The "murder" consisted of Falwell's critical view of the vast American welfare system and his refusal to recognize—in Gillon's incomparable words—"woman's right to decide what should happen to her own body and a person's right to seek sexual pleasure with whatever type of partner he prefers," that is to say, abortion and homosexuality. Evron further offended Gillon's sense of the fitness of things by suggesting that Goldberg's rescue by, and arrival in, a country called Israel had even the slightest importance in comparison with his political and military struggle against the South African regime.

In *Ma'ariv,* Dalia Ravikovitch, like Gillon a political columnist masquerading as a television critic, expressed irritation that, just because he loved humanity more than Zion, no government official had been waiting at the airport to welcome Goldberg, and no flags of triumph were flying. The previous governments of Israel, she alleged, stood shamed and disgraced because they had not gone to work earlier, more diligently, and at higher levels of diplomacy to secure Goldberg's release. He was, after all, a genuine representative of the noble tradition of Jews who fight on behalf of the oppressed of other peoples, a tradition powerful among Jews everywhere—except, alas, in Israel.

Having finished her ablutions at the shrine of Goldberg, Ravikovitch turned with rage on Falwell. (She was even revolted by the fact that Evron had asked a certified friend of the human species, a "prisoner of conscience" like Goldberg, to sit in the same chair that had been polluted by the presence of Falwell.) Falwell was another Flatto-Sharon (the former MK, who was a fugitive from French law); his holy trinity consisted of Jesus, Reagan, and Begin; he cared nothing for the plight of the Palestinian Arabs; his only abilities were those of deceit, distortion, and lying; and his philosophy was not that of the miracle-maker of Galilee but of General Motors.

Although many viewers of this much-discussed television program must have found it peculiar that Goldberg referred compulsively to his interlocutor as "comrade," the interview dealt primarily with nonpolitical matters and so kept alive in the hearts of Goldberg's Israeli sponsors the hope that they might yet conceal from the general public the ugly secret of his views about Israel and those who work for its destruction. But their hopes were soon dashed by the publication of an interview with Goldberg in the weekly magazine *Koteret Rashit.* Although a condition of Goldberg's release from prison had been his signed undertaking (over which he "agonized") that he would not "plan, instigate or participate in acts of violence for the achievement of political ends" in South Africa, he appeared to have no qualms about condoning and advocating PLO violence against the men, women, children, and babies of Israel. Not even the king of terror, Yasir Arafat, has been so brutally cynical as Goldberg in declaring that nearly every Israeli killed by a PLO bomb in a bus, supermarket, street, school, or nursery deserves his or her fate. According to this exemplar of moral sensitivity, "terror . . . is not a moral issue." As for justice, Goldberg found its perfect expression in the bombs the PLO places on Israeli buses because "most of the bus passengers and those wounded by explosive devices are not innocent, since they support the oppression of Palestinians." To these noble and touching sentiments he added the qualification that if by some unlikely chance there are innocent victims of PLO terror—perhaps he thought of the children of Ma'alot and Kiryat Shemona—they just "happened to be in the wrong place at the wrong time."

No sooner had Goldberg's espousal of PLO terror against Israelis become public knowledge than Israel's more flamboyant politicians reacted, in predictable fashion. Tehiya Knesset member Geula Cohen called for Goldberg's expulsion from Israel on the grounds that he had "justified the murder of innocent women and children" and might well be expected to lend his considerable skills in making bombs to the PLO just as he had lent them to the African National Congress. By contrast, Citizens' Rights Knesset member Yossi Sarid urged that Goldberg be given the honor of lighting one of the twelve commemorative torches during Israel's Independence Day celebrations in May. He also expressed the hope that Goldberg would one day learn "in what ways Israel is similar to South Africa and in what ways different." (Since Sarid has often likened Israel to South Africa, he might not be the best one to instruct Goldberg in his comparative studies, which in any case would have had to be completed very quickly since the unwilling student announced his desire to leave Israel as soon as possible.)

What is the significance, for Jews and Israel and Zionism, of the Goldberg affair? Is trouble so scarce in Israel that it must be imported from South Africa? Did someone in the Foreign Ministry take too much to heart the Jewish folktale in which a family miserably crowded into its tiny cottage is advised by a rabbi to take in, temporarily, its most obnoxious relatives (and perhaps a goat and cow, as well) so that after the unwelcome guests leave, the cottage will seem spacious and pleasant? Does the Jewish tradition of redeeming Jewish captives from gentile jails apply in a case where the captive has been imprisoned for reasons having nothing to do with his Jewish identity, does not in fact consider himself Jewish, and identifies strongly with the enemies of Jews? Is there perhaps a touch of what enemies of Zionism call "racism" in Israel's ransoming of the "Jewish" Goldberg rather than the black Nelson Mandela? Did the founders of Zionism fail to anticipate that "normalization" of the Jews in Zion might make their intellectuals as receptive to anti-Semitism as the intellectuals of any other people? Could even the most obtuse politician fail to guess that a rootless Jew deeply involved in Marxist revolutionism in Africa would have, where Israel is concerned, the brutal views and the blood lust of Denis Goldberg? Is the infatuation of so many Israelis with the Jewish enemies of Zion a demonstration of what is often called "Jewish self-hatred" or of a monstrous self-love that seeks gratification in the contemplation of its own image freed from the coils of time and space?

New immigrants living in absorption centers in Israel often insist that one cannot begin to fathom this country or to answer such questions without seeing Israel as another Chelm, formerly the Eastern European capital of Jewish folly. For the overwhelming message of the tales of Chelm is encapsulated in a Yiddish proverb that complements the one with which I began: "God never told anyone to be stupid."

16

NBC's War in Lebanon: The Distorting Mirror

I think the press ought to be arrogant.
—Reuven Frank, president,
NBC News (11 May 1983)

I never wonder to see men wicked, but
I often wonder to see them not ashamed.
—Jonathan Swift

Introduction

A word fitly spoken is like apples of gold in
pictures of silver.
—Proverbs 25:11

It probably took several centuries from the time that printing was invented for the superstitious belief that whatever is in print must be true, to die out. Now, in the age of television, we face a parallel danger in the widespread belief that "pictures don't lie." In fact, as I shall frequently have occasion to suggest in the following pages, pictures, like words, can and do lie, for pictures, like words, are created and manipulated by men, whose reputation for probity has been open to question since the expulsion from Eden. The injunction to "hold the mirror up to nature" sounds sensible enough until we remember that mirrors may be dirty or clean, concave or convex, cracked or whole; and that everything depends on which portion of nature is chosen to be reflected, how often it is reflected, and how much is revealed of the history of the reflected images. Not the least danger of distortion in the use of the mirror is the tendency of the owner to hold it up to himself and make it into the deceiving mirror of self-love, a mirror that reflects not life but the spectator.

If, as James Billington argued in his book, *Fire in the Minds of Men* (1980), the press, once known as the Fourth Estate,[1] has now "in many

217

ways replaced the First [Estate], the Church," we are under the most compelling obligation to ask whether journalists are using their enormous power for good or for evil, responsibly or recklessly. Americans have long assumed that their press, unlike the British and European versions, will clearly distinguish between news and editorial opinion. Even in the wake of the war in Lebanon we may still take some comfort from the fact that American journalists generally lagged far behind their European and British colleagues in the art of cloaking naked partisanship in tendentious reporting. But the tendency of our television news media to flout the conventions of balance, fairness, and accuracy in the interests of political ideology is growing, not receding. NBC's disregard for these conventions (and, in the case of "fairness," federal regulations) was by no means *sui generis;* but I have chosen to analyze NBC rather than its competitors because the malpractices common to the three major networks were drawn out into extreme or radical form by NBC. Neither of the other networks, for example, allowed so complete a monopoly on the expression of biased editorial opinion on the war as NBC did in making John Chancellor its sole editorialist. The closest NBC came to acknowledging that there might be a different view from the anti-Israeli one that Chancellor expressed several times a week was on 4 August, 1982 in the wake of Chancellor's intemperate outburst against "imperial Israel" on 2 August. Tom Brokaw read from three letters disagreeing with Chancellor's views, but apparently took care that the three selected were all by people with names readily identifiable as Jewish, and added that in any case reaction to Chancellor was about evenly divided between those who agreed with him and those who did not. NBC also outdid the other networks in its relentless insistence (for example, on 24 and 28 June and 2, 4, 12, and 13 August) that American public opinion was turning against Israel. Since NBC is one of the main shapers of public opinion, this insistence (based on the flimsiest of evidence) did little to shore up its reputation for impartiality. NBC was also the only network that consistently refused to acknowledge the existence of PLO censorship.

My discussion of NBC-TV's coverage of the war in Lebanon extends from 4 June through 31 August 1982, and is based on videotapes of every night of evening news during that period. My observations touch on six major subjects or problems in NBC's reporting and commentary: (1) the subject of censorship; (2) the question of civilian casualties; (3) deliberate falsifications; (4) the terminology of bias; (5) the missing background of the war; and (6) selective and tendentious interviewing.

Finally, a distinction is in order. On this subject as on most others, generalizations about an organization cannot authoritatively render the whole truth about every individual who works for it. Not everybody who reported the Lebanon war for NBC was engaged, as Mudd, Chancellor, Brokaw, Mallory, and Reynolds appeared to be, in a private war against Israel. Whatever objections one may have to particular reports and even the surrender to shared media clichés by Bob Kur, Rick Davis, or Martin Fletcher, it would be unfair to impute to them any such will to deceive as moved many of their colleagues. These men acquitted themselves honorably under very trying conditions; but their efforts in the direction of seeing clearly and telling what they saw in a plain way were nearly lost in the plethora of calculated distortions that comprised NBC's overall approach to the war in Lebanon.

The Subject of Censorship

> *In Lebanon, Palestinian commanders permitted camera crews and correspondents to move freely into areas under attack, but not to photograph military targets hidden among civilian offices and apartments.*
> —John Martin, ABC News

No theme, not even that of civilian casualties, was more relentlessly pursued by NBC-TV than that of censorship, that is to say, of Israeli censorship, for censorship by Israel's adversaries was blithely accepted by NBC as an aspect of the natural order of things. The opening salvo in NBC's campaign against Israeli military censorship came on 5 June and established the pattern that would be followed throughout the summer. Jessica Savitch, introducing a report by Vic Aicken from northern Israeli "settlements and villages," sternly warned that "It's censored by the Israeli military." Aicken himself stressed at the outset of his report that he could only show pictures "allowed by the Israel censor," and concluded the report with these words: "Vic Aicken with a censored report from northern Israel." Then Savitch, like a patient schoolmaster who believes in nothing so much as incessant repetition, remarked: "His report was heavily censored by the Israelis and half of the pictures he wanted to send out were cut." Then, presumably for the benefit of those viewers who are deaf or who can understand nothing unless it is repeated five times, NBC placed next to Savitch a large placard saying "ISRAEL CENSORSHIP," at the same time that she audibly and visibly inhaled her scarcely controllable outrage at this violation of NBC's inalienable rights.

In the days and weeks to follow it became clear that NBC was determined to retaliate whenever possible for the injury inflicted on its "right to know" by Israeli censorship. Not only did reports from Israel and from southern Lebanon begin and end with graphic and oral references to Israeli censorship, but reporting of the war was periodically punctuated with entire program segments devoted to the subject of Israeli censorship. Thus, what might have begun as a piece of valuable information about the difficulties of reporting the war soon became a means of editorializing, almost unceasingly, against Israel. The venomous tone and compulsive repetition suggested that people in the upper echelons of NBC News had allowed their sense of outrage to determine editorial policy. Reuven Frank and his colleagues had made resolutions in anger, and were not to be moved from them even after the anger had subsided, just as fiery volcanic eruptions harden into rock after they have cooled.

The anger was much in evidence in Roger Mudd's remarks of 18 June about Israel's censoring of two cassettes of interviews with PLO prisoners and "refusing" to say why, and in the furious outbursts of 23 and 24 June by Brokaw and Chancellor. Brokaw started the program of 23 June with the ritualized announcement that Israel had broken yet another cease-fire, then switched to Steve Mallory, whose voice came out of a blackened screen against which were boldly superimposed the words: "PICTURES CENSORED." Since NBC had decided (perhaps, even from its own point of view, unwisely) that no amount of repetitious haranguing on this subject was excessive, Brokaw followed up with a separate story on the Israeli refusal to transmit pictures of injured children, damage, and casualties in a Beirut neighborhood. The visual backdrop showed an Israeli flag, cassettes, and "Israeli Censorship." Then, in high dudgeon, Brokaw declared that the story had nothing to do with Israeli national security, and, in a voice dripping with sarcasm, noted that Menachem Begin had complained of "corrupt media."

The fury against Israel over the censorship spilled over that evening into a particularly egregious distortion of facts by Roger Mudd. Trumpeting what sounded like a spectacular revelation of yet more Machiavellian skullduggery by Israel, he reported that the war in Lebanon had been coordinated with a "campaign" against Palestinians in "Jordan's West Bank, which is occupied by Israel." When the picture switched to Martin Fletcher in said "West Bank," however, viewers got nothing more than a reasonably sober account of Israeli troops quelling demonstrations by Arab university students in favor of the PLO. Mudd's revelation proved to be mere wind. Mudd tried a similar stunt the following evening, 24 June, in his introduction to Steve Mallory's typically sensational report of blood, chaos, filth, and fire in West Beirut, caused in part by the explosion of powerful car bombs of unknown origin. Since not even Mallory was about to assign the blame for these to Israel, Mudd took it upon himself to do so by insidious juxtaposition: "The Reagan White House revealed today that Prime Minister Begin promised President Reagan on Monday that Israel would not try to capture Beirut. By making Israel's pledge public . . . the White House was bringing pressure on him to live up to it. But as we will see in a moment . . . sending in an army is not the only way to destroy a city. It can be shelled to death from without and within." But just in case there were viewers who did not get Mudd's message, Brokaw was ready with yet another blast at Israeli censors for allowing such scenes (which might reflect unfavorably on the PLO) to be transmitted while deleting material that had nothing to do with Israel's national security. Now that its anchorman had editorialized against Israeli censorship on two consecutive nights, one might suppose that the subject had been, for the moment, exhausted. But no, NBC's resident sage John Chancellor added a long editorial on the matter.

Chancellor began with the astounding remark that "Censorship in the Middle East is getting to be a real problem, and it sometimes makes it hard to cover the story." Chancellor did not remind his audience that Israel is the only democratic country in the Middle East, the only one in which there has always been a free press, or that censorship, ranging from authoritarian to totalitarian and employing methods ranging from persuasion to coercion to murder, has, time out of mind, prevailed in the Middle East. Had he done so, viewers might have wondered why Middle East censorship never became a "problem" for Chancellor and his colleagues until practiced, in the midst of a hard-fought war, by Israel. In the course of this diatribe he did mention that although Syria helpfully transmitted the tape that Israel had intercepted, Syria "enforces a total ban on stories about its own military." Yet Syria's far more stringent censorship was mentioned only casually and "incidentally"; it did not, for Chancellor, constitute a "problem." Exactly why this should be so is not clear, especially since Syrian censorship had earlier in 1982 effectively kept television cameras away from the Syrian city of Hamma (the fifth largest in the country) while the Syrian army ruthlessly massacred, with tanks and artillery, between fifteen and twenty thousand of its own, unarmed citizens, who had been guilty of refractory behavior toward the regime. Where then was Chancellor's concern for the American public's right to know, and for NBC's right to film? Was he not then, and is he not now, troubled by the "problem" that very little, if any, attention is paid by the news media to slaughters that cannot be photographed although they are known to have happened? We know that his boss, Reuven Frank, is not. For when the president of NBC News was taxed with this question, he responded, with his characteristic moral tact: "There isn't interest in the Copts or the Kurds, or the massacre in Burundi . . . so you don't cover them." To talk of what "should" be covered is impermissible because it suggests moral criteria, with which his profession is unconcerned. "You cover what you think is interesting for the viewers. I can't imagine anybody getting upset about the Copts"—as if it had never occurred to Mr. Frank that the absence of "coverage" explained the absence of "interest."

Although Chancellor acknowledged that Syria's censorship policy left something to be desired, he expressed no misgivings about PLO treatment of journalists and even went out of his way to remark that "There is no censorship in Beirut. . . ." This must have come as a stunning revelation to the countless journalists who in recent years have testified to what the *Guardian* of London (one of the most fiercely anti-Israeli papers in the world) called the "censorship by terror" that prevailed in Beirut, and the *Economist* named the phenomenon of "publish and perish." On 22 February 1982, John Kifner, the *New York Times* correspondent in Beirut, wrote:

> To work here as a journalist is to carry fear with you as faithfully as your notebook. It is the constant knowledge that there is nothing you can do to protect yourself and that nothing has ever happened to any assassin. In this atmosphere, a journalist must often weigh when, how, and sometimes even whether, to record a story. . . . There is a pervasive belief among the Beirut press corps that correspondents should be extremely wary of incurring the wrath of the Syrian regime of President Hafez al-Assad.

In February 1982 Zeev Chafetz, then director of Israel's Government Press Office, charged that substantial segments of the Western news media follow a double standard in reporting and commentary on the Arab-Israeli conflict because they fear and respect Arab terror, but take for granted and abuse the freedom allowed them in Israel's open society. He explicitly charged that terror prevented critical reporting on the PLO and Syria, and that ABC's wide-ranging attack on Israel (in the program "20/20") had a causal connection with the murder in Beirut in July 1981 of Sean Toolan, ABC-TV's correspondent there. (Toolan's sin, apparently, had been his contribution to a program by Geraldo Rivera on PLO terrorism). Chafetz also claimed that five U.S. journalists had, in 1981, been held for almost twenty-four hours by Palestinian Arab terrorists, and the incident was not reported in their newspapers for over six months (they had been released after their lives were threatened and their employers promised not to report on the episode).

Over a period of five years a series of threatening letters, assassination attempts, explosions, and murders by the PLO intimidated the Lebanese press to the point where, according to Edouard George, senior editor of Beirut's French language daily, *L'Orion Du Jour,* "not one of them dared to write or broadcast the truth." Peter Meyer-Ranke, Middle East correspondent for Germany's Springer chain of papers, said he had personally observed "self-censorship, self-restriction, and silence" by his colleagues in Beirut. Among those who, because they did not silence themselves, were silenced forever by the PLO are: Salim Lawzi, owner of the weekly, *Al-Hawadit,* arrested at a PLO checkpost in July 1978 and tortured to death in the village of Aramoun, after which photos of his body were distributed among Beirut's journalists as a warning; Edouard Saeb, editor-in-chief of *L'Orion Du Jour* and local correspondent of *Le Monde,* shot to death in September 1976 while crossing Beirut's Green Line; and Riadh Taha, president of the Lebanese newspaper publishers' union and part of an effort to form an anti-PLO front with Bashir Jemayel, murdered by the PLO outside the Carlton Hotel in Beirut. George claimed several foreign journalists were murdered by the PLO in West Beirut between 1976 and 1981: Larry Buchman, ABC-TV correspondent; Mark Tryon, Free Belgium radio; Robert Pfeffer, correspondent for *Der Spiegel* and *Unita;* Italian journalists Tony Italo and Graciella Difaco; ABC correspondent Sean Toolan.

Where, during the years when these outrages were perpetrated in Beirut by the PLO, were the voices of John Chancellor and NBC to decry censorship? Why is it that censorship becomes a Middle Eastern problem only when it is practiced (and hardly in a manner even remotely resembling the instances just cited) by Israel? No one with a passing acquaintance with human nature ought to have been surprised that the intimidation and terror with which the PLO censored journalists before June 1982 continued, *a fortiori,* once it came under direct attack by Israel. Countless witnesses told how PLO commanders—in the words of John Martin of ABC News—"permitted camera crews and correspondents to move freely into areas under attack, but not to photograph military targets hidden among civilian offices and apartments." In other words, the television reports coming from PLO-occupied West Beirut were indeed censored, contrary to what Chancellor alleged, and censored in such a way as to remove from sight precisely the evidence used by Israel to justify its siege. "What's more," observed the *New Republic,* "you weren't even told that you weren't seeing something important. So while television relentlessly repeated that dispatches from the Israeli side were censored by Israeli authorities, it didn't tell you of the PLO's censorship—which of course made the censorship that much more effective." Ann Medina, of the Canadian Broadcasting Corporation, showed rare courage in filming PLO censorship with a hidden camera. Her film proved, beyond any possibility of contradiction, how a PLO censor accompanied reporters in Lebanon "everywhere we go." This may help to explain the intriguing way in which *Newsweek,* in a rare burst of candor, sought to justify the "anti-Israel tone of many of the dispatches from the front" by disclosing that "many correspondents based in Beirut developed warm relationships with PLO leaders." Is it conceivable that fledgling reporters are taught in their journalism courses that cozy relationships with terrorist combatants afford indispensable aid in impartial reporting of wars in which those terrorists become involved? If so, perhaps they should be warned that in the business of war reporting, "warm relationships" may be a self-deceptive label for compliance with terrorist censorship.

The extent to which television became, in the words of Ted Koppel of ABC, a war-weapon in PLO hands, even forced two of the major networks—CBS on 9 and 12 July, and ABC on 12 July—to acknowledge the existence of PLO censorship; only Mr. Chancellor and his colleagues at NBC maintained their stony silence on this subject. They maintained it even in the face of what an observant viewer of their own pictures might well have construed as evidence of the contrary. Thus, on 12 June, just after Mallory's standard report on bombing in Beirut, viewers were shown several PLO fighters retreating into central Beirut. One of them pointed his gun menacingly at Mallory's cameraman, prompting the remark that "they *don't* like to be photographed." Inadvertently, NBC thus reminded viewers that the PLO is very much in the censorship business, but that its favored instrument for keeping camera crews from photographing military installations is the gun rather than the pen. This very same film sequence was used again, for reasons that perhaps only a Viennese doctor could satisfactorily explain, without comment as part of Jack Reynolds' report of events allegedly taking place on 29 June, and as a prelude to a Roger Mudd harangue against censorship—Israeli censorship, that is. By some subterranean psychological process, the fact of PLO censorship by the gun had insinuated itself into the minds of the NBC news staff but came out to the American public as an attack on Israeli censorship by the pen. And wherein lay the Israelis' offense against free expression? Jack Reynolds's sign-off words—"West Beirut"—were "inexplicably removed by Israeli censors." This, but not the PLO threats against reporters' lives, was yet another "problem" for Chancellor, Mudd, and company.

Following the line taken by Brokaw on 23 June, Chancellor, in his commentary of the twenty-fourth, generously allowed that "every journalist can understand when censorship is used by a government to protect the lives of its troops. But increasingly, in the Lebanese story, censorship has been used to protect Israel's image and to serve its political goals." NBC's commentators always know what is or is not relevant to Israeli national security, for which—so it is implied—they have the gravest concern; but no other form of censorship is permissible. At least it is not permissible to Israel, for it is well known that the British blackout of television coverage of the war in the Falklands, a war that, whatever might be said in its justification by the British, could hardly be said to have been fought in the protection of British national security, did not stir Chancellor, Brokaw, and Mudd to the rage they vented whenever Israel refused to transmit film via satellite. The arrogance that Reuven Frank recommended as the sine qua non for ambitious journalists has rarely been so much in evidence as in NBC's lectures to Israel on its moral transgression in failing to provide complete information services to its enemies in wartime. First, even the most careless viewer, watching NBC's relentless barrage of anti-Israeli stories, must have been surprised by Chancellor's temerity in saying Israeli censors would not pass stories "that make Israel look bad." Second, is Israel any more under a moral obligation to transmit from its Tel Aviv satellite interviews with Yasser Arafat or other PLO spokesmen than the United States in World War II would have been to disseminate interviews with Hitler conducted by foreign journalists sympathetic to his "cause"?

When Reuven Frank was asked about the vendetta his staff had carried on against Israel over the issue of military censorship, he replied that "Basically, the Israelis are treating the foreign press better than most of the other countries. We are picking on them." This is a typical reply from Mr. Frank, a man amply endowed with the quality that his surname describes, a man whose family coat of arms is probably emblazoned with the motto "unashamed." He is fond of parading his general cynicism, which diverts attention from his particular responsibility for NBC's misdeeds and from his own entire indifference to self-correction.

Throughout the summer, NBC continued to hammer away at Israel over the issue of censorship. The stress was always on the political nature of Israeli censorship, sometimes qualified by a fleeting reference to Syrian censorship, but never any at all to PLO censorship by terror. The program of 1 August appeared at first to give some semblance of balance by using background graphics referring to Syrian censorship in Rick Davis's report from East Beirut, and background graphics referring to Israeli censorship when John Hart appeared before a map of Lebanon and informed his viewers that during the preceding eight weeks many scenes had been "missing in the war reports from Lebanon. . . . Reports from West Beirut sent from Syria, subject to Syrian censorship; reports from East Beirut sent from Israel are restricted by Israeli censors." But all this was merely a prelude to yet another report, very detailed, on Israeli censorship that ignored the Syrians altogether. Bob Kur, a far more scrupulous journalist than Chancellor, made some attempt to explain Israel's rationale for what Kur condemned as "purely political" censorship: "Israel does not want to generate sympathy for the PLO or, some say, with good reason, provide a stage for its spokesmen." Kur also admitted that "Israeli censors never

tried to hide the damage in southern Lebanon, nor did Israel try to hide its
unprecedented antiwar demonstrations," and that "a degree of censorship
during wartime is not unusual for any country, and some have been more
restrictive than Israel." But any credit that might redound to Israel from
these acknowledgments was quickly erased by Kur's conclusion that there
was so much criticism from abroad of Israeli censorship that "Israel *could*
not easily have increased censorship." In other words, here as in all other
respects, Israel was just as mischievous as the world allowed it to be. Why
"the world" allows Israel's adversaries to be so much more mischievous,
with impunity, Kur did not bother to explain. Perhaps the answer is, as R.
Emmett Tyrrell, editor of the *American Spectator,* alleged: "Not all our
allies are . . . diabolized. The diabolizing comes down only on those who
actually oppose America's enemies."

The Question of Civilian Casualties:
"No Military Targets Here"

*Israel, by aiding Lebanese Christians
since 1975, has saved more civilian lives
than have been lost in this war. But a
television screen is easy to fill. . . .
Television in war is bound to suggest more
generalized destruction than has occurred.
Furthermore, had there been television at
Antietam on America's bloodiest day
(Sept. 17, 1862), this would be two nations.
Americans then lived closer to the jagged
edges of life, but even they might have
preferred disunion to the price of union,
had they seen the price, in color in their
homes in the evening.*
—George Will, *Newsweek,*
2 August 1982

On 2 August, a photograph published throughout the world showed
what was described as a severely burned baby girl, with her arms ampu-
tated, who had been wounded during an Israeli bombardment of West
Beirut. The photograph came to symbolize Israel's allegedly indiscriminate bombing of civilians. On 14 August, NBC's Fred Francis reported
Secretary of State George Shultz's endorsement of Ronald Reagan's view
that the "symbol of this war" was this same "picture of a baby with its
arms shot off." It was a symbol in more ways than Reagan and Shultz
understood, for by 20 August it had been conclusively proved that the
photograph had been deliberately misrepresented in the news media in
order to smear Israel. Doctors who suspected the veracity of the photograph sent a special team to find the baby, and discovered it to be a boy

(Reagan, Shultz, and NBC even had the sex wrong) with a broken left arm still in a cast, but otherwise healthy and intact. He was released from a Beirut hospital five days after his picture as a moribund girl made front pages around the world. NBC did not think it worthwhile, after Francis had reported the "story," to correct the misrepresentation, or, for that matter, to correct the impression given by the complementary story of 14 August by Steve Delaney in Beirut. This told of a West Beirut home for retarded children in which—allegedly as a result of frequent Israeli shelling—the children were found starving and lying in their own excrement. Mother Teresa was photographed carrying one of the skeletal children from the home. But Mother Teresa, unbeknownst to NBC viewers, said in a later television broadcast that the children had been kept in these wretched conditions for a very long time before the Israelis came, and that those responsible for the conditions not only got off scot-free but had the additional satisfaction of seeing their helpless victims used for their own propaganda purposes.

The doctored photograph and the stage-managed hospital visit of Mother Teresa were thus symbolic of the uncontrollable desire of many in the news media to depict Israel as a brutal power intent mainly on the destruction of Palestinian Arab civilians. That civilians were uprooted, injured, and killed in this war, as in all wars, no one can doubt; but they were not uprooted, injured, and killed to anything like the extent or with anything like the callous indifference or evil intent alleged by the journalists, NBC's reporters foremost among them.

Almost from the outset of the war, NBC's field reporter in Beirut, Steve Mallory, made it his special duty to insist, day in and day out, that Israeli bombing raids did not merely cause civilian casualties as a by-product of military missions, but were directed at civilian targets. On 4 June Mallory reported the Israeli attack on a sports stadium in southern Beirut used by the PLO as an arms depot; the attack, said Mallory, was "deadly accurate" and "officials said most of the casualties were civilians." Who these helpful "officials" were, Mallory did not say. On 5 June he reported the Israeli bombing of a "a school bus; fifteen died in the bus." He thus conveyed the impression to his innocent audience that those inside the bus were schoolchildren. In fact, nearly every other report on the incident said that the bus was not a school bus, and that its occupants were adults, not children. Some reports, crediting PLO claims, identified the men as construction workers, but Mallory suppressed even this half-truth lest it dilute the image of an Israeli massacre of young innocents. As for the larger attack on the "major coastal highway" linking Beirut to southern Lebanon, Mallory claimed that "Bystanders asked, 'Why? No military positions here.' " On 11 June, Mallory reported that "As the cease-fire was taking effect, Israeli warplanes streaked over Beirut. One dropped a bomb on a predominantly Moslem side of the city, hitting a civilian area. There are no military targets here." On 12 June, Mallory reported crews "looking for casualties or survivors of yesterday's Israeli bombing of civilian areas of central Beirut." On 17 June, Mallory described Israel's attack on Beirut International Airport and then sounded his standard refrain: "No military positions here." It was perhaps at this point that those viewers of NBC who had been in a war or read about one, or had been endowed with even the most modest portion of common sense, must have wondered whether there was anything that Steve Mallory did consider a military target, since he had already ruled out major airports and highways (so long as they were under Arab control). No matter how often he reported on Israeli attacks, it was the identical story: 21 June, "An Israeli round hit . . . in Central Beirut—primarily a civilian area" (and to show just how civilian it was, NBC followed the pictures of Israeli shelling with one of Arafat dandling a baby); June 25, "no military positions here" (a residential area of West Beirut); June 26, "Most casualties were civilians"; and June 28, "It's been . . . *civilians* who've lost the most."

The pattern of reporting the war from West Beirut established by Mallory was continued by Jack Reynolds, with the addition of strongly tainted political rhetoric and lurid emotionalism. On 9 July, one of the rare occasions when NBC allowed that somebody else besides the Israelis was firing, Reynolds noted that when "the Israelis responded—people were hit." On 10 July he gave his typically florid account of the day's shelling, followed by invocation of the Mallory refrain: "There are no Palestinian fighters here, they said." In this instance "here" was the area of the foreign embassies, an area that published reconnaissance photos showed to be replete with tanks, mortars, heavy machine guns, and antiaircraft positions; yet NBC saw no need for correction, retraction, or apology.

James Compton, who replaced Mallory in West Beirut in mid-summer, seemed torn between repetition of the Mallory-Reynolds formula and glimmerings of awareness of what virtually every disinterested observer of the PLO defense strategy had known for years, namely, that the PLO always places its troops and its weapons in and around schools, hospitals, and apartment houses, deliberately seeking to maximize civilian casualties in the event of an Israeli attack. (In many cases, PLO fighters hid behind rows of women and children when firing on Israeli forces.) As David Shipler wrote in the *New York Times* of 25 July:

> The P. L. O. was not on a campaign to win friends among the Lebanese. Its thrust was military. The huge sums of money the P. L. O. received from Saudi Arabia and other Arab countries seem to have been spent primarily on weapons and ammunition, which were placed strategically in densely populated civilian

areas in the hope that this would either deter Israeli attacks or exact a price from Israel in world opinion for killing civilians. Towns and camps were turned into vast armories as crates of ammunition were stacked in underground shelters and antiaircraft guns were emplaced in schoolyards, among apartment houses, next to churches and hospitals. The remains could be seen after the fighting, and Palestinians and Lebanese can still point out the sites.

Whether from ignorance, obtuseness, or cravenness, Mallory and Reynolds failed to mention any of this while expressing continuing wonderment and outrage at Israel's bombing of what they confidently declared to be "civilian" targets.

Compton began in the established NBC style. On 27 July he reported a hit on an apartment house "at least a mile from any Palestinian military concentrations." On 29 July he reported on a hospital hit by six artillery shells because Israel was "trying to get at an already destroyed tank that sits nearby." On 1 August, however, complications arose. As usual, it was alleged that Israeli "artillery [shells] fell in a seemingly random way in congested central neighborhoods," yet viewers were also told that "whole neighborhoods that held concentrations of Palestinian forces have now been reduced to rubble by the Israeli bombing." This must have come as something of a shock to viewers who had been assured by Mallory and Reynolds, week after week in the wake of Israeli shelling of these very neighborhoods, that "there are no military targets here." Then, in yet another paradoxical turn, Compton remarked on "the assumption here . . . that the PLO forces will now pull back into neighborhoods that hold concentrations of Lebanese civilians, forcing the Israelis to come after them in door-to-door fighting. . . ." On 5 August he was back to the formulaic postbombing refrain—"We could not find any Palestinian military targets"—but followed it with an apparently contradictory reference to the "tragic" situation in which PLO fighters had moved out of "camps" and into "civilian" neighborhoods, inviting Israelis "to come and get them."

Not all of the confusion here is innocent. At no point did NBC ever bother to inform its readers of what "camp" may mean in the Lebanese context. "Refugee camp" evokes the image of postwar DP camps and the miserable hovels in which the first wave of "displaced persons" the world over takes refuge. But very few PLO camps fit that description. What NBC referred to as "PLO camps" should have been called "armed bases," which were "protected" by maintaining the close presence of Palestinian Arab civilians and their families. They were also, as the *Times* of London reported on 21 August, "military training camps": "members of the Italian Red Brigades and the West German Baader-Meinhof gang were trained at the so-called 'European base' at the Shatila refugee camp in Beirut. The camp is one of those subject to recent heavy Israeli bombardment." Many of the "refugee camps" were in reality whole urban neighborhoods of high-rise apartment buildings, with not a tent or mud hut in sight. It was as if Mallory, Reynolds, and Compton had called General Custer's encampment and the Wild West's Fort Bravo "trading posts." This became abundantly clear, even despite what might be called NBC's own censorship system, on 11 August, when Compton reported Israeli raids on the refugee camps. A woman resident, sounding very much as if she had been coached by Steve Mallory, stepped forward to express the predictable denial, "there are no fighters here." But James Compton, to his credit, declared that the woman's statement was not the whole truth, for no sooner had she spoken than three PLO fighters emerged from hiding—"the truth is the Palestinian forces are mingled with civilians everywhere in this refugee camp," a truth it took NBC ten weeks to divulge.

The false testimony of this Palestinian Arab woman, testimony of precisely the kind so eagerly sought after and so uncritically regurgitated by Mallory and Reynolds week after week, should make us pause to reflect on the innocence of adult civilians injured in bombing raids on PLO concentrations. The PLO constitution, or "National Covenant," spells out, in thirty-three variations on a single theme, its members' commitment to the destruction of the state of Israel. No matter how diligently certain journalists seek to deceive themselves and others on this fundamental point, every Palestinian Arab is aware of it and no Palestinian Arab bothers to deny it except when whispering into the ears of journalists in cafes. Palestinian Arabs in Lebanon are not innocent of the PLO's merciless plans and procedures for the erasure of Israel from the map. How could they be, when they saw the wholesale deployment of PLO armaments in houses, schools, and hospital grounds? The degree of culpability of a person who harbors a killer is not the same as that of the killer; but it is not the same as innocence, either. Even in the "normal" circumstances of war, it has traditionally been assumed that the immunity of noncombatants must be qualified if military operations are to be possible at all. Should the fact that the PLO went to such lengths to mingle itself with the civilian population have made it as immune to attack by Israel as it made it immune to attack by the reporters of NBC?

Chancellor, reflecting and then magnifying the reactions of NBC's Beirut reporters, consistently damned Israel's siege of Beirut as exacting "a terrible human . . . cost" (7 June), "savage" (2 August), "horrifying" and "brutal" (5 August), and "inhuman" (6 August). Yet there is abundant evidence that Israel made greater, not lesser, efforts than most attacking armies to avoid injuring civilians, and increased its own casualties by doing so. Robert Tucker, professor of international relations at Johns Hopkins University and a careful observer of modern warfare, has stated that "The places attacked were almost invariably known or long-suspected PLO military positions. Civilian casualties were incurred in the immediate vicinity of such objectives. Moreover, from all that is known, these casualties were of an incidence to be expected when an attacking force is taking even more than reasonable precautions to spare the civilian population from injury." He also noted that even the severest bombardments of the war, those of 4 and 12 August, resulted in civilian casualties that, even if we accept the figures given out by PLO officials—not famous for their probity in such matters—"bear no real comparison in their magnitude with the indiscriminate bombings of cities in World War II" and "compare quite favorably with measures taken by American forces against civilian centers in the Korean and Vietnam wars." On 12 August, NBC reported tens of thousands of tons of bombs dropped on West Beirut. But the military historian U.S. Colonel Trevor N. Dupuy, Retired, stated that "on that day I spent about five hours observing this bombardment. During that time, it was apparent from my observation that no more than 150 bombs, probably 200 to 500 kilograms each, were dropped on Beirut. . . . To any veteran who has been under air or artillery attack in 'normal' combat situations, this was relatively modest harassment."

The truth of the matter, of course, is that for those who articulate NBC's foreign policy, *any* damage wrought by Israeli air attack in Lebanon would have been deemed disproprotionate in relation to the value of Israel's enterprise, for it is NBC doctrine that Israel (unlike Britain, for example) may not go to war unless its very existence is at stake. Former Secretary of State Henry Kissinger wrote on 22 June about the war that "No sovereign state can tolerate indefinitely the buildup along its borders of a military force dedicated to its destruction, and proceeding by periodical shellings and raids." But on 6 August Chancellor said that although Israel might have had a "genuine" concern about PLO actions from Lebanon, it was in "no mortal danger" and therefore had no right to go to war. NBC also laid it down from the outset that, whatever Israel or the Lebanese people might claim to the contrary, the sending of Israeli military forces across the Lebanese border was an invasion by what Chancellor on 2 August called "an imperial Israel which is solving its problems in someone else's country." The notion that Israel entered Lebanon, as the allies entered France in World War II, to liberate the country from a brutal, conquering regime, received no consideration from NBC's policymakers. When people in Christian neighborhoods of Beirut had the temerity to inform Steve Mallory (15 June broadcast) that they were happy to see the Israelis arrive, he heaped scorn on those who "welcome the invaders as liberators." Clearly, it is the reporters and not the inhabitants of Lebanon—after all, they just happen to live there, and are not "Palestinians"—who are entrusted with the task of deciding whether the Israelis are invaders or liberators. No wonder that one journalist, shocked by the behavior of many of his colleagues in Lebanon, expressed the view that not the Jews but the journalists consider themselves the chosen people.

Deliberate Falsifications

> *If the reporter has poisoned our imagination by his version of the truth, he brings us back to reality by his lies.*
> —Karl Kraus

The propaganda battle against Israel during the Lebanese war began with the invention by the PLO of the figures of "600,000 homeless civilians" and 10,000 civilians killed in the portion of southern Lebanon taken by Israel. On 10 June, Roger Mudd reported that "the Red Crescent, which is Lebanon's Red Cross, is quoted as estimating that more than ten thousand civilians have been killed or wounded since Friday." This statement did not merely transmit a wildly exaggerated figure; it contained a double falsification. The Red Crescent is not Lebanon's Red Cross but a branch of the PLO, something any conscientious reporter would have known and said; and—a fact Roger Mudd chose not to share with his audience—the Palestinian Red Crescent organization is headed by Yasser Arafat's brother, Fathi Arafat. Although on 16 June John Chancellor announced that "The Red Cross said today that approximately three hundred thousand may have been made homeless," Jessica Savitch on 19 June proclaimed the favored PLO figure of six hundred thousand without going to the trouble of inventing a "source": "It is now estimated that six hundred thousand refugees in south Lebanon are without sufficient food and medical supplies." The real Red Cross had, on 18 June, refused to endorse the six-hundred-thousand figure, but this did not trouble the intrepid Jessica Savitch, any more than she was troubled by the fact that her colleague Bob Kur had, on 17 June, said that seventy thousand had been left homeless by the war.

The figures that NBC disseminated so eagerly were of course ludicrous. Six hundred thousand refugees amounted to more than the total population of southern Lebanon under Israeli control. If, as was alleged by the PLO and its publicity agents in the news media, ten thousand had been killed, primarily in Tyre and Sidon, it seemed odd that the Mayor of Tyre reported to the *New York Times* that only sixty-two persons had died there, while the Bishop of Tyre said only fifty civilians had been buried as a result of the war operations. The official figures released by the local authorities in Sidon indicate that about one hundred were killed. In his story of 15 July in the *New York Times,* David Shipler (certainly no great friend of Israel) said that "it is clear to anyone who has traveled in southern Lebanon, as many journalists and relief workers now have, that the original figures of 10,000 dead and 600,000 homeless, reported by correspondents . . . during the first week of the war, were extreme exaggerations." When he was asked why NBC had knowingly disseminated these PLO-invented fabrications, Israel Bureau Chief Paul Miller replied petulantly that it was "not the job of the media not to report the figures" bandied about by various parties, so long as the sources of the figures were also given. We have already seen how scrupulous Roger Mudd and Jessica Savitch were in identifying their sources. What Paul Miller did not even attempt to explain was how his reporters could have been so ignorant of the country they were covering as blithely to pass on a figure of six hundred thousand refugees for an area whose total population, the vast majority of whom never left their homes, was less than five hundred thousand; or so contemptuous of their audience that even after it became, as Shipler wrote, "clear to anyone who has traveled in southern Lebanon" that the original figures were lies, they never retracted the figures or corrected them. In fact, they gave PLO supporters every opportunity to recite these bogus figures (see, for example, Steve Delaney's report of 28 June and Jack Reynolds's of 2 July) without challenging their accuracy.

The figure of six hundred thousand, a patent absurdity on the face of it, was irresistibly attractive to journalists hostile to Israel for the same reason that it was invented by the Arabs in the first place: it began with a six and facilitated the licentious equation of six hundred thousand Palestinian Arabs with the six million Jews who had been murdered by Hitler. At least since 1967 the PLO has made it a consistent practice to ride on the coattails of the Jewish experience of discrimination, exile, oppression, and murder by stealing the Holocaust from the Jews, presenting themselves as the "Jews" of the Middle East and the Israelis as their Nazi oppressors. Although NBC went to nothing like the lengths of von Hoffman, Cockburn, Oliphant, and other inhabitants of the dirtier sections of Grub Street in alleging that Israelis were doing to Palestinian Arabs what Nazis had done to Jews and others, their reports and commentaries were certainly tainted by this practice. John Chancellor claimed that he "kept thinking . . . of the bombing of Madrid during the Spanish Civil War." ("Was he there at the time?" asked Frank Gervasi. "The year of the bombing of Madrid by the Junkers 52s of Hitler's burgeoning *Luftwaffe* was 1936, when John was 12 or 13 years old.") James Compton artfully described the

Israelis (30 July) as "prepared to force a final military solution." Steve Mallory was always ready at hand when Yasser Arafat had something to say about Beirut's being the Arabs' "Stalingrad," and Jack Reynolds—true to form—went a step further by endorsing the equation (29 June).

Reynolds had already demonstrated his high respect for historical accuracy on 13 June in a report on the rush to volunteer for action among Palestinian Arabs in Jordan, where, according to Reynolds, they had been living in camps "since Israel took over Palestine in 1948." What inflames these would-be fighters "is inevitable . . . anger at the Israelis who pushed them out of Palestine." Not even Reynolds's most tendentious colleagues, during three months of broadcasting the war, had the temerity to go quite this far; but Reynolds is NBC's most devout believer in Oscar Wilde's dictum that "the one duty we owe to history is to re-write it."

By 1948 four-fifths of the territory known as Palestine under the British Mandate was already under Arab control, in the country known as Jordan. The United Nations had voted to partition the remaining section—western Palestine—into two countries, one Jewish, one Arab. Israel recognized the Arab part as the Palestinian Arab state, but no Arab country did or ever has done so. Instead, the Arab countries declared war on the Jewish state and attempted to destroy it. The attempt was unsuccessful, but Jordan did succeed in occupying eastern Jerusalem, which the United Nations had intended to be an "internationalized" city. And this was how Israel "took over Palestine in 1948." Reynolds's version of why many Arabs left Palestine in 1948 is exactly the PLO version, but no reputable historian would endorse it. Even the anti-Zionist historian Christopher Sykes wrote that "there is no evidence of a long-standing and agreed Jewish policy to evict the settled population; on the contrary in the first half of 1948 there is considerable evidence that the Jews tried to prevent the flight. . . . When the war was over, Arab journalists and broadcasters asserted on several occasions that the exodus was a planned Arab manoeuvre, the main object being to clear the land and thus give freedom of action to the invading armies" (*Cross Roads to Israel*). It is anticlimactic to note that, having uttered these bold-faced lies, Reynolds also failed to ask, as any normally curious reporter would have done, why these refugees of 1948 had been kept in such wretched conditions by their brother Arabs for thirty-five years. Even John Chancellor was willing to admit (9 August) that "when Arabs attacked Israelis they [refugees] ran away" and that their present plight was more the fault of the Arab countries than of Israel. To anyone who wondered why Jack Reynolds's every broadcast from Lebanon was a condemnation of Israel and an exoneration of the PLO, the broadcast of 13 June was a revelation, the key to an enigma. PLO "anger" at Israel is, according to Reynoldsian psychology, "inevitable"; if it is inevitable, then no moral blame can possibly be attached to the actions that it brings in its wake, however merciless and bloody they may be.

As this discrepancy between Chancellor and Reynolds suggests, the rewriting of history appears to be a freelance affair at NBC; reporters are free to distort as they like, so long as what they like is not what Israel likes. Roger Mudd, for example, took it on himself to refuse recognition of Jerusalem as Israel's capital city. NBC's staff was, in general, chary of locating events in Jerusalem that happened to have taken place there. Paul Miller and Martin Fletcher were usually "in Tel Aviv" even when the scenes they described and the stories they narrated were recognized as having originated in Jerusalem by anyone who had ever been there (6 and 7 June, 25 and 30 July, etc.). But at least they could justify this practice by claiming that they were transmitting their reports from a Tel Aviv office. With Roger Mudd, however, the problem was either spectacular ignorance or an attempt to distort facts to fit policy. On 29 June, Bob Kur reported on a debate in Israel's Knesset, which meets in Jerusalem, and concluded with, "Bob Kur, from the Israeli Knesset," specifying no location. Roger Mudd promptly helped out by locating it in Tel Aviv, saying, "While Tel Aviv debates, Beirut waits." On 19 July he announced that the "focus of the Middle Eastern crisis shifted from Tel Aviv and Beirut to Washington today." The Lebanese seat of government is Beirut; the American seat of government is Washington; and the Israeli seat of government is Jerusalem. Why, then, Tel Aviv? On 5 August Mudd introduced Jim Bittermann, reporting "from Israel's capital"; perhaps by this time someone at NBC had told Mudd that it was unseemly to adjust geography so blatantly to fit bias, but that if he felt so strongly about the matter, he could substitute ambiguity. (When Shakespeare's Macduff asked his countryman, Ross, on the latter's return to England, "Stands Scotland where it did?" was he really worrying about his country's suffering or fearful that some eleventh-century Roger Mudd had relocated Caledonia in Wales?) Although NBC did not go so far as explicitly to consign Jerusalem to the rule of those who were daily proclaiming their resolve to "liberate" the city, it did refer over and over again (see Savitch, 31 July, or Mudd, 23 June) to "Jordan's West Bank," and it is hardly a secret that the city of Jerusalem is included in the Arab definition of "West Bank." It was as if NBC had decided, on its own, to assign sovereignty over this disputed area to the country that invaded it in 1948, a sovereignty not even Arab nations have ever granted to Jordan.

Some observers believe that such falsifications result from ignorance. Martin Peretz of the *New Republic* wrote in October 1981 that "NBC can't persuade its 250 affiliates to air one hour of network news instead of the present half-hour. Thirty minutes is preferable to sixty, since TV news come to us from men and women who know little and understand even less. But if you haven't seen them improvise, you have not really seen ignorance in full flower." This seems to me an overly charitable interpretation. Those who believe that Roger Mudd, for example, blundered innocently should pay particular attention to the broadcast of 2 July, a typical example of NBC's double standard in conveying statistics to the unwary viewer. A Lebanese-American doctor who gained international celebrity for her fiery flow of anti-Israeli rhetoric in interviews by most television reporters in Beirut recited to Jack Reynolds the PLO estimates of civilian deaths (those "extreme exaggerations" referred to in the *New York Times*) while the respectful reporter nodded his head in agreement. Mudd, entering the ring to deliver the second part of the regular NBC one-two punch against Israel, then announced:

> Prime Minister Begin claims the Israeli army has picked up sixty-six children aged twelve to thirteen and armed with submachine guns who were recruited into the PLO. . . . Later, however, a spokesman for Begin said that he had made a mistake and read from the wrong paper, and that the correct number was either two or twenty-two child soldiers.

NBC, suddenly very conscientious in sifting the evidence for statistical claims, was doing its best to suggest that Begin was a liar or a fool. Nevertheless, in subsequent days it became irresistibly clear that, as the *New York Times* reported on 25 July: "An extensive P.L.O. conscription program drafted Palestinian boys as young as 12 and mobilized all male students for one to three months of duty a year, according to some Palestinians. During the invasion, Israeli soldiers said they found themselves in combat with 12-year and 13-year-olds shooting rocket-propelled grenades. More than 200 youngsters from 12 to 15 were captured and have been released. The P.L.O.'s draft apparently stirred resentment, for Rima Shabb told of checkpoints being set up to catch young Palestinians who were trying to run away. . . . Sister Alisse Araigi, headmistress of a Maronite school in Nabatiye, said, 'Families came to us and asked for certificates that children were sick and couldn't be drafted.' " That Begin's statement of 2 July was essentially true, and that he had erred on the side of caution rather than exaggeration, were facts rigorously concealed from NBC viewers. Showing up Menachem Begin clearly had a higher priority for NBC News than telling the truth about the PLO's exploitation of Arab children.

As if this were not enough for one evening, NBC also gave an account of "a growing feeling of anti-Americanism" in West Beirut because of injuries caused by U.S.-made cluster bombs and shells, dutifully displayed for the cameras. But, as Joshua Muravchik pointed out in *Policy Review* (Winter 1983), NBC neglected to mention that the story was based on information provided at a PLO press conference at which the shells were displayed. "In contrast, one of the other networks ran the same footage with the simple announcement that it was a PLO press conference. There was a remarkable contrast between the abundant cooperation that NBC gave to this PLO public relations effort and the deep skepticism that it showed to Israel's slightly bungled public relations effort the same night." (Another aspect of the cluster bomb story not made public by NBC is that its chief non-Arab disseminator was Franklin Lamb, a certified fraud with a criminal record who had earlier invented out of whole cloth a horror story about an Israeli "vacuum bomb," a type of bomb that does not exist.)

NBC was often so eager to impute monstrous, destructive evil to Israel that it disregarded even the visual evidence it placed on the screen and so fell into ludicrous self-contradiction. On 5 July Reynolds reported that Beirut was being "slowly reduced to rubble" and said that "almost all the civilians here have fled" except the few who had no place else to go. Yet on 6 July, one day later, because he was eager to do a story on the "amazing resiliency" of the people in West Beirut, Jack Reynolds showed Beirut returning "to its own sense of normalcy [sic]." By 8 July Reynolds had effected a miraculous transformation and resurrection of a city that three days earlier was little but "rubble." "Almost overnight," he exclaimed, "West Beirut has begun to change for the better and things look fine now. People are crowding into supermarkets." On 9 July Reynolds continued his rapid repopulation and rebuilding, but apparently not without a suspicion that some viewers might wonder whether total evacuation and nearly total destruction can be fleeting phenomena. He therefore hastened to explain that "parts of West Beirut are still deserted and destroyed." Reynolds's antics provide a shocking example not merely of the way selective camerawork can be used to support virtually any assertion, but of the way journalists can persuade themselves that destruction exists in the lens of the camera; cities can be emptied and filled, destroyed and resurrected, by tendentious reporters more readily than by the mightiest historical forces or the most powerful machines.

NBC repeated the same cycle at the end of the month. On 31 July Jessica Savitch, with characteristic hyperbole, said, "You've got to wonder what is left in West Beirut to be destroyed." If the photographs of Beirut that flashed across the screen two minutes later, showing a city essentially intact, did not raise several million eyebrows, then surely John Chancellor's commentary of 2 August must have done so. For Chancellor spoke against a background showing a majestic city of brightly shining high-rise buildings stretching as far as the eye could see. Apparently, NBC's reporters, by a judicious turn of phrase and an opportunistic direction of the camera, can destroy and restore cities at will. Whether they can also restore our confidence in their honesty, having first destroyed it by such unscrupulousness of statement and sleight-of-hand methods, remains to be seen.

The Terminology of Bias

> *And let us bathe our hands in . . . blood*
> *Up to the elbows, and besmear our swords.*
> *Then walk we forth, even to the market place,*
> *And waving our red weapons o'er our heads,*
> *Let's all cry "Peace, freedom, and liberty!"*
> —Shakespeare, *Julius Caesar,*
> III, i, 106–110.

More pervasive, more effective, and more insidious as an instrument of persuasion than outright attack on an object of a journalist's dislike is the repeated use of biased and highly charged language. As the English novelist Arnold Bennett once wrote, "Journalists say a thing that they know isn't true, in the hope that if they keep on saying it long enough it *will* be true."

A listener attuned to the subtleties of language could recognize the tendentious drift of NBC reporting in the early days of June. Mudd began by referring (on 4 June and again on 7 June) to Israeli action taken after the shooting of Ambassador Argov in London as "an eye for an eye and a tooth for a tooth," thereby implying not merely that Israeli action against terrorist bases was taken solely in response to the shooting, but that it was morally equivalent to it, and that the whole nasty business was an atavistic irruption of unredeemed, "Old Testament" Jewish ferocity into the modern, civilized world. References to PLO shelling of Nahariya on 4 and 7 June depicted it as a "settlement south of the Lebanese border." Nahariya is a town fifty years old; one might as well refer to Bellingham, Washington as a "settlement" because it is south of the Canadian border. The choice of this label was not innocent error, for it had the effect of suggesting that Nahariya and other northern Israeli towns that came under PLO fire shared the questionable and disputed status of the "settlements" in Judea and Samaria (the "West Bank") of which Americans have heard so much (and none of it good) in recent years.

On 6 June Paul Miller referred to the approximately forty thousand Syrian troops in Lebanon as the "Syrian peacekeeping army in Lebanon," an expression Senator Daniel Moynihan called "an Orwellian triumph." On 7 June NBC referred to the "PLO coastal town of Sidon," but by 26 June it had become "Israeli-occupied Sidon." In fact, no sooner did Israeli troops take over an area than it was referred to as "Israeli-occupied Lebanon" (thus Martin Fletcher in Tyre on 19 June). At no point in its three months of covering the war did NBC find it necessary to inform its viewers that Syria, in addition to having had those forty thousand troops occupying half of Lebanon, including half of Beirut, for seven years, has never in its history had an ambassador in Beirut because it does not recognize Lebanon as a sovereign country but considers it part of Syria. Whereas Syria's troops, which had made very substantial contributions, through savage shelling of Christian population centers, to the figure of one hundred thousand people killed in Lebanon between 1975 and 1982, are for NBC a "peacekeeping army," Israel's soldiers are part of a "war machine" (Mallory, 15 June, Brokaw, 16 June) representing "a warrior state" (Chancellor, 16 June).

NBC developed certain fixed Homeric epithets that it applied throughout the war. Its reporters attached the label "moderate" to Saudi Arabia, for example, so regularly that many Americans watching NBC must have come to think it a geographical term. On 13 June John Hart said that despite King Khaled's death no change was to be expected in Saudi Arabia's "reliable" supply of oil and "stable" prices, and Marvin Kalb prognosticated that the "Saudis may now encourage moderation in Lebanon." On 14 June Paul Miller reported the Mubarak-Fahd meeting as one of "moderate Arab states," adding that Fahd is "known for his peace proposal to recognize Israel" (a disingenuous piece of puffery that disguises the fact that Fahd's proposal did not specifically mention recognition of Israel at all). On 27 June Miller was finding more evidence in London of Saudi moderation and a desire for a "diplomatic solution" in Lebanon. On 16 July Chancellor expressed fear that Iran might turn its guns "on its moderate Arab neighbors." These endless hymns of praise sung by NBC to Saudi moderation may have gone far to make NBC's viewers forget that this is the same Saudi Arabia that consistently advocates *jihad* ("holy war") against Israel; that massively supports the PLO; that holds the oil cartel together; that practices public beheadings; and that rejected the Camp David accords, the Reagan peace plan, and the Lebanese-Israeli accord worked out by the United States in 1983. Nevertheless, it is an article of faith at NBC that King Fahd is always busily working behind the scenes for "moderation" and peace.

The "moderate" label was conferred on Jordan's King Hussein by NBC and most of the news media long ago, but it seems to have taken the Lebanese war for NBC to transform Yasser Arafat into a moderate. Although Jillian Becker, the English writer on terrorism whose study of the Baader-Meinhof gang (*Hitler's Children*) gained world renown, has said that "to speak of international terrorism without mentioning the PLO would be like describing the circulation of the blood without mentioning the heart," no one at NBC dared to use the word "terrorist" in connection with Arafat and the PLO. It was as if no one at NBC had been looking when the PLO murdered Israel's Olympic athletes (1972) or invented the fine art of hijacking by blowing up all forty-seven passengers in a Swissair plane (1970), or slaughtered Christian pilgrims arriving at Tel Aviv airport from Puerto Rico (1972), or murdered the U.S. ambassador in Khartoum (1973) and the Egyptian diplomat in Ankara (1979), or attacked the kibbutz nursery of Misgav Am (1980). An organized ignorance or else a collective amnesia seemed to have taken hold of Reuven Frank's staff, so that none of the hundreds of outrages committed by Yasser Arafat's organization against innocent human beings of every nationality (including Arabs) could be allowed to cast the slightest shadow over NBC's idyllic picture of "guerrillas" fighting for their homeland and freedom and (this above all) "honor" in Lebanon.

On 20 June Steve Mallory reported that Arafat was "trying to work out a compromise peace settlement." On 22 June Chancellor worried solemnly over the danger that as a result of Begin's "success" in Washington Arafat "will lose out to the extremists" (this was said by Chancellor against the background of NBC's picture, also used on the previous day, of Arafat kissing a baby). NBC's reporters not only insisted on the term "guerrilla" and refrained from using the term "terrorist" for Arafat and the PLO; they were forever suggesting the bias, if not downright bigotry, of those who did call them terrorists. Judy Woodruff reported from Washington on 12 July (on the basis of evidence yet to be uncovered) that the administration was threatening to deal directly with the PLO, "which *Israel* considers a terrorist organization." Tom Brokaw, interviewing Israeli Foreign Minister Shamir on 6 August, referred to "the PLO, or the terrorists as *you* call them." In a later report, 16 August, Brokaw allowed by implication that some members of the PLO might be less devoted to moderation than Arafat when he said that "even hardline factions of the PLO are willing to leave."

Whereas NBC classified Arab nations and the various factions of the PLO according to their greater or lesser moderation, Israelis were classified ornithologically, as hawks or (less frequently) doves. Typical was James Compton's (17 July) reference to Ariel Sharon as popular with the "hawky sector of Israeli society." For Roger Mudd even this epithet was not strong enough; on 9 June he averred that "Israel's decision to go after the Syrian missiles undoubtedly means that superhawks are now in the ascendancy in Tel Aviv" (to which city Mudd had previously moved Israel's seat of government). Since nearly all Israeli factions in and out of government were in agreement on the necessity for destroying these missiles, viewers might well have concluded that Israel is a society made up of these predatory aggressors, an impression frequently reinforced by

NBC's automatic references to "Israel's aggressiveness" (Brokaw, 12 August).

The gentlemanly reticence about using the term "terrorist" when Yasser Arafat and the PLO came into view disappeared altogether when NBC went after Israeli leaders. On 19 July Martin Fletcher reported on documents Israelis captured in Lebanese camps, several of which "Israel hopes" will show that the PLO was the center of internationally supported terrorism. But John Chancellor, determined to make NBC's viewers remember the real terrorist in the Middle East, introduced, in the midst of a commentary having nothing to do with the war, the following: "Menachem Begin, a terrorist in Palestine, went on to become Prime Minister of Israel." NBC's reporters showed remarkable diligence in transmitting those speeches by Communist members of the Israeli Knesset that referred to Begin and Sharon as "terrorists." This was no doubt one reason why Chancellor, on 13 August, recommended to the U.S. Congress that it emulate the forthrightness of the Knesset in speaking out against Israel's role in the war. (Christian leaders opposed to the PLO fared little better than Israel with Chancellor; Bashir Jemayel was identified in Chancellor's 24 August commentary as "this bloodthirsty young Christian.")

The epithet most frequently applied to the PLO in the course of NBC's reporting of the war in Lebanon was "honorable." On 25 June, Walid Jumblatt, the leftist Druze leader who became one of NBC's favorite interviewees, claimed that Israeli bombing did not allow time to talk or the chance for an honorable solution. Steve Mallory, acting as the dutiful puppet of Jumblatt's intention, then asserted that "without some honorable solution" the "Palestinians" would continue to fight. Two days later, 27 June, Mallory bridled at the notion that the PLO should leave Beirut without some quid pro quo, because "the Palestinians want to leave with some honor." (He claimed that "Israelis have rejected the compromise" agreed to by the PLO and the United States, an agreement that seems to have existed exclusively in Mallory's head, for no evidence of it could ever be discovered.) On 11 July Jack Reynolds (sounding very like a PLO spokesman) declared that "the PLO will resist unless an honorable withdrawal can be arranged." On 13 July Reynolds again pleaded that "what he [Arafat] wants most is an honorable withdrawal and a continuation of the struggle for a Palestinian homeland." In June and July, PLO "honor" was constantly invoked by NBC as an argument against the continuance of Israel's siege of Beirut. Such "honorable" men could hardly be expected to agree to negotiations for their withdrawal so long as the siege continued. (No attempt was made to explain why Israel should continue the siege if the PLO was ready to leave, or why, if the PLO had showed not the slightest sign of willingness to leave until the siege had commenced, it should be more willing to leave once the siege had been lifted.) In August, PLO "honor" was as sacred as ever; only now it was the bombing that prevented these honorable men from negotiating their withdrawal. It seems never to have occurred to anyone at NBC that a main reason why the quickly defeated PLO forces stayed in Beirut during the many weeks of Philip Habib's patient efforts was not their "honor" but the fact that the Arab states refused to take them in, and therefore they had nowhere to go. Both Lebanese and PLO officials have stated that the bombardments of 4 and 12 August had the effect of persuading the Arab states to change their mind and of dissuading Arafat and his followers from holding out for political victory despite military defeat. Nevertheless, on 16 August, Brokaw asserted that now, having fought the Israelis for two months, "they can leave with honor. They believe the world is more sympathetic to their cause" (as well they might, given the efforts made on their behalf by NBC and like-minded journalists).

The Missing Background of the War:
The PLO in Lebanon

I rather choose
To wrong the dead, to wrong myself and you,
Than I will wrong such honourable men.
—Shakespeare, *Julius Caesar*
III, ii, 127–29

Who, then, were these honorable men and why was Israel going to such lengths to expel them from Lebanon? NBC had short and ready answers to these questions. Homeless "Palestinians" (in NBC's lexicon, only Arabs, not Jews, can be Palestinian, an excellent means of implying that Palestine belongs exclusively to the Arabs), out of desperation, had organized themselves in Lebanon into fighting units that sought to regain a usurped "homeland." Their "chairman," Yasser Arafat, was a beloved leader (see, for example, Reynolds, 16 July) who spent much of his time kissing children (so much, in fact, before NBC's cameras that viewers might have wondered how he had time for anything else) and proclaiming that "We resist to protect the children, the next generation." NBC followed this vignette on its 12 July broadcast by freezing the picture of Arafat kissing a little boy, as if this were the image of him that it wished forever to keep before the mind's eye, although on 16 July he was kissing adults for NBC cameras.

NBC's frequent glimpses of PLO members showed them as devoted to their families, eager to avoid destruction, given to volunteering to clean up neighborhoods in their spare time, and having no desire to kill Jews. The weakness and essential "powerlessness" of Arafat's forces were constantly stressed in NBC battle reports. "Sophisticated Israeli warplanes" were always flying "too high, too fast" (23 June, 22 and 23 July). One could never have guessed from this relentless stress on PLO powerlessness that its forces had in fact amassed gigantic quantities of weapons: rocket-launchers, antiaircraft guns, tanks, thousands on thousands of light arms plus ammunition supplied from nearly every arms merchant in the world, and enough matériel from the Russians to equip an army of three to five divisions. NBC viewers rarely saw pictures of PLO weapons being fired from the midst of civilian areas because pictures of antiaircraft batteries and tanks within apartment houses or hospitals would have seriously damaged NBC's portrait of the Israeli attack as an onslaught against civilians.

Ironically, the only time during NBC's version of the Lebanese war that viewers saw an impressive display of firepower by the PLO was during the last week of August, when they daily "celebrated" their withdrawal from Beirut. Even these fiery occasions, so lavishly covered by NBC, were deceptively presented. When "salutes" were given "with everything from small arms to tank fire" (Vic Aicken, 22 August) one was curious about where the bullets and shells were landing. NBC yielded to its curiosity so far as to note (23 August) that two people were killed by these salutes. The truth is that over one hundred people were killed or wounded in these demonstrations of PLO pride and honor, but NBC chose not to mention the fact once it became known. The stress had to be on PLO "rejoicing" and on the universal devotion of Arafat's men to their leader. When, in 1983, violent mutiny against Arafat's leadership broke out, many viewers must have been puzzled.

Israel, on the other hand, was presented as an imperialist power "solving its problems in someone else's country" (Chancellor, 2 August). Its prime minister, Menachem Begin, was usually pictured with a scowl on his face and a *Never* under his chin in a photograph placed alongside a smiling Arafat (see, for example, 27 July) forever searching for "peaceful settlement" (3 July) and tirelessly "signaling . . . willingness to leave Beirut" (30 July). Israel's leaders were nearly always "hardened," "defensive," and "militant" (Brokaw, 11 August); its minister of defense was "boisterous," "uncooperative," and "intransigent," and also appeared with a *Never* under his chin (Fred Francis, 27 August). Israel's stony intransigence and unwillingness to compromise found expression in its reliance only on force. Rick Davis, to the sound of blasting guns, declared on 31 July: "This is the tactic of persuasion—Israeli style." This already powerful imperial "war machine" was, moreover, supported by the mysteriously "powerful Israeli lobby" (Mudd, 28 June) in the United States, where the Congress's reluctance to take a bold stand against Israel might well be due to "the influence of Jewish voters" (Chancellor, 13 August). It was even possible, according to NBC, that "the power of the American Jewish community" had been responsible for a long-standing "pro-Israel bias" in news coverage. Since this particular sentiment had been expressed by none other than NBC News's own president Reuven Frank (interviewed 8 August 1982), it came as no surprise that Roger Mudd should imply sympathy with those Arab-Americans who hoped to persuade the news media to be more "fair" to them (28 June).

NBC's reporters often sounded as though they were under instructions to assume that Israel was guilty until proved innocent and to treat all utterances by Israeli officials with a caution and circumspection nowhere in evidence when Arabs were quoted. Brokaw (30 June) warned that Rick Davis would report from Sidon on how Israelis presented "what *they* called evidence of an international terrorist ring" that the PLO operated. Judy Woodruff (12 July) said that the U.S. administration threatened to deal directly with the PLO, "which Israel considers a terrorist organization." Martin Fletcher (19 July) reported on "documents Israelis *say* they captured" in Lebanese camps. On 1 August the cautious Fletcher said that "Sharon produced aerial reconnaissance photos he *said* showed PLO tanks and heavy machine guns near Western embassies." In itself, such caution about accepting official pronouncements is admirable, but NBC's caution, like its morality, was very selective. NBC invariably took at face value condemnations of Israel by unnamed U.S. government "sources," that convenient formulation that provides license for every tendentious speculation of the journalist. More to the point, it invariably assumed the PLO to be innocent until proved guilty—or rather, even after proved guilty, for when PLO casualty statistics, for example, were shown to be utter fabrications, NBC continued to allow pro-PLO Arabs to repeat them without challenge or correction. NBC invariably accepted PLO claims that Israel had broken the cease-fires, though even President Reagan blamed the PLO for this. On 1 August, one of the extremely rare occasions during the entire war that NBC showed civilian casualties in *East* Beirut, Rick Davis said, "One report said Palestinian mortar hit two apartment buildings. . . . But some of the people here say it was a misplaced Israeli bomb."

In order to arrive at this conception of the adversaries in this war, still more to persuade their viewers to share the conception with them, NBC's news staff had to conceal from view both the immediate background of the war and much of the history of the Arab-Israeli conflict. American citizens who were so unfortunate as to rely on NBC News for their information about Lebanon between 1975 and 1982 would know little, if anything, of the PLO occupation of southern Lebanon, of the Syrian occupation of half of the country, and of the bloody civil war that had raged for seven years. In June 1982 NBC exposed viewers to pictures of spectacular devastation and damage in Tyre, Sidon, Damur, and southern Beirut, but rarely bothered to tell them that a war had been going on in these places for seven years. Television cameras zoomed in on damage, but television reporters were not overly scrupulous about specifying when the damage had occurred. John Chancellor's "history" of the conflict leading to the 1982 war (7 June) included not a single word on the seven years of PLO-Syrian occupation and civil war; viewers were simply told that "Israel is trying to buy a few years of peace at a *terrible* human and political cost." If viewers had just seen Israeli tanks firing on a devastated Damur, Chancellor's anger might seem justified. Similarly, if the news media had begun their coverage of World War II on the day of the allied invasion in June 1944, and had not taken the trouble to recount what the Germans and the other axis powers had been up to since 1939, the landing in France and the ensuing carnage would have seemed monstrous acts. The truth of the matter was that Damur had been a Christian township whose population had been massacred and its survivors exiled by the PLO in the fighting of 1976–77.

The PLO, generally pictured by NBC as powerless, besieged, idealistic freedom fighters longing for a land and state of their own, had in actuality for six years "had something closely approaching an independent state" in southern Lebanon. These were the words of *New York Times* reporter David Shipler in a lengthy dispatch from Sidon on 25 July. The PLO "had an army, a police force, a crude judicial system, . . . a civil service and a foreign policy. Those who lived within its rough boundaries said they were too terrified then to describe it to outsiders. Now, for the first time, they are describing what it was like, telling of theft, intimidation and violence." NBC viewers who took time away from their screens to read Shipler's report must have been stunned to discover that "the major tool of persuasion" of this organization whose yearning for peace NBC regularly contrasted with Israel's aggressiveness "was the gun." NBC's "guerrilla" fighters looked very different to those who lived under their reign of terror. "Both Lebanese and Palestinians describe . . . outright theft as a common practice of the P.L.O. . . . They often took things from shops without paying, Miss Raad and others complained. Youssef Alifreh, a young Palestinian resident of the Burj al Shemali camp, near Tyre, confirmed it. 'Now we are happy because the armed P.L.O. left,' he declared. 'When somebody wanted to buy something, he would take it and not pay, and if someone would complain, he would shoot them.' " Although NBC's reporters were mightily impressed by Arafat's devotion to children, many Palestinian Arab refugees in camps took a dimmer view, and told Shipler,

"Our children were working in the lemon groves, and then the P.L.O. forced them into service.' " For the majority of Lebanese under the PLO rule, NBC's honorable men were terrorists and thugs. " 'Life was terrible,' said Khalil Hamdan, who owns a gas station in Harouf, a Shiite Village near Nabatiye. 'They never used their brain, . . . They used their Kalashnikov. Even in the car, they used a machine gun to open the road for them.' "

This aspect of the Lebanese picture was not confined to the *New York Times*. David Ignatius, reporting from Damur for the *Wall Street Journal,* described how, on the night of 17 January 1976, "Palestinian guerrillas and their Lebanese Moslem allies attacked the northern part of the town . . . crying 'Allah-u-akh-bar'—God is great—as they stormed into the houses of Christian civilians. The screams of the attackers and the victims could be heard a half-mile away. . . . About 300 of the people of Damur were killed." Martin Peretz, writing in the *New Republic* (2 August) related that "Lebanese of all persuasions and origins have expressed—I heard it myself dozens of times—gratification at their liberation from the PLO." John Laffin, writing for the *Catholic Herald,* described (10 September 1982) how "White flags are beginning to show on many a house in southern Lebanon—but not the white flags of surrender. In this region the flags indicate that the family has an unmarried daughter—and naturally a virgin. The Lebanese found that the traditional signal was merely an invitation to rape by the PLO and the custom went into abeyance. Whatever the PLO was defending it was not the sanctity of the Lebanese home." Nevertheless, Roger Mudd on 28 July lamented that the "war has rekindled old hatreds" between Christians and Moslems (if so, this was a classic case of carrying coals to Newcastle).

It is scarcely necessary to remark that some awareness of the fact that, in the words of the *New York Times,* "The P.L.O. established a de facto capital in west Beirut" or that "the camps became the P.L.O.'s political and military centers, where they shared control with the Syrian Army," would have given NBC's innocent viewers a very different impression of Israel's bombing of west Beirut and of the camps than the impression they very likely received from NBC's presentation. There were exceptions to the rule among NBC reporters. On 13, 17, and 21 June, Bob Kur transmitted reports from southern Lebanon that included interviews with Arabs thankful to Israel for liberating them from the PLO's reign of terror, and he also once mentioned (21 June) that the PLO habitually positioned their guns near schools and hospitals. But for every such report by Kur there were two dozen by Mallory, Reynolds, and Compton that reiterated the PLO version of past history and present events, which also was the version accepted and propagated by Chancellor, Mudd, and Brokaw on the home front. On occasion one could sense the conflict between sense impressions—the witness of one's eyes and ears—and ideology, as when Martin Fletcher, on 28 July, reported from Damur how returning Christians were trying to restore homes and lives ravaged by the PLO and then—in a jarring non sequitur—asked, "How hard will it be for Christians to shake off Israeli patronage, and for Christians and Moslems to learn to live in peace again?"

If NBC viewers got little of the immediate Lebanese background of the war, they got nothing at all (apart from Jack Reynolds's grotesque travesties) of the larger background of the Arab-Israeli conflict since 1948. They were never told that the neighboring Arab states, with the exception of Egypt since it signed the peace treaty in 1979, have been formally at war with Israel since 1948. In that year the state of Israel was established; the Arab states declared war against it and sent five armies across its borders, an act of aggression that was recognized as such by many Security Council resolutions adopted between 1948 and 1951. Arab aggression continues down to the present day, so that the Lebanese war is but the latest in a series of six major battles (1948, 1956, 1967, 1969–70, 1973, and 1982) of a prolonged war. Israel, confronted with a thirty-five-year state of war, decided in 1982 that if the Arabs wanted perpetual war, they could no longer expect Israel to wait for a time of attack convenient to the Arab rulers and commanders.

The PLO, too, has a history. In 1964 the Arab League created it in order to carry out terrorist attacks against Israel (Israel, of course, in its pre-1967 borders). Although rent by factionalism—Syria, Iraq, Algeria, and Libya financed their own factions within the PLO—and at the service of Saudi, Soviet, and Syrian foreign politics, it was united by a covenant. The PLO National Covenant stipulates in Article 6 that no Jew who arrived in Palestine after the "Zionist invasion" (dated by Arafat from 1882) has the right to live there. Article 19 declares that "the partitioning of Palestine and the establishment of Israel are entirely illegal." Article 20 denies any "historical or religious ties of Jews with Palestine" as "incompatible with the facts of history." Arafat declared in January 1980 that "Peace for us means the destruction of Israel." In May of the same year his Al-Fatah organization announced, in Damascus, that its purpose remained "the complete liberation of Palestine, the liquidation of the Zionist entity politically, militarily, culturally, and ideologically." Although the cold-blooded murder of infants and children figured very prominently in the record of PLO exploits—the Avivim school-bus ambush in 1970, the abattoir at the Maalot school in 1974, the machine-gunning of the babies at

Kiryat Shemona in the same year, and the smashing of the head of three-year-old Galit Haran of Nahariya against a rock in 1979—NBC did not shrink from presenting Arafat as especially attached to children.

NBC's presentation of the PLO as a valiant band of "guerrillas" seeking to regain their "homeland" resulted either from organized ignorance or the will to deceive. Is it conceivable that no one at NBC recognized the distinction between guerrilla actions, which inflict injury on an enemy by whatever means possible and result in innocent casualties, and PLO terrorist actions, which do not even recognize the concept of innocence among the Israeli population but assume that every man, woman, child, and infant, is deserving of death? Is it conceivable that no one at NBC wondered why, during the nineteen years when Jordan controlled what Jessica Savitch and Roger Mudd called "Jordan's West Bank," there was not only no call for an independent "Palestinian" state in that area but no peace in the Middle East? Is it conceivable that no one at NBC wondered how an apparently rational man like John Chancellor could present the Lilliputian state of Israel as a predatory Brobdingnagian warrior extending its imperial reach over an Arab world composed of twenty states sprawled over fourteen million square kilometers and controlling resources beyond the dreams of Croesus?

During its three months of broadcasting the war in Lebanon, the closest NBC came to an acknowledgment that it might have blotted out the background essential to an understanding of the conflict came on 6 August. Tom Brokaw, now in Israel, mentioned in a bemused fashion that some Israelis had asked him, "Where were you when the PLO was killing thousands of Lebanese over the past seven years?" But since NBC's willingness to admit error is nonexistent, and its belief in its infallibility is unshakable—"the press," according to Reuven Frank, "ought to be arrogant"—no program of self-correction was ever undertaken.

Predictably, NBC lingered uncritically, admiringly, even affectionately over the PLO's riotous departure from Beirut and the arrival of its various factions at their several destinations. The evacuation was the ultimate "media event" of the war, for it is not difficult to imagine how different it would have looked if the cameras had not been there. Vic Aicken was especially touched by the "pride as well as sorrow" of George Habash's men, and offered mournful threnodies over the wounded, and rhapsodic accounts of tearful farewells and of Arafat on yet more kissing sprees. His tone turned acerbic, however, when he noted that U.S. marines "got lost" because their maps included places that had been wiped out by Israeli aerial bombardment. Tom Brokaw did say that although "Arafat left Beirut today like an Arab head of state at the height of his glory," "in fact he was being driven out of Beirut by a massive defeat." Yet none of NBC's resident sages could bring himself to name the real truth that was concealed by this masquerade, as Bill Moyers did on CBS (23 August):

> Watching scenes of the Beirut evacuation this weekend, I was struck by how it is possible for the cameras to magnify a lie. The Palestinian troops left town as if they'd just won a great victory. Arafat, they praised as a conquering hero. In fact, they are leaving town in defeat. And in fact, Arafat led them to this cul-de-sac where they made their last stand behind the skirts of women and among the playgrounds of children. . . . It could have been otherwise if Arafat and his allies accepted the reality of Israel, if they had not established within Lebanon a terrorist state sworn to Israel's destruction, and if Arab governments had not found it useful to nurture the PLO in the bloody illusion that Israel can one day be pushed into the sea.

Selective and Tendentious Interviewing

> *Jack Reynolds, NBC: "Is the American attitude toward the PLO changing?" Yasser Arafat: "We hope so. I began to touch it through the mass media . . . I began to touch it."*
>
> —(16 July 1982)

On 30 July NBC's Roger O'Neill offered a special report on what was alleged to be a "spirited and bitter debate" within the American-Jewish community over the war in Lebanon. Yet it soon became apparent that this was a debate in which, so far as NBC was concerned, only one side was permitted to speak. By way of showing its viewers the substance of this debate, NBC offered two people at a synagogue who took identical positions on "Israel's wrong path to peace"; this was followed by glimpses of the anti-Israeli protests of "New Jewish Agenda," an extreme left, pro-PLO fringe group; finally, O'Neill commented that "to make sure voices of dissent don't get too loud Israeli military commanders are now speaking to American Jews about the war." Apparently these military commanders despatched to stifle dissent did not do a very good job, since Roger O'Neill seemed unable to locate a single Jewish voice to speak for Israel. He concluded this survey of the "bitter debate" with the observation that the "war has split the American-Jewish community like no issue before" and quoted an unidentified rabbi who (bravely defying those Israeli military commanders sent to silence him) told the interviewer that "If we forget about Palestinian humanity, we may soon lose our own." If there was anywhere in America an articulate Jewish voice that supported Israel's action in Lebanon, NBC took special care that no one heard it.

On the next evening, Rick Davis interviewed three officers of an organization called World Relief about the Israeli blockade against supplies going into West Beirut. They expressed anger against Israel because, they insisted, their food was meant only for civilians. Also, by happy coincidence, these dispensers of charity (and strong opinion) had met with an Israeli officer who, just like the American rabbi interviewed by Roger O'Neill the night before, alleged that Israelis were losing their own humanity because of their inhuman treatment of the Palestinian Arabs. "The three men said they asked an Israeli officer where his humanity was, and he said 'I left it behind when I came to Lebanon.' . . ."

Two nights later, Roger Mudd interviewed Israeli Foreign Minister Shamir in Washington. He asked Shamir whether President Reagan would pull Habib out of his negotiating role "if you don't lower the level of violence," an expression Mudd was so taken with that he repeated it a few seconds later: "also, if you don't lower the level of violence, won't President Reagan force you to negotiate with the PLO?" Mudd also took it on himself to suggest—as if he had already replaced Habib as the chief negotiator—that Israel pull back five or ten miles as a "sign of good faith." As if this were not enough to indicate NBC's powerful disapproval of Israeli policies, Mudd followed the interview by saying, "Shamir would not acknowledge that Israel is having a credibility problem in the United States, but he also said that if there *was* one, it was not justified, because, he said, Israel tells only the truth." Mudd's arrogance, hostility, and rudeness toward Shamir must have come as a surprise to viewers who remembered his manner in the interview he had done (20 July) with Saudi Foreign Minister Prince Saud al-Faisal, a manner that can most charitably be described as one of oily sycophancy. On that occasion Mudd not only kept putting into the prince's mouth the idea that "the Middle East crisis can't be solved unless Palestine is recognized" (whatever this means) and that Syria dare not take in the PLO for fear this will give Israel an "excuse" to attack Syria; he also interjected engaging laughter by way of tacit approval whenever the prince referred to Israel's malignant designs on the region.

These three interviews, coming within a period of four days, were only too representative of the way in which NBC sought to buttress its hostile view of Israel's actions in Lebanon by an artful selection of hostile witnesses and a double standard of behavior in cross-examination. One could watch NBC for weeks on end without hearing a single pro-Israeli voice, while Arafat and such fervid supporters of Arafat as Saeb Salam and perfervid Israel-haters as Walid Jumblatt performed day after day. It was not merely that they were interviewed frequently (more than seven times as often as anti-PLO Lebanese) but always in a respectful, admiring, even affectionate manner. There were no hard questions, no abrasive challenges, no snide remarks, all of which were standard in interviews with

Israeli officials. To watch an NBC reporter interviewing an Arab official was to be reminded of Swift's adage that crawling and climbing are done from the same posture. A particularly egregious example of oleaginous fawning on PLO spokesmen was James Compton's interview with Arafat on 21 July. In response to Arafat's indicating that in addition to already existing UN resolutions on Palestine he would like "a new one," Compton helpfully proposed a Madison Avenue formulation: "If America will say yes, Palestinians have legitimate rights, is that everything you need?" and was mightily pleased by Arafat's sweet reasonableness in replying, "Oh, yes." On none of the many occasions when Arafat was interviewed by NBC did any of the network's reporters dare ask him what his own responsibility might be for the civilian dead of Beirut and other places. As a *Wall Street Journal* writer remarked on the very next day, 22 July: "The American media still has the sense not to glorify a gunman who uses hostages to shield himself from the police, but everyday they are making Yasser Arafat out to be a plucky little hero, even as he hides behind the innocent civilians of West Beirut." And who can know by how much Arafat prolonged this hiding (and multiplied the attendant casualties) because of the favorable publicity NBC's reporters and their colleagues gave him? If by 16 July, as he told Jack Reynolds, he had begun "to touch" American hearts "through the media," was it not plausible for him to believe that he might eventually capture those hearts entirely?

Everywhere a double standard was in evidence in the selection and treatment of interviewees. On 14 July Bob Kur reported on Israeli soldiers refusing to serve again in Lebanon, and interviewed an Israeli soldier who urged his countrymen to "talk" with Palestinian Arabs instead of fighting them, after which Yitzhak Rabin, also interviewed, criticized Israel's "political" goals in Lebanon as illegitimate. On 17 July James Compton mentioned that a rally reported to be twice the size of the antiwar rally so lavishly covered by NBC on 3 July had taken place in Tel Aviv, but in this case none of the people involved was interviewed. While Jumblatt and Salam appeared so regularly to castigate Israel that it was easy to believe they had been hired as NBC field reporters, Bashir Jemayel, the Lebanese Christian leader soon to be elected president of the country, was interviewed only twice, and since, as noted above, John Chancellor had tagged him with the label of "bloodthirsty young Christian," it did not much matter what he said. PLO representatives were interviewed fourteen times in July and August, but Major Sa'ad Haddad, whose forces then controlled southern Lebanon, was not considered worthy of NBC microphones and cameras. When he was referred to, it was invariably as the leader of a right-wing "Christian army" (Fletcher, 28 July), although 60 percent of his militia was Shia Muslim.

In July several U.S. congressmen visited Lebanon. One was Charles Wilson, a Texas Democrat who had voted for the AWACS sale and intended to vote for the Jordanian arms sale,· but nevertheless brought back from Lebanon impressions of "the universal enthusiasm with which the Lebanese welcomed the Israeli army. . . . I mean it's almost like a liberating army. . . . It was astonishing. I expected this, somewhat, from the Christian population. But I didn't expect it from the Muslim population. . . . And in talking to a group of people, some of whom had lost their homes, some of whom had lost relatives, they said it was awful. But they said that all in all, to be free of the PLO was worth it." This was a remarkable and newsworthy eyewitness American reaction to the Lebanese war, but it did not appear so to NBC, which never reported it to its viewers. But when five U.S. congressmen, led by the anti-Israeli crusader Pete McCloskey, called a press conference to announce (falsely, as it turned out) that Arafat was ready to accept Israel's right to exist, the story (or nonstory) dominated NBC's Middle East news for three consecutive nights and brought a Tom Brokaw interview of McCloskey on 26 July. Congressman McCloskey's announcement that "Arafat accepts all UN resolutions relevant to the Palestinian question" was, as I have noted earlier in this book, a transparent farce. Arafat did not, of course, specifically recognize UN resolutions 242 and 338, which do not refer to the Palestinians or the Palestinian question at all; and he said nothing about Israel's right to exist. Nevertheless, Tom Brokaw, exhibiting NBC's characteristic amenability to PLO balderdash, not only failed to ask McCloskey any hard, skeptical questions, but noted irritably that "debate" over the meaning of Arafat's statement "didn't keep Israel from pounding West Beirut for the fifth straight day." How unreasonable of the Israeli air force not to be as impressed as, say, Roger Mudd by the familiar PLO masquerade. At no point did NBC provide identification of McCloskey as an anti-Israeli activist who had long worked to cut off U.S. aid to Israel and had been a regular performer on the PLO lecture circuit.

During its three months of reporting the war, NBC never succeeded in discovering a single interviewable American who supported Israel or opposed the PLO. It never interviewed any Lebanese Americans who opposed the PLO, and indeed went out of its way to give the demonstrably false impression that Lebanese Americans supported the PLO against Israel. (The most casual reader of American newspapers would likely have known that the American Lebanese League publicly castigated the PLO for holding much of Lebanon and West Beirut hostage and asked them who gave "the PLO authority to insist that Lebanese civilians die with them?") Also, by a remarkable coincidence, every one of the ten Americans (not counting government officials) NBC interviewed condemned Israel and supported the PLO. Although over two hundred U.S. generals and admirals signed their names to newspaper advertisements stressing the "extraordinary significance" of the defeat of the most advanced Soviet arms by "Israel-modified American weapons and tactics," NBC, despite the fact that it consistently took the view that Israeli actions had damaged U.S. policy and interests in the Middle East, felt no obligation to interview a single one of them.

Conclusion

It is not easy, nor is it the aim of this study, to say what is the underlying cause of the deplorable lack of self-critical professionalism in NBC's reporting of the war in Lebanon. As I have noted elsewhere in this volume, Israel has, since she won a war in 1967 that, if lost, would have meant her destruction, incurred the visceral hostility of many journalists, including the majority of those who reported the war in Lebanon. Jay Bushinsky, Cable News Network's man in Jerusalem, described the foreign press as "enraged" and "bitter and resentful" toward Israel, and David Bazay (Canadian Broadcasting Corporation) referred to a "get Israel" attitude among his colleagues.

It would take me beyond the boundaries of this analysis to speculate on the moral and intellectual causes of this rage, bitterness, and resentment. It is, however, an aid to reflection to remember the disservice done to truth by the American press in an earlier conflict of this century in which the Jews were crucially involved—the Second World War. In her detailed study of how the American press treated the Holocaust, Deborah Lipstadt[2] has demonstrated that, in its collective blindness, arrogant "skepticism," failure of imagination, and indifference to the loss of Jewish lives, the journalists were as culpable as the American government for America's refusal to accept refugees from Hitler or to initiate efforts to rescue the Jews of Europe. Few readers of her book will fail to notice some remarkable resemblances between the jaundiced reporting of the war against the Jews from 1933 to 1945 and the widespread hostility to Israel that has been a feature of American journalism since 1967.

When, after 1945, the press received irrefutable confirmation of what it had for years denied—namely, that the Nazis sought to murder all European Jewry—very few journalists acknowledged error or apologized for having deceived the public. The years that have passed since the Lebanese war have brought many revelations of journalistic derelictions of professional duty during that conflict, but no corresponding movement of contrition from the offenders. Apparently, most journalists still believe themselves to constitute what Robert Heilman has called "a private body which claims unconditional freedom to determine what the public body shall be informed about; which cries aloud at any suggestions of limit or restraint; which seems to believe its practitioners free from common human frailties, and hence to begrudge admissions of error.[3]

Notes

1. In constitutional law, an "estate" denotes an organized class of society with a separate voice in government, such as the clergy, nobility, and commons (knights and burgesses) in Europe starting in the thirteenth century.
2. Deborah Lipstadt, *Beyond Belief: The American Press and the Coming of the Holocaust 1933–1945* (New York: The Free Press, 1986).
3. Robert Heilman, "Writers on Journalists: A Version of Atheism," *Georgia Review,* 39 (Spring 1985): 51.

Index